Mustn't
Grumble

Also by Joe Bennett

A Land of Two Halves

Bedside Goats and Other Lovers

Fun Run and Other Oxymorons

Mustn't Grumble

JOE BENNETT

SIMON &
SCHUSTER

London · New York · Sydney · Toronto

A CBS COMPANY

First published in Great Britain by Simon & Schuster UK Ltd, 2006
A CBS COMPANY

Copyright © Joe Bennett, 2006

5 7 9 10 8 6 4

Simon & Schuster UK Ltd
Africa House
64–78 Kingsway
London WC2B 6AH

www.simonsays.co.uk

Simon & Schuster Australia
Sydney

A CIP catalogue record for this book
is available from the British Library

ISBN 0-7432-7627-2
EAN 9780743276276

Typeset in Palatino by M Rules
Printed and bound in Great Britain by
The Bath Press, Bath

Mustn't Grumble

Contents

Introduction 1

1 Going, Oh My God, Home 3
2 In Pursuit of a Bowl 10
3 Walking to Swans 22
4 Wheels 34
5 Old Stuff and Rooney 49
6 Conceal Your Wants 62
7 Writer Way 74
8 Hoe Hoe 87
9 Nice Place 98
10 Banging in the Rain 106
11 The Bloody End 116
12 Dead Poet with Golf 127
13 Afternoon Toggles 134
14 Crusties and Teacakes 143
15 The Tethered Goat of Happiness 153
16 Cider with Romance 161
17 Back to School 171
18 Pork Juice 182
19 Democratic Yawn 192

20   Where they Borrow Whippets   199

21   What a Lovely Pier   208

22   Football for Girls   218

23   Look What They've Done to Mah-Jong   225

24   I Will Nae Have a Headache Tonight   232

25   Across the Neck   241

26   Wot Larx   250

27   Up the Stump   263

28   I Twitch   270

29   Whatever You Do, Don't Smile   276

Introduction

I am English, but I have spent most of my adult life abroad. When a publisher asked me if I would like to come back, travel around England for a bit and write a book about it, I said yes.

Here in New Zealand, I bought a road map of England and spread it out to plan a route. But there was too much England. Every inch of the map was dotted with place names I knew and should visit. It was impossible to be comprehensive. Any route I took would miss infinitely more than it hit. What I needed was a frame for the journey, a skeleton to which I would add the flesh.

I thought of several skeletons, but discarded them because they felt factitious. Then I thought of H. V. Morton. He felt bang right.

I read Morton's *In Search of England* when I was sixteen. It told the story of his travels around England some time between the wars. I loved it. As I read, I decided that I too would travel around England. Morton drove, but I would walk.

I never made the journey, of course, but I did write a synopsis of it, sitting up in bed, propped by pillows in my Sussex bedroom. That synopsis filled two sides of foolscap. The pen I used was one of those clear-barrelled Bic ballpoints with a little plastic bouchon in the end. When writing, I used to prise the bouchon out with my teeth and suck it.

Though I can remember the act of writing, only one detail of what I wrote remains in my mind. It was an image of walking through flat fields of potatoes in Lincolnshire. I was steering towards the spire of Lincoln Cathedral that rose alone from the level horizon. I cribbed the image straight out of Morton.

Thirty-one years later in New Zealand, it did not take long to find a second-hand copy of *In Search of England*. The bookseller had read Morton. So, I soon discovered, had many people of my age and older. They all spoke well of him.

Rereading a book at forty-seven is very different from reading it at sixteen. Morton's prose felt dated now, as it hadn't then, but I still admired his zest, and his neat, light touch with a story. More movingly, I could sense what it was that first excited me when I read him. Somewhere down in my guts, the ghost of romantic adventure stirred its limbs and shook off the dust.

Morton set out from London in April 1926. He drove west as far as Land's End, stopping more or less at random at villages and market towns and cathedral cities. Then he went north to the Scottish border, across the top of the country, and back down the east coast. His purpose, openly expressed, was to find the real England, the core of Englishness. He duly found it. It was an England of rural stolidity, drenched in the past. It seemed unruffled by the recent world war.

By following Morton's route I would have a constant standard of comparison. He would give my journey shape and purpose. I would be able to see how the England Morton found has altered in eighty years, to see what has endured and what has perished. Like Morton I would talk to people at random. Like Morton, I would meet the unexpected. Like Morton, I would peep briefly into other lives. But unlike Morton, I would not drive. I would hitchhike. It has always been my preferred way to travel. It dishes up a greater range of people, a fatter slab of chance, and it forces me to lower the barrier of my English reserve.

Feeling more excited than I had for a while, I booked a flight to England.

1

Going, Oh My God, Home

The smoking lounge at Singapore airport is a rooftop balcony of sunflowers. It's 8 p.m. and eighty degrees. The air smells of carbolic, as if the whole island had been recently disinfected. The hot wind bends the sunflowers close to the point of snapping. Around the beds there's a line of yellow paint beyond which you are not allowed to smoke, presumably for fear of poisoning the flowers.

3

I am there for three hours. I spend most of them smoking, drinking beer and half-heartedly engaged in conversation with a Scot and a Cornishman. They have both worked on oil rigs in the North Sea. Killing time, they try to find a mutual acquaintance.

'Do you ken that sparkie, tall guy?' asks the Scot. 'We used to call him Streak of Piss.'

The Cornishman does not ken Streak of Piss.

Undeterred, the Scot lists several other people that he kens, but the Cornishman kens none of them. Nor, remarkably, does the Scot ken any of the guys the Cornishman kens.

The Cornishman tires of the game and asks me what I'm going home for. When I tell him that I am going to hitch around England, he cocks his head. 'You'll be lucky,' he says. 'How long since you've been back?'

'A year or two.'

'The place has changed, mate. It's gone paranoid. And you're not exactly a dolly bird, are you?'

He isn't the first person to suggest that hitching will be hard. Last week in Christchurch I went to buy the trousers I am wearing now, a pair of the multiply zipped and pocketed things that are in fashion with the young. They are the nearest contemporary equivalent to the knee-pocketed army-surplus trousers that I habitually used to hitch in.

The shop assistant was young and Irish. When I told him what I wanted the trousers for, he suggested I bought something warmer.

'Why's that?'

'You're going to be standing by the road for one hell of a long time,' he said and he laughed, and I laughed with him.

It is early April, just the time of year that Morton set off on his travels. But amid the tropical heat of a Singapore night, it is Browning who rings in my head, and in particular his line about the elm-tree bole in tiny leaf. I am not sure that I can identify an elm tree. I am not even sure that any elm trees remain after the Dutch disease. But I can picture with a twang of nostalgia those tiny and tender elm leaves, translucent as baby skin, sprouting, somehow, from the tree's barked and bulbous base.

The plane is crammed, the doors are shut, the safety video plays and nothing happens. We just sit on the tarmac. The cabin grows slowly warmer. People fan themselves with newspapers and menus, looking around, seeking a reason for the delay, for the heat. The sense of frustration turns to a sense of suppressed alarm at the rising temperature. People sit like nervous antelope, sniffing danger, alert, instinctual. The great god of technology seems to be faltering. Something is wrong with this ship of the sky.

'What the fuck's going on?' asks a loud Scottish voice. It's the oil engineer. He's a couple of rows behind me. A stewardess scuttles to his seat, leans over to him, talks inaudibly, as if to an errant child.

The pilot comes on over the public-address system. But that too seems faulty. It crackles between loud and low. And his Asian English is hard to interpret. The cabin has become seriously warm. My forehead bristles with sweat. A baby wails. The wail cuts through the cabin like a saw. The noise is almost enough to provoke anger. I consciously keep myself in check, being English, being proper. But it would take only a couple more degrees of temperature, a couple more baby wails, to crack the reserve that still governs the cabin, to set people talking to unknown neighbours. And from there it would not be far to revolt, to people rising from their seats and insisting on being released from this sealed metal tube. Civilization is on the point of crumbling. Instinct is regaining the supremacy that it has held for most of the brief history of our species. I can feel in myself exactly the sentiments that are springing in every heart and mind on the plane, regardless of race or language. Seated in the most advanced product of human reason, we are regressing swiftly to something entirely unreasonable, something atavistic, and we are all doing so at the same time at the same rate. You can see the faces of the stewardesses battling it too, their selves struggling with their training. It would take only one dramatic event, a whiff of smoke, say, to trigger panic.

A sudden whirr and the air-conditioning kicks back in. Within a minute the temperature is comfortable. The aircraft gives a tiny lurch and starts to move. And faith in technology instantly regains sway. The beast that was becoming an oven is now going to hoist us into air too thin to breathe and carry us at more than half the speed of sound for several thousand miles and provide for all our needs, and we are comfortable with that. We trust.

The plane takes off. We settle down to eat and watch and breathe and wait, in limboland. I reflect that when my foot next touches soil, it will be in England, my native lump of rock. I feel a little fizz of zest. For though I have lived abroad for all but two of the last twenty-five years, I remain English and will die English. And I am happy with that. In a primal way over which I have no control, I still love the place.

Few airport names are romantic, but fewer still are as unromantic as Heathrow. Or as inaccurate. The only rows are of rental cars, and if ever there was a heath it's buried now beneath a monstrous acreage of concrete. Artificially lit in the darkness before dawn, the concrete is busy with low-cabbed vehicles.

As I pass through the rigmarole of disembarkation, luggage collection, customs and immigration queuing, I recognize the tone of everything. The ceilings are lower than in other airports, the porters grudging, the air-conditioning in the corridors less efficient, the noise greater, the officials more bored, less smiling. The English have never done this international stuff well. The Americans do, the newly ambitious tiger nations do, but the English manage to infect the whole with an air of shabbiness, of slight grudge. I don't mind. It is how it is.

Although the country is supposed to be alert for terrorists I whisk through immigration, my purple European passport getting only the briefest glance from an official in a turban with a face like ravaged sandstone. It is six in the morning.

The Arrivals Hall at Terminal 3 is too warm and absurdly busy. We travellers emerge, still fogged with sleep or sleeplessness, into an identity parade. Beyond the barriers the greeters stand three deep, scanning us in search of the one familiar face, dismissing the dishevelled rest.

A girl is waving to me. She is wearing a strangely outmoded cloth coat, like a doll's coat, or something from the fifties. I had not expected her to be there. She is a cub journalist on one of the free newspapers that you find in sodden dispensers about central London, a publication aimed at ex-pat Kiwis and Australians. She emailed me last week, wanting to interview me about a book of mine. I told her that, as it happened, I was about to come to England. But, I added, I would not be spending time in London, nor could I promise to be anywhere at any particular time except Heathrow at six on this Wednesday morning. I thought that would put her off.

She is called Maike. I tell her I must smoke and we go outside to where the coaches park. The air is thick with diesel. The sky is lightening from black to slate grey and the pavement is slippery with what is not quite rain, just a pervasive damp. There are no elm-tree boles. Only traffic and admin buildings and a multi-storey car park and the strained faces of travellers and the flat faces of people going to work too early in the morning.

I grind my butt out with a hundred others by a bin and we go back inside. On the cafe table beside me there's a copy of the *Sun*. While Maike fetches coffee I turn to page three. Breasts still, pert, primped and smiling just as they were when I lived here a quarter of a century ago. I compute that in the years I've been away, about 9,000 young women have rolled up their

T-shirts for the *Sun*. That's 18,000 breasts. The ones I saw in my youth will be sagging now, unphotographed.

Across the way a newsagent's is stacked high with the morning papers, all of them national, all of them aimed to gratify a particular reader. It's the caste system in print. To carry a newspaper under your arm in this country is to wear a badge. I was brought up with the *Telegraph*.

Maike asks when I am setting off and I say now, right now, and she says she'll come too. She wants to take a photo of me hitching.

You can't leave Heathrow on foot. The only exit is through the tunnel and that tunnel is forbidden to pedestrians. Maike and I board a bus at random.

'We just want to get out of Heathrow,' I say to the driver in his cage of plastic.

'You and everyone else,' he says and charges us nothing and I am absurdly pleased. With patient skill he rumbles the huge double-decker through the metropolis of traffic and round the too-small roundabouts and through the pedestrian-free tunnel. Maike and I get off at the first stop beyond the droop-nosed Concorde, which has been guarding Heathrow for as long as I've been catching planes, presumably because Britain hasn't invented anything to replace it, apart from, perhaps, the Dyson vacuum cleaner. Opposite us stands the slab-sided Holiday Inn. It would be hard to imagine anything looking less like a holiday. Or, indeed, like an inn.

Planes take off every few minutes and disappear into the mattress of cloud. That cloud compresses the air and muffles the world. We walk west, past a terrace of wet houses with plastic double glazing screwed over every window frame. There's a dead pram in the front yard of one and a pink bed. We pass a scrappy forgotten field, the last remnant perhaps of Heathrow's heath. I stop to study the remains of a hedge. It's a traffic-soiled straggle, a grim parody of the hedges that Morton motored between in 1926, or indeed of the hedges that lined the lanes of Sussex during my childhood. But beneath the grime is the vegetation that I grew up with, that I can name. Here is alder, holly, a stunted horse chestnut, hawthorn, nettles, cow-parsley and the browned stems of last year's thistles. In defiance of the gloom and the dirt and the incessant traffic, the buds on the horse chestnut have burst to expose intimate fronds of leaf like tiny tongues, of a green so fresh it aches.

The road is unhitchable. There's ample traffic, but for one thing the cars are travelling too fast, and for another they are forbidden to stop. The road is officially a clearway, the illegality of stopping stressed by fierce red lines beside the kerb. Here you have no choice but to move. I tell Maike that we may have a little walk ahead.

'A little walk?'

'A longish walk.'

I hoist my pack to my shoulders and we're away. An old iron sign says Bath Road. It is too small and low for these speeding drivers to notice. Its modern equivalent is a hundred square feet of post-mounted metal, offering drivers the choice of the M25 or Slough. The road is straight and daunting and we are the sole pedestrians, obvious aliens in vehicle-land.

A mile or so along the road I stop at a rutted driveway leading down to a shop. 'Palms, reptiles, birds and accessories,' says a hoarding at the top of the drive.

'This'll do,' I say.

It won't do. I know it won't do. But though Maike is sweet and good company, I am keen to be shot of her. I want to be alone.

Maike takes a photo of me with my thumb hopelessly extended in the exhaust-rich air, wishes me luck and heads back towards Heathrow. I wait till she is out of sight, then pick up my bag and head into England, on foot and on my own.

2

In Pursuit of a Bowl

In April 1926, Morton set off, presumably along the road that
I am on now, driving a bull-nosed Morris, a Bertie Wooster
car. And he had Bertie-Woosterish encounters that he reported
in Bertie-Woosterish style.

For example, outside a pub at a spot which he identifies
only as 'The Place where London Ends', Morton met an old
man:

'Good morning,' said I to the ancient man.

'Straight on,' he replied.

'Good morning,' I ventured again.

'About seven miles,' he retorted.

I felt that we were going to be great friends.

'Will you have a drink?' I asked.

Even this failed to bring us together, so I went right into his silver side-whiskers and shouted 'Beer!' whereon he sprang smartly to attention and walked into the bar.'

It's a style of writing that is of its time. It smacks of bound copies of *Punch* and a private income, but it remains fun to read.

From 'The Place where London Ends' Morton sped off down 'a green tunnel of a lane' and went 'in search of England'. That search was of its time too. Memories of the First World War were fading and the internal-combustion engine was opening England to the casual tripper. Morton brought good news of the country they had fought for. The England that Morton wrote of was not the urban or industrial England where most people lived even then. It was an England of villages, duck ponds and thatch, of churches and markets and slow-dropping peace. It was an England drenched in history, where the ghosts of kings, monks and heroes stalked the cathedral aisles, and where the feet of ancient armies echoed on the cobbled streets.

And his picture of England has proved remarkably durable. It remains in the collective mind, and is reproduced on a million calendars a year, and in countless brochures and magazines.

That enduring image of enduring England does not include the M25. On a bridge across that motorway I stop to smoke. Beneath me six lanes of traffic speed on undisclosed errands, a roaring river of engines. I drop my butt. It bounces from the top of a lorry and is caught by the fearsome turbulence of the air and dances a few seconds before I lose sight of it. I walk on. I have yet to meet another pedestrian. I can find evidence of only two who have ever passed this way. One came to spray litter. The second sprayed the litter with grime.

I stop to hitch beside a pond. By pond I mean a small area of reeds, sludge, petrol-rainbows and plastic drink bottles. But the local birds are presumably not spoilt for choice, for here, stalking among the reeds like a gangly animated spear, is a heron. I lay my bag at my feet and hitch for real.

In my youth I hitched thousands of miles through Britain, Europe and North America. More recently I hitched around most of New Zealand. I am familiar with hope, boredom, excitement and fear. But in all that time by the road I have never once felt as I feel now. I feel invisible.

Your presence as a hitchhiker always has an effect on the traffic. Some drivers smile or scowl or accelerate or look pointedly away or even steer slightly towards the centre of the road in order to ensure that you don't leap onto the bonnet. Other drivers signal that they are about to turn off, and a few of them may even be telling the truth. But now, on this dismal stretch of urban road beside a pond containing refuse and a heron, I have no discernible effect at all. I seem simply not to register. I'm not there. It's not encouraging.

But then finally, after perhaps an hour of hitching so fruitless it would make the Gobi look fertile, I make contact with the people of England. There are two of them. They are young men driving west in a white Transit van. They have shaven heads. And they both, with transparent glee, salute me. To do so, each raises two fingers and then lowers them. Not once but many times. Up and down the fingers go with a thrusting, almost sexual, vigour. Both young men are grinning. Indeed, the passenger enjoys the business so much that he goes at it with both hands, as if milking a cow, and when the van speeds past and away from me he is so keen to maintain contact and to convey his message that he lowers the window and leans out of it to carry on milking. He even bellows something at me that I don't quite catch but that I am confident is of an unsupportive nature. The van fades to a dot and I become invisible again. Five minutes later I pick up my bag and walk on.

I hope to find a more suitable spot to hitch, or a more minor road where the drivers are less imbued with haste and urban alienation. I find Slough. Even without a knowledge of Betjeman, it would be hard to expect much of a place called Slough.

Slough seems to have no definable edge. I find myself inside its boundaries without having noticed it begin. Slough just sort of happens.

On a huge, immaculately mown roundabout where the M4 and A4 converge, a bed of red plants has been planted to form the word HONOR, spelt that way for no reason that I can discern. On the roundabout a man is exercising his dog. Man and dog are encircled by constant traffic. The dog is an ancient Bill Sykes bulldog with a muzzle like a horse. Its fur is worn in patches and its teats brush the grass. It squats awkwardly to piss on the second O of HONOR.

On the walls of a subway under the M4, a scattering of graffiti holds more meaning for others than it does for me. 'Fuck UR SELF' has an appendix: 'Wrong context you pakie knob' it says, right next to 'Donna is a pengwin mother fucking telly tubby'. Beyond the subway stand the first tower blocks of Slough and a huge headquarters for Honda.

It's a trek to the centre of Slough, an unenthralling trek along an unhitchable road. Morton didn't do Slough. He drove on to Bucklebury, and a heath 'aflame with gorse', where he chanced upon a bowl-turner. The bowl-turner could have come straight out of the Middle Ages. I don't find a bowl-turner in Slough. I find dispiriting semi-detached houses with low walls and damp front yards. I find the Queensmere Shopping Centre, where there is no mere, no queen and as far as I can see no smiles. I find the Brunel Bus Station of a design that would have brought Brunel out in boils. I find 'Don't flash your cash' signs, and 'Street Crime Initiative' signs, and a vast

Tesco Extra currently under construction, and I begin to feel discouraged.

I don't need thatched cottages, but I wouldn't mind being somewhere I can see green, or some buildings that make at least some gesture towards aesthetic considerations, and some people who don't look like the walking dead and who reply to my cheery good morning with something more than a grunt. For I have been cheery. When I left Heathrow I felt like a kid at a funfair: so many places to go, so much time to spend, so much freedom. But the impossible hitching, the buildings, the dispirited dogs, the bent people in fawn anoraks, these are already bending my mood. And now late morning is late at night in New Zealand. I last got into bed two days ago and I can feel my lids lowering as I walk. I could find a bed in Slough, but I don't want to wake up in Slough. Nor do I want to do the long walk out of Slough's suburbs to somewhere it is possible to hitch. So I take a train. I buy a ticket to Thatcham, which, as far as I can tell from my road map, is only a stroll from Bucklebury.

'Charles, this is Stephanie,' says the woman over the back of my train seat. I can't see Stephanie, but from her voice, her name and her manner I can picture her. She will be wearing boots and trousers, a modish blouse, a modish coat, a thousand pounds' worth of clothes. 'Charles, look, I'm sorry, but your fabric hasn't arrived yet . . . I know, I know . . . no, Friday, we're hoping to have it by Friday. Pierrot is on to it. I've got to go to Glasgow tomorrow but Pierrot's on to it and Pierrot and I and – did I tell you I've got a new assistant, Mandy? – we'll be down on Tuesday . . . Yes, Charles, I know, I know.'

Beyond the window the urban world of elephant grey and too many battered people gives way to a rural one of hedges and irregular fields, unpeopled, soothing. The trees are tinged with spring green, their skeletons still evident. The grass is as lush as hope. On the banks of a cutting, brambles straggle, looking half-dead as always, but thick with the ugly vigour of weeds. Over the rolling mounds of farmland stretch flowering fields of rape, the out-of-keeping crop, the only primary colour in misty England.

As if to echo my relief from the urban boil the sky begins to break like an ice-cap. Cracks in the laden clouds widen to crevices of weightless blue. Suddenly, starkly, we pass a vast and faultless palace, belonging to Microsoft, but not to the land. It stands apart from any settlement, announcing itself as a new beginning, a company that can trade in nowhere, sufficient unto itself. The building has the architectural taste of an oil-rich Texan.

I change trains at Reading, 'where medieval churches share the horizon with breathtaking modern architecture'. Or so says a poster published, astonishingly, by Reading Borough Council. From it I learn that Reading is a place 'where old coaching inns find space in one of Britain's leading modern shopping centres'. The prettiness of Morton's England, in other words, is wedded to the convenience of Tesco's England. And there at the end of the platform, installed I presume by the council to affirm the continuing existence of Olde England, is a train-spotter. He is faultless, binoculars round his neck, his anorak as colourless as you could wish, his hair as flatly lank and his Thermos flask dented.

All I know of Reading I got from a school friend called Sid. Sid came to university here in the late seventies and lasted a month. But that was long enough for him to send me a postcard which featured a snap of an accommodation tower. On top of the tower was a hand-drawn stick figure depicted in the act of jumping. The figure was labelled 'me'.

I alight one station short of Thatcham, partly because I am in danger of falling asleep and partly because I am keen to walk among fields for a bit, but mainly because I hope to prove to myself that the thumb still works. I station myself by a lay-by.

The drivers on the road between Midgham and Thatcham are mainly alone, which is how I need them, and are not travelling too fast, which is also how I need them. And with the spring sun now high in the sky they are able to see me from some distance and discern that I am not entirely disreputable and also that I am considerate enough to have stood where they can safely pull over to make my acquaintance and perform their act of generosity. And then they can feel good about themselves for having done both a good thing and a slightly risky thing, for having dipped a toe in the waters of chance.

In short, the place, the time, the weather, the conditions are perfect. I can't go wrong.

I end up walking to Thatcham. Not a single driver has so much as acknowledged my existence.

The first pub I try in Thatcham advertises accommodation but doesn't do it. The second doesn't but does. The landlady leads me up a squeaking staircase to a first-floor room. Resisting the lure of the single bed, I dump my bag and head for Bucklebury.

Morton stopped his Morris at random on Bucklebury Common and met a man carrying a wooden bowl. The man told him the thing had been made by William Lailey, the last traditional bowl-turner in England, who just happened to be at work round the corner. Morton duly turned the corner, met the bowl-turner and rhapsodized about the virtues of traditional crafts, the happiness of honest work, the soullessness of modern industry and so forth. The bowl-turner shared his views. Morton told him that he could make a lot of money out of his bowls.

'Money,' he said with a slow faun-like smile. 'Money's only storing up trouble, I think. I like making bowls better than I like making money.'
'Will you say that again?'
. . . I wished to hear for a second time the voice of the

craftsman, the lover of his job, the proud creator of beautiful common things; a voice that is now smothered by the scream of machines.

The lane climbs up Hart's Hill to a view across Berkshire that could have been a frontispiece for Morton's book – lush, small, irregular fields, black cattle lying in ear-tagged ease, their legs folded, the vegetative green fading with distance into some darker namelessness of colour, patches of woodland, rooks in the air like wheeling black smuts, the light softly diffused, the air somehow afternoon rich and heavy and over-oxygenated, almost cloying – a small-scale, domesticated, inimitable landscape. I stride with new energy, not tired any more.

Bucklebury Common is an area of woodland and heath, crisscrossed by paths and dotted with hamlets.

Two women are coming up the road with retrievers on extendible leads. Before I reach the women they turn onto a pathway through the woods. 'Hello,' I shout, 'excuse me,' and am about to quicken my pace towards them but they glance back at me then pretend that they haven't glanced back. They hurry down the path, jerking their dogs along. I leave them be.

Another woman comes round a corner with another dog. I approach more cautiously, making a point of smiling and trying to look nicely educated. 'Excuse me,' I say when we are too close for her to skedaddle, 'I'm sorry to trouble you, but . . .'

It's a phrase that I doubt I have ever used in New Zealand.

The woman is country-dressed, in fawns and greens, and she is wearing what I am confident she would call wellies. Her accent is public school. No, she hasn't heard of H. V. Morton, but yes, she has heard something about bowl-turning in these parts. 'But Olive would know for sure.'

'Olive?'

'She was the schoolteacher here for I don't know how many years. Though she might be having one of her cranky afternoons.'

And we set off for Olive's place. When I ask the woman what she does for a living she says, 'What, me?' with a voice of genuine surprise. And then, after a pause, 'I do nothing.' Her dog is of a breed I don't recognize, a sort of giant and lolloping spaniel.

She leads me down one wooded lane after another, into little valleys where what were once cheap cottages are now expensive houses. Ivy hugs them. The gardens are luxuriance made neat. Collared doves and wood pigeons maintain a constant background purring, a noise as smug and richly contented as the deep green peace of Bucklebury Common. I find the place enchanting. The houses lie buried in green; the human presence is benign and mature. 'Beware!' says a notice nailed to a tree. 'There were recently two burglaries in Bucklebury. Little Lane was targeted.'

Olive's cottage is the smallest of several in a clearing. The guttering is shot, the roofline far from horizontal. As we approach, a squat deer leaps off the front lawn, over the box hedge and flees into the woodland. 'Muntjac,' says the woman. 'They're terribly common round here. Some people think they're pests.' Her voice drops to a stage whisper. 'Olive may tell us to go away. She's ninety-something, you know. You will go away if she tells us to, won't you?'

It's four in the afternoon. Olive is reading in her sitting room. She opens the casement window. 'Yes?'

She is seriously old. Her eyes are sunk and reverting to liquid, her gait is stooped, her upper lip crowned with a moustache of close to squadron-leader density. But her voice is imperious. She could walk into a classroom today and still teach. The kiddies just wouldn't dare. And they would learn to spell.

I tell her that I'm looking for any traces of a bowl-turner called William Lailey.

'George,' she says in a voice that does not entertain the possibility of error, 'George Lailey. Wait there.' She turns, her body cranked with age but its movements still fiercely decisive, and pads into another room.

'She always makes me feel,' whispers my companion, 'like I'm being told off.'

Through the window Olive hands me a wooden bowl. 'Turn it over,' she instructs. On the base in black ink, 'Geo Lailey June 1920'.

The bowl is shallow and crude, the size of a dessert plate, devoid of decoration. I run my fingers over its slight concentric ribs where it span on the pole lathe eighty-five years ago and the chisel gouged at it, and I feel like Sherlock Holmes.

'It's damp because I washed it yesterday,' says Olive. It's a statement, not an apology. 'Is that all?'

'Didn't he live here,' says the woman with the accent and she waves a vague arm, 'on this green?'

'No,' says Olive. Her tone is withering. 'That was the scythe-and rake-maker. George Lailey had a workshop at Turners Green.' And she looks at the woman and then at me with those sunken watery eyes as if to ask whether she really has to cope with any more of this. I would love to ask her more but her stare makes me mute. I return the bowl. Olive closes the window, the woman with the accent says goodbye and trundles off with her dog, and I wander back into the boggy woods in search of Turners Green. I meet another dog-walking woman.

She too is cautious when I hail her. But when I tell her I'm from New Zealand she says she thought she detected a twang and she had spent time working in Dunedin and how long is it since I came back to England? A year or two, I say.

'Oh, so you won't be too shocked by the changes.'

'The changes?'

'The violence. So many murders. I used to go anywhere any time, but I wouldn't walk through Reading now, not after nine o'clock at night, even with my gentleman friend.'

'Oh, come on.'

'No, really, the place has changed.'

Turners Green does not appear to have an apostrophe but does have a small memorial plaque. 'On this site stood the hut of George Lailey 1869–1958, bowl-turner of Bucklebury.'

I knock on the door of the gingerbread cottage next door, its fruit trees airy with blossom. The woman of the house is the first not to seem nervous of me. She invites me in, makes me a coffee, and summons her son from the garden. He fetches another of George Lailey's bowls, by which I am slightly less excited than I was by the first one, but about which I say excited things, and then the boy unearths a school project he did on George Lailey for which he earned six house points.

At his mother's bidding, the boy fetches his bike and his helmet and cycles with me across the common to the allotments and his grandma. She is burning garden rubbish in a supermarket trolley and is wearing a sort of fisherman's hat with a brim, a sturdy coat and wellington boots that I bet she doesn't call wellies. As a child she was close friends with George Lailey's niece, but recalls little of the uncle and knows nothing of Morton. She considers Bucklebury 'the best place in the world to live' and lurking in her voice are the remains of a rural accent, a soft rolling of r's and a richness of vowels that seem appropriate to this place. I leave her burning her rubbish, the smoke adding to the thickening mist of early evening, and traipse back over Hart's Hill to Thatcham, pleased by the ease and success of my detective work. I feel a slight and unexpected thrill from having trodden so closely in Morton's eighty-year-old footsteps.

Thatcham, though no metropolis, is spoilt for eateries. Five Chinese restaurants, two chip shops, a curry house and a kebab, pizza and chicken palace, where I buy a traditional English doner kebab. It would feed two and is entirely meat. I eat in the market square, then join half a dozen drinkers in the pub watching a European football match. The game doesn't excite me, but I like the placard borne by a Dutch supporter and addressed to his English counterparts. 'You're all as ugly as Camilla,' it says. I feel my eyes drooping and go to bed at nine o'clock, in England.

3

Walking to Swans

I wake at four and sleep has gone. It's jet lag, I suppose. I make an instant coffee and tip two individual portions of UHT milk into it, both of which take twenty seconds to open, their tabs too small for my clumsy early-morning fingers. I climb back into the narrow bed. The eiderdown has the same reddish paisley pattern as one I remember from childhood. It looks like highly magnified sperm. It smells faintly of must and less faintly of former sleepers.

On the bedside cabinet there's a copy of *Five On a Hike Together*. The front cover shows the Famous Five paddling a home-made raft. All but Timmy the dog are wearing bright orange life jackets. 'Now on TV' announces a green and yellow flash across the top.

I open it at random. 'Some grown-ups are so jolly decent, thought Julian.' The last chapter is called 'An Exciting Finish'. Chapter 19, 'Maggie and Dick are Annoyed'.

It's a pre-industrial literary Eden. Good prevails, morality is king, adventure is innocent and people walk safely through a graffiti-less world after nine o'clock at night in search of Reading's single bad guy. He proves dumb enough to be unmasked by a bunch of goody-good sexless middle-class kids with a passion for crumpets and a vocabulary that's simply wizard.

Was life ever like that, even in Berkshire? If not, then was Enid Blyton deluded or was she wilfully deluding her readers? She presented an England of villages, churches, dusty millers, plump millers' wives, moustachioed station-masters, whiskered grandfathers, honest servants, hoary gardeners and dithery squires, all of them snug in a benign and sparsely populated countryside. Class, stability and a fundamental human goodness. The good got what they deserved and were content with what they'd got. No one envied or aspired. Everyone just was.

I wonder whether Olive the schoolteacher gave her tough little charges Enid Blyton to read. And if so, did she think it good for them? I don't know. What I do know is that in the early sixties when the Great Train Robbers were greatly robbing trains, when London was swinging and the Kray twins were running its East End, I was ingesting Miss Blyton. And it was Miss Blyton's image that prevailed, that formed my template of ideal and essential Englishness, an image that endures however much experience may contradict it. It sets village above town, town above city, Bucklebury above Slough.

It is that same image, I suspect, that drives stockbrokers to buy houses in hamlets deep in the woods of Surrey. The village as the heart of English life is a notion that even the Industrial Revolution, a couple of centuries old by now, has failed to dispel. And it tallies with the England that Morton went in search of in 1926.

The bedside light is too low and weak for comfortable reading. I try to return to sleep but fail, and just lie silent in the darkness waiting for dawn. It seeps slowly over the rooftops and through the window, sharpening outlines, infusing the bits and pieces of my room with colour: a small chest of drawers crudely fronted with pink rose-patterned wallpaper masking who knows what blemishes; a cheap fire-sale wardrobe on a slight lean; ancient double-twist electric cable painted over and stapled to the skirting; a chromium tea trolley holding the kettle and the little plastic pitchers of milk; a no-smoking sign; and a cellophane-wrapped pair of buttersnap biscuits. A plate from Mallorca hangs on the wall showing parrots and a woman in local costume in colours too vivid for England, alongside a pencil drawing of the head and shoulders of an Alsatian. The whole tiny room is misshapen. There isn't a right angle in it.

Despairing of sleep and keen to smoke, I dress and creak down the stairs but find both external doors locked. Back in my room I prop open the sash window with the Famous Five. I lean head and shoulders beyond the sill and light a duty-free Rothmans, flicking the ash into the yard below and blowing smoke over the tangle of tiled roofs and outhouses. I feel like a bike-shed schoolboy, then notice that in the gutter beneath the window lie half a dozen butts.

Footsteps on the stairs and I emerge from my room smack on cue to startle the landlady. She does a little jump of surprise, emits an involuntary gasp and then says sorry at the same time as I say sorry. She lets me past the Alsatian whose portrait I slept beneath, and out into early morning Thatcham.

I like watching places wake up. The birds are hard at it. A

wise thrush is singing each song twice over on the tiled roof ridge of a Chinese restaurant. Doves and wood pigeons burble. In Wyatt's of Thatcham the white-hat-and-striped-apron butcher seems straight out of Blyton, rolling bloody roasts of beef on his hollowed wooden block and deftly tying them with string. The greengrocer's is open-fronted and ready for trade, its pyramids of English cauliflowers and Chilean apples new-built and impeccable. The three women are togged up in thick green jerkins and fingerless gloves, stamping their feet for warmth and blowing into their hands. Just around the corner, behind the plate-glass windows of Waitrose, the workers stacking the displays of fruit and veg are in short-sleeved shirts.

Few vehicles are about yet. I catch a glimpse through a ground-floor window of a woman buttering toast. Her plate is white with a wide blue ring. I love the intimacy of such detail, the mundane rendered rich by its randomness. For me it's one of the pleasures of travelling, and only possible when travelling alone. I feel good, free, and I am buoyed too by yesterday, by the discovery of so many traces of Morton's bowl-turner. I turn at random down the roads, see people in housecoats bending to collect milk from doorsteps, or setting out for work, locking doors behind them, putting cats outside for the day, starting cars with beads of moisture on the bodywork. In the newsagent's, a labourer buys ten Benson & Hedges and lights one immediately and a man with a terrier buys his *Daily Mail* without saying a word to the newsagent because this is the paper he always buys. It is all orderly, quiet, diurnal and English.

The churchyard is deep in grass and dew. An old man walks his mongrel among the graves. By the gate stands a pile of grass clippings smelling sweetly of corruption. The noticeboard advertises Rockmass. It's 'a eucharistic church service with some of the best rock music around . . . Take a centuries-old church building, add a powerful sound system, lighting effects, candles and a fantastic band and get a unique experience' runs the tag line. 'Be early', it adds, 'to ensure a seat' and I am unsure whether this is honesty or sales hype or just good old hope. In the High Street twelve-year-old girls totter to school in clinging mini-skirts and clumping heels, pouting sex and toting cellphones.

My breakfast is served in the bar amid the foetid legacy of beer and smoke. The table is vestigially sticky, the curtains still drawn, the coffee instant, the bacon fatty and the light barely adequate to read my paper. The football ended 0–0, and is labelled a triumph and was the third round first leg of the National Bank Interleague European Championship Cup or whatever. I don't know the names of the players any more. When I went to live abroad, many of them were unborn.

After breakfast I go to buy my superstitious staples for hitching, a bottle of soft drink and a packet of 'fun-sized' Mars bars, neither of which I expect to touch but which I always carry as my charms against disaster. I try to convince myself that their absence from my bag yesterday caused my failure. Back to the pub to collect my bag and the place is locked again, front and back. As I try the gate to the yard the Alsatian leaps at it, looking less endearing in the flesh than it did in pencil. I tour the town centre once more. It's now fully awake and with the soft magic of half-light dissolved like mist. The pyramids of fruit have been vandalized by commerce. Waitrose has a smattering of customers. There are women whose coats and headscarves and little shopping bags on trolleys are unchanged from my childhood. I am keen to be on my way, to lollop in short and easy hops to Newbury and then on to Winchester.

As I return, the landlord is emerging from the pub with rubbish bags and the Alsatian.

'You,' he says. It sounds like the jab of a finger in my chest. 'You were meant to be out by nine o'clock.'

It's ten past.

'Sorry,' I say with my usual combativeness. 'But the place was locked.'

'That's as maybe,' says the landlord, which is not an easy

argument to counter. He snorts and goes huffily about his business. I fetch my bag and walk out of Thatcham.

It's a comparatively minor road, but there is traffic enough. I take up position by a gate and a horse. The horse leans over the gate. I pat and rub its bony muzzle, study its shivering nostrils, like huge and bristly valves. Its eyes are vast brown marbles, its docility remarkable. After a while the horse loses interest. The traffic never starts to show any. I don't know why.

As far as I am capable of looking good, I'm looking good. I may be male, forty-seven and bald as a turnip, but my clothes are clean, my backpack is small and new, my position by the road is inviting, and, crucially, I'm feeling cheerful. I know from experience that drivers pick you up when you feel good and don't when you don't. It's as if you radiate goodwill that registers even through the toughened glass of a windscreen and above the noise of a quadraphonic stereo system.

Cheerfulness is hard to fake. Today I don't need to. I stand by the road like the angel of merriment, barely containing my infectious chuckle of delight in simply being alive and here, right now. The Volvos and BMWs are unmoved. Their stream-lined grilles swerve neither an inch towards me nor an inch away from me. I am litter.

It is twenty years since I hitched anywhere in this country. Back then, most lifts came from former hitchers who had graduated to car ownership but not forgotten their less affluent days. Is that over? It feels that way. And if so, what has snapped the thread? Is it affluence? Does everyone now have a car, or two cars, or three cars, with the result that a hitchhiker must, by the very fact of his carlessness, be odd or dangerous, an outsider, a ne'er-do-well, a pirate of the road whom one would be ill-advised to ask on board? Or is it more fundamental still? Has something snapped the bond of trust, the assumption that people mean well until they prove otherwise? In short, has fear won in a *Daily Mail* world? Or am I just ugly?

I don't know. All I do know is that in the end, over the course of a couple of hours, and with several stops at likely hitching points, I walk the half-dozen miles to Newbury.

Until I reach town I see no other pedestrians, though I do pass a 'Police Warning' fixed twenty feet up a lamppost.

'Laptop? Mobile Phone? Handbag? Where are yours?' it asks the crows and chaffinches.

Fields give way to guest houses and an estate of 'beautiful new Barratt homes'. They look like fresher versions of the house I was raised in, brick, with tile fascias and white window frames. But these homes offer 'Barratt living', which wasn't around in my youth. We had to make do with football in the park and Marmite on toast and jeering at the jittery local paedophile, none of which sounds very Barratt.

Newbury introduces itself with a string of home-supplies stores, B&Q, MFI, Comet, Currys, all accessible only by car and offering everything needed to stuff a Barratt home with happiness as advertised. The stores are cuboid, glass-fronted, car-parked and reeking of impermanence.

Morton called Newbury a 'knowing-looking, bandy-legged town', presumably because it has a race track. I see no bandy-legged knowing-lookers, but I do see a gentle mud-green river. Before heading out to find the A34 to Winchester on which I have pinned my dwindling hopes of hitching a lift, I take a seat by the towpath. It's midday. The sun is beginning to split the clouds.

There is a class of person who prides himself on knowing the collective nouns for birds. I belong to that class of person. Apparently these collective nouns were all invented by some nineteen-century Hampshire clergyman who suffered from a surfeit of rural boredom, but that doesn't stop me dropping a murder of crows into the conversation, or a murmuration of starlings, whenever the chance arises. But I don't know what the bored reverend came up with for swans. A pride of swans, perhaps? A regatta?

It is so easy to forget how big swans are. They are also bul-
lies. On a bench by the water a woman with blotched and
swollen ankles is eating a pie. Bits flake off and a single swan
lumbers from the water and across the towpath to suck them
up, its neck like the hose on a vacuum cleaner. The bird then
just stands before the woman and stares down its beak at her.
Its head is higher than her head. She looks up, starts, and tosses
the bird what's left of her pie. I'd do the same. The swan is the
size of an ostrich. Look an ostrich in the eye, however, and
you'll see scatter-haired lunacy. Look a swan in the eye and
it'll go for you.

A swish Volkswagen people-carrier draws up and the swans
immediately make for it. Pavlov would have made notes. They
glide across the flow with ruthless elegance, driven by webbed
feet wider than the span of my hand. The more distant ones
beat the water with colossal wings, half flying, half walking
across the surface, before letting their wings and meaty bodies
fall, driving a bow wave that slops against the bank. The VW
disgorges a four-year-old in a pus-coloured puffa jacket. Under
pregnant Mum's supervision he tosses bread. The swans eat
and keep coming, lumbering out of the water, an advancing
tide of feathered bulk. The child can't strew the bread fast
enough. The swans close in on him and Mum whisks him off
his feet at the exact moment that he bursts into tears. The swans
slide back into the water with utter impassivity. One hunches
its wings, lowers its head and pursues another, pecking fiercely
at its fleeing tail feathers.

Lunchtime Newbury slowly unfolds. Office workers lunch
by the river on burgers or little packets of sandwiches, loosen-
ing their ties in the spring sun. It's sweet here and I am in no
rush. Though Morton spent no time in Newbury I decide to
stay the night.

I rent a room at a bed and breakfast run by an elderly
woman from Poland. She is half-crippled by a damaged knee
but relentlessly cheerful. She was 'taken' by the Nazis as a girl,

likes to see a man smoking and has been in this country for almost sixty years. Her late husband worked for Berkshire County Council. So did my father, briefly, before I was born.

'I don't know vy I have accent,' she says. 'I leave Poland 1946. I live ever since here and hereabouts.' And yet in her pronunciation of hereabouts you can hear a soft rural burr, the sort of accent that has been squeezed out by the Estuary English that I have heard everywhere since I landed, except in Bucklebury. In Estuary English, this part of England is the Sow Feece.

In the peaceable centre of Newbury, policemen on the beat go in pairs and wear flak jackets. The paraphernalia of enforcement on their belts looks like a wall display of kitchenware. I study the stuff as closely as I dare and can't see a whistle. Blyton would be disappointed.

Though Newbury's shops, I know, are repeated in every high street in the country, they are novel enough to me to be of interest. The shoppers too, the older men especially. So many of them are dressed in ties and jackets from British Home Stores or M&S, zippered to the neck even on this warm afternoon, sober, balding men in fawn and grey, silent, zombieish, not disturbing the orderliness, looking to a man like Philip Larkin on one of his less exuberant days. I enjoy watching them in a low-temperature sort of way. England is not just a football team, or the Lake District, or Shakespeare. It is also an elderly man in Boots in Newbury comparing tubes of pile-cream.

The sweet little museum tells me that Thatcham may be the longest continually occupied settlement in the country. It was apparently a camp seven thousand years before Christ, and a thousand years before the English Channel became wet. I spend an hour or more following the familiar pattern of invasion, occupation and assimilation that is the story of these islands. I particularly enjoy a range of ferocious weaponry and a display about the Battle of Newbury in the Civil War.

Just as I'm about to leave, I come across an exhibit on the

bowl-turners of Bucklebury. Here's a photograph of George Lailey, and another of his father and grandfather who were wood turners too and both called William, so Morton may have been right after all. 'The first two generations of Laileys made bowls as a side line,' says an information board, 'but after 1927, when a romantic description of their work was published, George was able to earn his livelihood by turning bowls.'

The romantic description can only have been Morton's. His book must have led hundreds of people to do as I did yesterday, making the pilgrimage to Bucklebury Common in search of an older England. Effectively Morton made Lailey into a saint of sorts, his hut a shrine. And saintly George, it seems, was happy to sell every pilgrim a hand-turned wooden relic.

The museum is set close to the river and housed in a former granary. But the river is actually a canal. It was a prime trade route before the roads and railways won. The canal fell into disrepair. Its buildings rotted. In the fifties, a preservation society rescued it and its associated buildings and the result is a pleasure spot, where the conscienceless swans trade their beauty for bread. Where barges once brought coal and grain, narrowboats now put-put up and down on endless holiday. It's all benign and pretty and purposeless. I ask the woman behind the museum counter, who is a dead ringer for my sister, what else there is to see in Newbury. 'Not much,' she says, 'the rest's, well, modern.'

It's the tourist mantra around the world but especially in England. Old is good and modern is bad. Today is an unenchanting mess. Yesterday was a mess too, once, with its poverty, suffering and violence, but time has composted it into sweet-smelling stories. Like, for example, the romantic Battle of Newbury. On a fine September morning three hundred and sixty-two years ago, twenty-eight thousand Royalists and Parliamentarians faced off on the hills around this town and spent the day gloriously hacking each other to bits. Three and a half thousand men died. Neither side won. It's one of the battles that the Civil War Society, or whatever it's called, dresses up to re-enact from time to time, getting every detail as accurate as possible except for the blood, the dismemberment and the three and a half thousand deaths.

Suddenly at half-past three the roads fill with giant Volvos on missions to collect the boys and girls from the nicer schools. The boys and girls from the less nice schools walk, tyrannizing the pavements and being allowed into the sweetshops only two at a time. The girls are dressed like slappers. The boys are smaller, the crotches of their trousers low, their shirt-tails immemorially flapping. Will time subdue the slappers into women with wheeled baskets? Will it dress the feral boys eventually in reticence and zippered jackets? I'm not sure.

Sam is lecturing friends on the Enlightenment, which seems an odd way to treat them over pints of lager in the pub. He's giving them the gen on David Hume and Samuel Johnson. The friends, one male, one female, are pretending to listen but all the while the male fingers are sliding down the female spine and burrowing like a vole beneath the waistband of her jeans to explore the land below.

Sam's Scottish, in his mid-twenties. He has the look of the perpetual student, with John Lennon glasses and Steve McQueen hair. While he's on the Enlightenment, I merely eavesdrop from a nearby table. But when he mentions chronic tonsillitis, I interrupt. For I've had chronic tonsillitis and I know the cure and I tell Sam that it is penicillin.

'I'm allergic to penicillin,' says Sam.

He's about to go to Canada and he's terrified of the journey. It's not the flying he minds but the inevitability of terrorism. 'I just know,' he says, 'that when the cabin crew seal the air-tight doors, the bloke sitting next to me will be wearing a tea towel and sweating.'

I laugh. The friends laugh. The highly educated Sam doesn't laugh. He believes it.

I tire early again. Mid-evening I stop for one last beer at a pub run by an ectomorphic relic. His lank hair is ruthlessly combed, his spine rigid with morality, and he wears a buttoned blue blazer. An emblem in heavy gold thread weighs down the breast pocket. He clearly stands for standards but his customers don't. They are young and slovenly, swearing loudly, a couple of them so hopelessly pissed they are beyond standing, others dourly watching a televised football match between a European side and a Scottish one, while drinking pints of lager with bogus foreign names. The landlord stands erect at the bar and surveys them with the disdain of a battered eagle. As I leave I bend to pat the pub dog, a terrier as ancient as its owner, and it gums me.

4

Wheels

I've given up. I'm on a train to Birmingham.

Across the aisle a woman from Florida is trying to find someone to talk to, but the English are thwarting her.

Five minutes ago she caught the eye of the woman diagonally opposite and immediately threw out a weather remark. The Englishwoman was horrified. She emitted a mirthless laugh, ostensibly of pleasure, but to any middle-class English

34

ears it was a howl of acute discomfort. The American woman persisted, which is how I discovered she was from Florida, and that it was her first trip to England and that the country was far cleaner than she'd expected, but the Englishwoman was a mussel clamped tight against the air. She blocked the American's every move with monosyllables of agreement.

It wasn't the conversation itself that the Englishwoman shunned. It was the publicness of the conversation. Within a minute Miss Florida had been silenced, and Mrs England was flicking just a little too quickly through a magazine.

The morning began fine. I woke early again. For some reason the door to my room was wide open, giving onto the well-kept sitting room of the doughty Polish landlady, with its vast television and array of family photographs. I felt odd to be the only one awake in someone else's home, like a licensed burglar.

In the large modern kitchen I made myself an instant coffee, my bid for silence thwarted by a plump blonde Labrador. Its fat stubby tail thumped the whiteware. I drank in darkness in the garden, the pre-dawn air scented, the Lab circling me devotedly and, at the least touch of a calming hand, rolling onto its back and squirming on the wet grass. With nothing else to do until the landlady got up, I took the Lab out through the early streets of Newbury, without a lead but confident of its chubby loyalty. I passed a paper boy, myself of thirty-something years ago. A milk float whirred with its eerie electric whine, still delivering its milk in glass bottles and furnishing me with a sense of sturdy continuity.

Mrs Poland was up and about when we got back. 'Vy you banging around in the night?' she said. It wasn't an accusation. Despite the odd wince as pain flared in her knee, she was indomitably cheerful.

'Not me,' I said. 'I was back and in bed by ten.'

'No, two o'clock in ze morning. Bang crash bang.'

I shrugged. She laughed. 'How you vant your eggs?'

When I paid her she made a receipt out for more than I gave her, telling me to claim it as expenses and to buy myself 'a little zomething nice'. I thanked her, kissed her and headed out to find the A34. It was marked on my map in fat arterial red.

The road signs led me uphill to a cutting. The cutting had no roadside footpath. I had to climb off to the left. The path led away from the road and into silent suburbs. I steered by a general sense of direction, following a lane out of town. Cresting a hill, I heard the A34 before I saw it. When I saw it, I stood still.

It was effectively a motorway. On either side of a median strip flowed imperious lanes of traffic. The inside lane was an unbroken line of lorries doing the speed limit. The outside lane was an unbroken line of cars exceeding the speed limit. It was quite unhitchable.

I stood and looked at it awhile and thought a bit and gave up. I turned, walked back to Newbury and rang Mark in Birmingham.

I went to school with Mark. Of all my school friends he was the one who left school with fewest qualifications, and of all my school friends he is the one who's done best. Perhaps that 'and' should be 'therefore'. Mark now employs a dozen people, inhabits a huge house and still grins like the eleven-year-old I scuffled with in 1968.

'Mark,' I said, 'have you got a car I can borrow?'

'I think so.'

'You think so?'

'Yeah, I don't think I've sold the Audi.'

I had to change trains at Reading again. A substantial crowd was waiting at the designated platform when a train drew in at another. A couple of people made a move towards the train. Others followed. The rest of us picked up our bags in uncertain readiness.

'Oi,' bellowed a guard. 'And where do you think you're going?' It was magnificently peremptory. Those who'd led the charge shuffled back like guilty third-formers. The guard scowled with a mixture of contempt and delight.

The train is not like the ones I caught to school in the seventies. It's more like an aircraft. It's clean and air-conditioned. The seat cloth is fresh and untorn. The public-address system works and is comprehensible. It's so obviously non-smoking there isn't even a non-smoking sign. And a running light display on the luggage rack indicates which seats are booked between which stations, though it still doesn't make eviction easy. At Oxford a woman got on and battled up the aisle to find her seat. A youth in a tracksuit was sitting in it, his ears plugged with an iPod. The woman stood beside the seat-back and checked the running light display above. The youth did not look up.

The woman took her purse from her handbag, opened it, extracted her ticket, and checked the seat number twice with exaggerated movements of her head from seat to luggage rack. The youth did not look up. With obvious pained effort, the woman said, 'Excuse me.' The youth either didn't hear her or pretended not to. Meanwhile all who could, watched while pretending not to.

The woman leaned into the sight line of the youth and indicated her ticket.

The youth looked up. He did not remove his earplugs. 'Yeah?' he said, too loudly.

'Sorry, but I think this is my seat.' The 'sorry' was exquisite.

The youth removed one earplug and said, 'What?'

It was almost too much. I felt the bloke next to me tense, either because he was readying to intervene on behalf of the woman, or because he knew he ought to intervene but didn't dare.

'Sorry,' said the woman again, 'but . . .' and she pointed at her ticket once more, then let the sentence trail. The youth looked at the ticket, then at the running light display, sighed, replugged his ear, levered himself from the seat in grudging silence and moved along the carriage. The man next to me breathed out. The woman sat and settled like a nesting bird, keeping her eyes down, waiting for the spotlight that had so cruelly singled her out to dim and die. The trains may have changed but other things haven't.

Including the land. Beyond the train window, for much of the journey, it could be 1970. Were it not for the cars it could be Morton's 1926. North Oxfordshire looks as gentle as sleep. Irregular fields and hedges, patches of woodland, docile stock, brick villages on mounds rising to spires and a web of mud-brown waterways easing between banks of knee-deep lushness. It's the green tumescence of central England. Every inch of the land bears the imprint of *Homo sapiens sapiens*, but so old an imprint that it has come to seem natural.

This compressed and domesticated prettiness has always been my template of countryside. It is in comparison with land like this that I have instinctively assessed all the other land-scapes I have lived among, the moonscape of Aragon, the pines and mist of Canada's west coast, the rugged vastness of the South Island of New Zealand.

Mark's wife meets me at the station. Jenny has the looks of a fortune-teller and the zest of an entertainer. She takes me shop-ping in the multi-levelled fluorescent endlessness of shops that is the Bull Ring. It's mid-afternoon and the place is packed. Outside, the spring breeze has an edge, but in here the American ice-cream shop is doing good trade. The mall is the old high street made warm and comfy. It is easy to condemn but the people come. They like it. It sucks them in from the suburbs, from pensioner flats, from grim terraces, to a bright-lit world of safety, hygiene, consumption and convenience. It could be Singapore or New York.

Jenny is at home here. She shops with energy, riffling through clothes racks, holding stuff against herself and dis-missing it in seconds, buying a dozen unplanned presents for her daughter's birthday, clothes, toys, games, and anything she can find that relates to dolphins, all the while maintaining such a flow of chatter, self-mockery, questions, gossip, arm-touches, and sudden gales of gypsy laughter that I find myself infected by her gusto and am happy. Jenny enters the shops I would never enter, whose profitable existence I cannot under-stand: the fashion shops that I cannot distinguish from each other; the shops of trendy kiddies' clobber; even the gift shops whose very title confesses that you wouldn't buy their stuff for yourself.

The underground car park is brightly lit and doesn't smell of piss. As we emerge from the ramp into Birmingham traffic, the late-afternoon dullness comes as a shock. Through the brick-and-leaf suburbs we drive to Mark and Jenny's place.

When Mark opens the garage door and shows me the Audi I am alarmed. I was prepared for a solid and plush saloon. I was not prepared for a soft-topped sports car. The two seats are technology-laden armchairs upholstered in leather as soft as skin. The gear knob is the size of a stiff penis. The polished metal bulb at its tip indicates that this car has six forward gears. I am no driver. Speed and big engines scare me.

I have always travelled in a spartan fashion, moving, sleep-ing and eating as cheaply as possible. It's a form of snobbery, I suppose, but also a legacy of youth when the excitement of abroad was so intense that I would go with next to no money. This car affronts my notion of travel, or rather my notion of me as a traveller.

I know, however, from three days of fruitless thumbery that I need a car and this one's free. Moreover it is apt. Morton's car was a two-seater sports job as well. In rural villages in 1926 its arrival would have caused a fuss, and urchins would have sprinted alongside it in excited admiration. I doubt that the Audi will set today's urchins sprinting, but there is still some-thing of the same patrician feel to this beast.

*

Saturday morning and I shake Mark's hand, hug Jenny, say cheerio to the kids and nervously nose the Audi out of the drive. I feel that I'm sitting only inches from the tarmac, as if in a hugely costly go-kart. There are dials, in what I believe is called the binnacle, that I do not understand. Mark has shown me how to lower the roof but even as he showed me I knew that I would never dare. I'd be afraid that I would never get it back up.

I crawl through the suburbs, ceding the right of way to anyone who wants it – battered vans, bicycles, limping women with wheeled baskets. As I near the motorway I sense my hands tightening on the wheel, a drip slipping icily from my armpit to my shirt. That shirt was bought in the South Island of New Zealand, which is as big as England but which holds just a million people. The only motorway around Christchurch is two lanes in each direction for a few miles and then shrinks to one.

On the slip road the cars accelerate at a tangent to the wall of lorries. The acceleration is counter-intuitive, but gaps open with magical politesse and the two streams merge like the teeth on a zip. Most of the cars flick deftly through the lorries and into the hurtling lanes beyond. I don't. I am relieved simply to be part of the streaming stream, behind a Sainsbury's truck covered in close-up images of water-beaded oranges and in front of a car transporter. My rear-view mirror captures only the bottom third of its giant chromium face. I feel like punctuation between capital letters.

In the lane beside me the boredom of drivers and passengers is impressive. They are travelling at speeds that render this statistically the most dangerous activity of their week by far, yet their faces show only indifference.

I note without embarrassment that I am an object of slight interest, sat in the slow lane in a low-slung car that sings of speed. Passengers idly looking through their glass do a hint of a double-take as they pass me. What are they thinking, these people I shall never speak to but at whom I am free to stare from my cocoon of glass and steel? That I have stolen the Audi? That it is sick? Or that I am?

After a while, when I sense that I am being stared at, I turn and smile at the starer. Sometimes they smile back, or say something to the other occupants of the car and more eyes swing my way. I try different expressions. I try looking horrified and bewildered, and from a minivan of lads I get an excited riot of silent laughter, at me not with me. I try scowling and get a V-sign.

But the behaviour of the cars themselves is impeccably polite. The unspoken, unconscious fear of collision makes the motorway as courteous a place as a formal ball. The vehicles behave like well-bred adults. Everyone indicates his intentions. Those intentions are acknowledged and accommodated. Metaphorical doors are held open for those who wish to pass through them. Brakes are rarely touched, horns even more rarely. I have become a member of the most civil society in the land. Everyone does unto others as they would wish to be done unto.

I enter Warwickshire. A sign calls it Shakespeare's County. The motorway presents Warwickshire as if on a cinema screen. I hear nothing except car-noise, smell nothing except car-smell, touch nothing except bits of car, but I see a rolling stationary pageant of hedges, fields, stock, farmyards. Sheep graze untroubled just the other side of a post-and-rail fence, but the fence is an uncrossable barrier. It separates two utterly alien worlds. The country roads and lanes pass over or under the motorway, excluded from its devotion to movement. The lanes are somewhere, the motorway is nowhere, a placeless parallel kingdom with different rules, different police, different purposes. Its signs are different. No fingerposts here, no forgotten milestones half buried among grass and weeds. Here the signs are the size of rooms, written not in English but in international pictograms, gargantuan and simplified: fuel, food, toilets, beds.

When I was a kid, the county of my birth seemed a whole world. Now I cross Warwickshire in twenty minutes.

The service station where I stop for fuel is shielded from the rest of England by bulldozed hummocks of land. It's busy. The constantly fluctuating population must be that of a small village. But it is not an Enid Blyton village. A sign by the petrol pump warns me to lock my car before going ten yards to pay. And the sight of my fellow drivers grants a slight shock. These are the people who formed the faultless society of the road, as after-you courteous as a royal garden party. But now I watch them one by one as each stills his sleek vehicle and breaks its aerodynamic shape by opening a door and emerging to stretch. Each slowly spreads arms as if crucified, then jams knuckles into the lower back and arches the spine, rediscovering a pedestrian self. It's like a dragon-fly hatching in reverse. The driver goes from glorious chevalier of the road to lumbering grub, a slow flawed creature with a stained dress or a limp or a beer gut, a creature who stops without warning, or blunders into the path of others.

The main building is like a space station. Constantly resupplied from a different world, it offers everything to maintain the space travellers. Food for everyone, games for the kids, and a vast labyrinth of shining lavatories where listless workers are at it round the clock with a trolleyful of mops and cloths and disinfectant. Time is almost without meaning here. The Full-Monty Mega-Breakfast is always on and always popular. Eggs spit. A scrawny chef refills the serving vats with glistening sausages, a twenty-pound tangle of bacon, and a cascade of bread triangles, fried to snappability and the colour of ripe wheat. The people shuffle along the counter then sit to eat and smoke. No one knows anyone except the people they came with and will leave with. Beneath its low synthetic ceiling the place heaves with anonymity and noise.

It's Saturday. A huge double-deck coach pulls up and disgorges a throng of males. Most are unattached, twenty- or
thirty-something, but among them are sons with fathers and
grandfathers. The sons, the fathers and the unattached are all
wearing white football jerseys with a wide red V where a mayoral chain would hang. The grandfathers are wearing informal
chain-store clothes. All are St Helens Rugby League Club sup-
porters, heading I don't know where to watch a game against I
don't know whom. The unattached are carrying lager and are
morning-beer boisterous, happy, loud, pushing at each other
like schoolboys. All are white. Most have tits. They head as
one for the gents then the breakfast. The last man off the bus is
the driver. He drags two massive clear sacks crammed with
cans. It is ten in the morning. I drive on.

M5, M42, M40, road names without places, complete unto
themselves, carving through the land, through hills, with me
growing braver and inhabiting the middle lane. It's the middle
of the road for middle-of-the-road people.

The outside lane is like the back of a classroom. It's where
the unruly dwell, the ones less familiar with fear, the ones
whose cars say something about them and whose speed says
even more. The Audi suits the outside lane, but I don't. When
circumstance forces me out there, I feel like a fish in air and am
anxious to flip back to my element.

In less than two hours I am bypassing Newbury on the A34.
Each road has merged with the next. I've traversed four counties and not once have I been obliged to stop, or even to drop
below fifty.

The A34 is indeed unhitchable. What distinguishes it from a
motorway I can't tell. Just beyond unseen Newbury I turn off,
conscious as I do so of a warm slug of pleasure, for now I can
follow Morton's route more intimately. I shall start with
Coombe Gibbet. I've never seen a gibbet.

According to Morton, 'On March 7th 1676, a man and a

woman were hanged on this gibbet and their bodies exposed as a warning to all sinners. Their names were George Browman and Dorothy Newman, and they were hanged for the brutal murder of two children which the woman had borne to a former husband. The children's bodies were discovered in the little hill-pond near the gallows.'

When Morton visited the gibbet, 'the wind tore through it, screamed past it, so that I had to hold on to it.' It won't be like that on this balmy day, but if it still stands I am keen to find it. All places of death are of interest, and a place of premeditated judicial death feels especially juicy.

After the unrelenting pace of the motorways the lanes of Hampshire salve the mind. They are so narrow, so empty, so greenly quiet. A cock pheasant struts into the road and then turns to walk down the middle. I slow twenty-thousand-quid's worth of German engineering to the pheasant's pace. The bird is like a Chinese vase with wings. Nearby, its hen is head-down dowdy, creeping businesslike in the hedge's foot.

Little patches of copse are bright with bluebells and prim-roses. The lanes wind like loose string, baffling my sense of direction, leading me away, I feel, from Coombe. I pass through two villages, both drenched in midday silence, and offering me no one to ask directions of. In Aldmansworth I draw up beside a man in a quilted green vest. Even as I brake I can tell that he likes the Audi, is happy to speak to me because of it.

His accent is not of place but of status. It purrs with income and I hear my own accent revving up through the tax brackets to meet it. I always do that in England, approximately matching the class of anyone I'm with. It's a form of social chameleonship that is rooted in cowardice. In New Zealand I don't do it.

'Ah, yes, Coombe Gibbet,' he says. 'Fuck 'em then straight on.'

'I'm sorry?'

'Just along the lane there, turn right to fuck 'em, then straight on.'

'Fuck 'em then straight on?'

'That's right. You can't miss it.'

There's a sign at the entry to the village of Faccombe. 'SLOW', it says. 'Drive carefully. Children playing.' There are no children playing. There are no children doing anything else either. Faccombe is so achingly well kept, so stockbroker lovely, it seems unlikely that any children live there, and that if they did they would be discouraged from playing. I see only flint garden walls, spent daffs and a man and a woman tending the pretty graveyard. Both straighten backs to watch the Audi pass. Both are wearing quilted jackets.

A little beyond Faccombe I pull over onto a rutted car park. I seem to have missed the unmissable gibbet. The Audi, built for autobahns, graunches on chalk. I wince, ease the car forward and stop. A middle-aged couple turn at the graunch and hold their heads still like interrupted cattle, staring, assessing. They are several income brackets below a quilted vest. Their car is a modest thing, a middle-lane car, a suburban ordinariness. They have binoculars and thick socks and day packs and walking sticks like ski poles and a dented Thermos flask with a dense crisscross pattern on its body. I recognize the Thermos. We had one of the same design when I was a child.

'Is there a gibbet round here?' I say, aware as I speak not only that my accent has once again sought to match the imagined income of the addressees, but also that 'Is there a gibbet round here?' is a sentence I have probably never spoken before. Furthermore I am not confident that these people will know what a gibbet is, and if they don't, I'm not sure I want to go through the bother of explaining. But I needn't have worried.

'You mean Coombe Gibbet?' says the man.

I want to ask if Hampshire offers an array of gibbets, but don't.

The man directs me up a track. Thirty yards on I'm thrown forty years back. I'm on the South Downs of Sussex in shorts and a Terylene shirt with my mother and Rebel the dog, hunting for flint arrow heads and never finding any, and hunting too for wild flowers which my mother would unfailingly identify. For this is downland and only downland is like this. This is the turf for which the adjective springy was coined. Black-faced sheep on delicate legs graze audibly at its springiness. The track across it is worn to mud and chalk and knobbles of flint. Air comes no fresher than this air and the watercolour sky is alive with sky larks, insignificant birds that climb to a thousand feet and trill like dripping strawberries. It's the sweetest bird noise in the world and it doesn't matter that what they're trilling is the avian equivalent of fuck off.

Awash with nostalgia I climb a crest and suddenly I am not alone. It's Saturday and here, where three tracks meet, I see hikers in hiking gear and bikers in biking gear and signs announcing that this is a take-off point for hang-gliders in hang-gliding gear.

But there, on the ridge ahead, stands the gibbet. It is stark against the sky. I'd expected an inverted L, like the shape you draw when playing hangman. But this is a T, its upstroke maybe twenty feet tall, its short cross beam supported by a pair of struts. The thing looks about as forbidding as a stick.

And, according to a laminated information board, a stick is what it is. This gibbet never hanged a man. The original did, but it has since rotted and been replaced, not once, but several times. But the worn track that leads to it suggests it has retained enough gruesomeness to attract plenty of visitors. The information board tells those visitors all they need to know about the gibbet and the Neolithic barrow on which it stands but I doubt that Hayden, Paul, Becki and Toni read it. For 'Hayden, Paul, Becki and Toni woz ere,' it says in clumsy marker pen, '14 Feb 2001.' The 14th of Feb is Valentine's Day. Love and death, those sturdy old companions. But I can't say that I get a gust of either.

I gaze down over the small chequered plain of north Hampshire for a while, say good afternoon to dog walkers who say good afternoon back, say good afternoon to hikers who say good afternoon back, say good afternoon to Coombe Gibbet and head back down the hill to the Audi, Fuck 'em and the A34.

Winchester's a pretty nightmare. The streets are thick with traffic. I want to stop. The one-way system wants me to move. I circle the town centre twice, growing hot at the neck, feeling my fingers clench on the wheel, then find a queue for a multistorey car park. I manage the ramp and ticket business at only the second attempt, spiral up through the building's damp and underlit heart, spiral back down through its damp and underlit heart, start up it once more, find a space, and, with my skull screaming warnings about the Audi's lustrous body work, I execute a deft seventeen-point parking manoeuvre, blocking as I do so a stream of cars like a jam jar of wasps, all frantic to continue spiralling.

It's a relief to open the Audi door a foot and slither through the gap, edging past a concrete pillar that's been nibbled and decorated by a hundred car doors, and make footfall into England's original capital. The place is thronged. It takes half an hour to find the information centre and an hour for the information centre to find me a bed.

'Why so busy?' I ask the charmingly frazzled woman.

'It's the weekend,' she says, which explains everything. She eventually finds me a room at a hotel by the railway station. I walk there. The room is tiny but the bed looks good. I stretch out on it to test its softness. When I wake up, it's dark and I'm hungry.

I dine on three pounds ninety-nine's worth of fish and chips, which I eat at the feet of King Alfred. He is carved in bronze and acting as a traffic island. His statue reminds me of someone I know. It's only as I mop up the last vinegary flakes of cod and the brittle salty shards of chips that I realise that King Alfred, scourge of the Danes, uniter of the English, is a dead ringer for Billy Connolly.

5

Old Stuff and Rooney

Remember *Ask the Family*? The bumptious Robert Robinson put questions to a couple of families that each comprised two parents and two children. Presumably there were other children left at home and what that did to their psyches isn't hard to guess, but the ones at home were the lucky ones. The kids who appeared on screen, hair smarmed, ties tied, spectacles planted with concrete permanence on the nose, were hard

49

to endure and harder to forget. Even the Famous Five would have wanted to beat them up.

It wasn't the kids' fault of course, the parents being profoundly culpable for exposing their darlings to the glaring light of ridicule before they had the self-awareness to say no, but oh it was awful. My recurrent nightmare was that my parents might write to the BBC and enter. I know now that they would never have been such fools, but at the time it terrified me, because I knew, just knew, that in front of the camera I would have behaved precisely like the know-alls I so despised. If I'd got an answer right, I would have tried to look modest but would have looked smug. If wrong I would have argued or sulked. Or rather argued then sulked.

But anyway, *Ask the Family* is back, apparently. And according to the *Daily Mail* it reveals the state of the nation. In 1974 Robert Robinson asked questions such as, 'What is the connection between Rugby School and "Sohrab and Rustum"?' and, 'Travelling due north from Accra, what is the first capital city you would meet?' In 2005 Robert Robinson's successor asks, 'How many children would a woman have if she had quintuplets?' and 'In what year did Muffin the Mule make his final appearance on television?' Firm evidence, says the *Mail*, that England is in terminal social decline.

At half-past six on a Sunday morning in April, Winchester doesn't look in terminal social decline. It looks lovely. The air is breath-misting cold. The sky is as clear as peace of mind.

Morton got a similar morning. 'It was that lovely time in early spring', he wrote, 'when the world, it seems, is swept and garnished for a festival. As I walked through the empty streets, I wondered when the citizens of Winchester, now snuggling down into that last self-indulgent half-hour of bed, would realise their folly and, opening their doors, come tumbling out to go a-Maying.'

I don't wonder quite the same myself, partly because I'm not sure what's involved in going a-Maying and partly because it is

April, but I can see what he was getting at, and 'swept and garnished' is bang right.

On either side of Parchment Street the plumbing is starting to gurgle, but only the street cleaner is about, driving his little tractor with its rotating walrus moustaches that efficiently shift the cigarette butts from one point in the gutter to another. I follow Morton's footsteps inevitably to the cathedral close. Just as in his day it is dotted with limes, their leaflets a gauze of green that the sun might dissolve. That same low sun turns the cathedral's flank to honey and flashes suddenly off buckled windows. My shadow is long on the dew-bright grass and my footmarks are black. I go and stand on Jane Austen.

Her marble tombstone is set in the cathedral floor. '. . . the benevolence of her heart, the sweetness of her temper, and the extraordinary endowments of her mind obtained the regard of all who knew her . . .' No mention of her novels but I bet they got her this plot.

When Morton came here he got a guided tour from an animated verger. I don't, and don't want to. Instead and delightfully, I have the football-pitch-sized cavernousness of the cathedral to myself, but for a single cleric who clip-clops past me in a surplice on his way to attend to some candles. At a distance he looks like a black shuttlecock. I sit on a chair over the grave of Nicholas Pyle who died three days before Christmas in 1715 and has been here since. I try to identify what I like about this place.

I like the way my cough echoes beneath the ancient roof, is magnified, then swallowed. I like the uneven medieval floor tiles, a cloppy sea of frozen stone. I like the effigy on the tombstone of Bishop Fox who had been secretary to Henry VIII. It shows him lying naked, withered and either agonized or dead, with one hand on his crotch. I like the sense of separateness, the invitation to sit and think. And I like the unfrantic temperature, the unshopness, the nave as wide as a motorway, the dwarfing waste of space between me and the ceiling. If this were a car park it would have a dozen storeys. Above all, I like the sense of sousedness, of steepedness.

In this and similar buildings Morton saw a pageant of the past, endowed with romance and mysticism. He saw the first Christian missionaries, the Saxon kings, the Norman builders. I don't. I just get a sense of insignificance and of sanctuary. For me, it's Larkin's 'serious house on serious earth'.

I poke around for a bit, not stepping over the purple rope that cordons off the altar, reading plaques, noting famous names and elaborate carving and ancient shrines and the bones of kings, but I learn nothing I'll retain. I leave through the monster door and am back in the morning where the clock restarts.

I leave and walk down past King Connolly to a bridge over a river so shallow-sweet and clear and rippling that I turn along the towpath in the hope of glimpsing fish. The river turns out to be the Itchen, perhaps the most famous and expensive trout stream in England. I see no trout.

The lane is flanked by a tall flint wall, and basking in the sun on top of it a single duck, a mallard drake, its folded wing tips a magenta brilliance, its head and neck like feathered petrol. Nearby stands a house made famous by having Jane Austen die in it. A handwritten, sun-faded postcard, Blu-tacked to the window, explains that this is 'a private home and not open to the general public'. You can see the exasperation in the tautology and even in the handwriting. I don't know what the general public would hope to find inside. Hairs on the pillow, perhaps, or ink stains? Or anything at all to give a little thrill by proxy, to suggest something greater than the here and the now and the dull.

I follow the Itchen out of town and through water meadows where the nettles are rimed with frost, the buttercups profuse and the Private Fishing notices ignored by the moorhens. The morning feels fresh-minted. I bounce through the wet grass. In the not-too-great distance I can hear the rumble of the invisible

M3, already busy, but the water meadow remains a lazy sweetness.

I pass the playing fields of Winchester College, and with a
jolt of recognition I realize that I played cricket here once as a
schoolboy for a junior county side. I could still recite the team
list more or less. I am in touch with none of those team-mates
now, the threads all broken between us, all of us making our
way separately and as best we can, all of us riveted into each
other's memory as sixteen-year-olds with hair and zest and
unlined faces, and all of us now approaching fifty, our skin
gone pouchy, our hair gone west. If we met in the street we
wouldn't recognize each other.

I can't remember the result of the game, or who we were
playing, or even whether I scored runs or took wickets. But I do
remember a catch. There, by that tree, I ran to chase a skyer, my
hair an orange oriflamme, my lungs unkippered by smoke, my
eye as keen as a kestrel's, and I remember knowing with concrete certainty that I would make the catch. It was more than a
knowledge; it was a body-sense, an absolute security, that right
now I can still feel the ghost of. I duly took the catch.

A few months ago in New Zealand a similar skyer went up.
I was keeping wicket so I had gloves to make the catch easy. I
will not go into detail. All I will say is that one or two of my
team-mates were kind enough not to giggle.

I cross a walled field where a woman calls a joyous retriever
to keep away from me, and I am outside the Hospital of St
Cross and Almshouse of Noble Poverty founded in 1136.
Morton wrote of meeting a foul-mouthed tramp hurrying
along this path to this hospital to claim his 'wayfarer's dole', a
handout of bread and beer, free to anyone who asked for it. I
wouldn't mind some bread and beer myself, having left the
hotel without breakfast, but a notice at the gate declares that the
hospital is closed on Sunday.

I stand a while and stare through the gate at a silent flint and
stone courtyard and mossy roofs. There's a rich and settled

contentment here, a deep-sunk rootedness. Land and buildings have settled together like an old couple in the hollow of a
mattress. It's lovely to look at but I couldn't live here. I find it
somehow cloying and oppressive. It puts me instantly in mind
of a school I taught at for two terms perhaps a hundred miles
from here.

It was a private school. The kids were fine but the staff
depressed me. I suggested once to the deputy head that we
change some detail of the organization of cricket. 'Joe,' he said,
his vowels emphatic, 'I've been doing it this way for twenty-
five years,' and it was clear that he considered his argument to
be both satisfactory and conclusive. I went to New Zealand.

Back in town the streets have filled. In the cathedral close are
gaggles of white-haired women dipping their beaks into history and towing mute husbands. Subdued Labs and collies
walk on leads at Sunday pace, stride for stride with their
owners' Englishness, tails swinging like slow rudders. The sun
has dried the grass and groups of the young are sitting on it,
creating a pretty image like a prospectus photograph of a university campus. I pass within earshot of a group of lounging
undergraduates. 'If I'd of fucking went,' says one, 'I'd of ended
up fucking spewing.'

'Fuck yeah,' replies another.

There are small mobs of French schoolchildren who contrive
to be simultaneously boisterous and bored, but most of the
crowd is English. A chromium obelisk has drawn the attention
of the young. It proves to be an interactive artwork installation.
Its surface is dotted with bulbs. When you send it a text message it lights up. Some children are repeatedly sending it text
messages. It is repeatedly lighting up. It is terribly exciting.

On the other side of the cathedral stands a Barbara
Hepworth sculpture called *Homage to Mondrian*. 'The red, white
and yellow colourings form a pattern evocative of pain, purity
and deity,' says an informative plaque. 'Notice the dynamic

balance of the whole achieved through the various parts. The
partial openness of the work draws the cosmos into its scope
and allows us to rest within it.' About which I shall say only
two things. One is that before being inscribed on the plaque,
these words must somehow have passed the scrutiny of I don't
know how many people and subcommittees without a single
person stopping, slapping the table and saying, 'Oh, come off
it.' The second is that any art requiring an explanatory plaque
does not deserve one.

The close is sprinkled with graves, on most of which the
words have been blanked by time and air and friction. But one
remains fresh. 'In memory of Thomas Thatcher a Grenadier in
the North Regt. of Hants Militia who died of a violent fever
contracted by drinking Small Beer when hot the 12th of May
1764. Aged 26 years.' The words remain fresh because the stone
has been replaced three times, most recently in 1968. The reason
this stone has been replaced is that time has transmuted this
young man's death into something delicious. It's the gibbet
once more.

I tread the streets a while, drawn like everybody else to the
older bits that shout their quaintness: Elizabethan casement
windows, so heavily lead-lighted they seem close to opaque, an
eroded market cross, the pub that claims to be the oldest in
England. In the Great Hall I gaze, as Morton gazed, on the
Arthurian Round Table that isn't Arthurian. It's an impressive
thing weighing over a ton, but it's a Tudor fake. Myth-making
to impress visitors is nothing new.

A nearby jeweller's window has a display of Lilliput Lane
ceramics. They are porcelain recreations of English rusticity, all
thatched cottages and hollyhocks and duck ponds and
Elizabethan casement windows and Mrs Bumcleft the baker's
wife. They evoke John Major's vision of England in which spin-
sters cycle to evensong past cricket on the village green. Lilliput
Lane ceramics are deemed collectibles but are more honestly
religious icons. They represent an ideal. To what extent Morton

is responsible for confirming that ideal in the English psyche, or even for establishing it, I'm not sure. All I am sure of is that Lilliput Lane ceramics are terribly expensive and, to my eye, hideous.

Winchester was the first capital of what was more or less England, and its ruins sing of power. Hard by the cathedral stand the tumbledown fortifications of Wolvesey Castle. Though heavily fortified it was the official residence of the bishop. Further up the hill stand military museums, law courts and the remains of a later castle. In other words, the throne, the church, the law and the army were all gathered in the one place, and who is to say that they don't all represent the same thing? And who is to say that it isn't the vestigial power of authority that draws the crowds to Winchester this spring weekend to poke around its crumbling relics like peasants paying homage? And who is to say that even the cathedral wasn't built as a boast and a warning, an assertion that the King had a friend with a capital F with whom it was wise not to tangle? And who is to say when I've asked enough rhetorical questions? I am.

By late afternoon the day has clouded, its spring gloss all gone. I'm foot-weary and thirsty. The pub is not the oldest pub in England, but a Victorian thing that has undergone a sleek modern refit. The floor is polished pine. There are sofas to lounge on and knee-height tables to stand drinks on and a computer to surf the Net on. I type Lilliput Lane into the search engine and discover that these visions of hollyhocked rusticity can be acquired direct from the manufacturer at an enchanting little spot called Kingstown Industrial Estate.

On the big screen I catch the last ten minutes of the FA Cup semi-final between Manchester United and Newcastle. It's already decided. The Manchester fans are singing like a huge cathedral choir. 'There's only one Wayne Rooney,' they sing. Uniqueness is an attribute that Rooney shares with, among other people, God.

I have never met Wayne Rooney, so what I am about to say is based on appearance and manner only and is therefore probably unjust. But this footballing prodigy looks to me to be exactly the sort of paste-faced brute that no teacher wants to find at the back of his fifth-form class.

The pub has won an award or two for something or other. The landlord is bright, efficient, well-spoken, industrious and absurdly young. When I tell him that the pub doesn't fit my image of a pub, nor he my image of a publican, he is delighted. He believes, he says, in hard work and ambition though these have become unfashionable. Class too. 'What's wrong with class?' he says. 'Gives you something to aspire to. This accent of mine was paid for by my parents.'

He is overtly keen on politics. 'Maggie gave the country purpose. Since then it's just drifted. Blair's all fart and no shite.'

I tell the landlord that I see him becoming a Tory MP. He reminds me of Sebastian Coe. 'Who knows?' he says. 'One thing about the English is we apologize for having opinions. We're self-effacing. That's good in a way, of course. It means we're confident of our skill bases, because of our education system, though that's another thing that's going to shite. Did you see that thing in the *Mail* about *Ask the Family*?' Even though I say yes, he goes upstairs to fetch it.

By the time he's back I'm in a round with Charles and Tony. Both were privately educated. Both once belonged to a regiment that guards palaces and wears bearskins. Both have the confident voice of class. But Tony is Welsh. 'I cried when Wales won the Grand Slam,' he says in his English accent.

Charles is drinking treble gins. He is within twenty-four hours of becoming a father. He keeps saying he must return to his wife, then orders another drink. To take his mind off the plunge into the deepest waters of life I ask him about bearskins. Apparently they are still the skins of bears. To be precise, they are the belly skin of the Canadian brown bear, and nothing else will do.

Moreover, in combination with the red tunic, bearskins are a passport to sexual success. 'You just can't go wrong,' says Charles in a wistful manner. Then, as if a switch has been flicked in his head, he bangs the last glass of irresponsible living down on the bar, turns with the smartness that befits a former Guardsman, opens the door, shuts it again, comes back to the bar and says, 'Just one more.' He has two more. He has to. The second one is his round.

I had almost forgotten about the iron-clad fixities of the English round system. A round is a tightly defined group but it is not referred to. It grows organically. One can join it only by buying into it. It is an unspoken point of honour that no glass in a round should ever be empty. And it is an infallible method of ensuring that you spend more than you drink. How that works out I don't know, but while it always seems to me that there is nowhere in a round to hide, a glance at the wallet in the morning reveals that someone who wasn't you was drinking your money.

It is also a means of exclusion. It is possible to refuse a drink from a third party because you are 'in a round'. The expression is spoken to mean, and understood by all but the most obtuse to mean, piss off.

Charles eventually forces himself to go. As he turns to leave, James takes his hand in both his own and shakes it. For men in a pub it's an extraordinary expression of emotion.

The moment the door finally closes on Charles, we talk about him. 'I've never seen him so nervous,' says James. But we agree that having a child is a huge step, heaving you permanently one rung up the evolutionary ladder, endowing you with an investment in the future. 'It changes your whole world,' says James, 'the way you work, the way you think, the way you vote.'

'Increase or dilution?' I say, paraphrasing a line from Larkin, more to myself than to James. It happens so often that Larkin pops into my head when the big and simple things arise.

'Ah, Larkin,' says James, astonishingly, and then, even more astonishingly, 'what will survive of us is love.'

I am delighted, but I have to put him right. Those words, so often quoted by the squidgy-hearted, most recently by the Archbishop of Canterbury at some high-up funeral, are invariably wrenched from their context. The line that precedes and undercuts them is never mentioned.

But it's a joy to share a pleasure in a writer. We enthuse about Larkin and then about Waugh. James loves *Brideshead*. 'It's brilliant but flawed,' I say. 'It isn't the Catholic apologia that Waugh was trying to write. It's a love story. And only the first third truly works.'

'I want to fuck Sebastian,' says James, who is clearly as straight as a motorway. 'But not Julia.'

'Exactly,' I say. 'My round, I think.'

I am often asked if there is anything I miss about England. There isn't. I have lived so long abroad that I don't yearn. If I did, I'd come back. But there are some things that I relish when I do come back and one of those is pubs. The first pub I remember was the Eight Bells at Jevington. I never went inside it, but my mother and father did after my father had played cricket. My brother and I were left outside, sitting on a flint wall that overlooked a field of huge pigs.

Every so often the door of the pub would open and release a belch of smoke and rich adult laughter, unrestrained and wholly good. Sometimes I would make out my father's laugh. He wasn't a man much given to laughing. What happened inside the Eight Bells was a mysteriously fine thing.

When I grew old enough to pierce the mystery, I was not disappointed. I liked pubs from the outset. I liked the neutrality of the territory. It was somewhere you went with friends for no purpose but to be with friends. I liked the extra intensity of emotion generated by the gradual ingestion of a drug, I liked the laughter and I liked the honesty that came with it. In short I was and am more often happy in the pub, overtly, smilingly happy, than in any other place.

I also liked the beer. I began with shandy, went on to bottled Guinness, graduated to bitter and stayed there.

Beer in the rest of the world is fine. It does the job. But it isn't bitter. It is yellow, too fizzy and too cold. Even when small breweries overseas claim to have replicated English bitter, they still serve it too cold. For me, the taste of a warm, flat, thin pint of bitter is the thing that tells me I am home.

When my sister read my last book she said that it underlined a gulf between us: I drank and she didn't. It made us different types of people. She may be right.

I rarely drink in my own house, but I do go to pubs, both at home and when travelling. I can't imagine what other travellers do in the evenings, though I have seen a million tourist couples sitting in restaurants and looking bored to within an inch or two of death.

Because I shall go to many pubs on this trip, I shall get a skewed view of English people. I shall meet more men than women, and those men will not be representative. But for one thing I don't care, and for another I am more likely in pubs than anywhere else to mine a little deeper into people, to get beneath the carapace of courtesy and into the quick of honesty. For alcohol lowers defences. And especially in England those defences are stout, and the passing visitor rarely penetrates beyond them. But in pubs, 'Good evening', can mean 'Let's talk'. In pubs, 'How are you?' can actually be a question.

Much has been written about the English pub. A lot of it is romantic tosh, a sort of Enid Blyton for drinkers. Many pubs are dire – foul-smelling, poorly staffed, televisioned and juke-boxed. The walls are lined with fruit machines, and the bar with louts. But in good ones, like this one in Winchester, they remain what they began as, places to mix, places to be without restraint, vents for truth and laughter, the necessary flipside of an ordered and civilized society and the social awkwardness that comes with it. I can think of no other venue where Charles and James and I would have fallen so easily into conversation, or learned so much of each other in so short a time. Pubs please me. I have a lovely evening.

6

Conceal Your Wants

All pleasure must be paid for. I wake at six and run a health
check without moving. The body seems sound, though
granular with hangover. I shake my head slowly. On the worst
mornings it feels as if the brain is moored in some gelatinous
fluid and it bumps slowly against the side of the skull. This
morning it just feels shrouded in a fumbling gauze of inaccu-
racy. I run through the events of last night, checking for

misdeeds, for the regrettable. Nothing. I remember lurching happily back up Parchment Street, lit with booze and singing. I was drenched once again in the sense I have always loved when travelling, a sense of being alone and insignificant and unstoppably free. The insignificance is as important as the freedom. I like the fact that nobody knows I am here, that I am beholden to no one, bound by no relationships, no duty, no expectations. I am free simply to rove and look at and taste the world. I can still feel the ghost of that feeling this morning, though the legacy of booze deglosses it a little.

I get up to piss. There is a flesh-coloured cellular blanket thrown over the toe of the bed. It wasn't there yesterday, but it evokes a little pang of recognition that I can find no reason for. We had blankets like that at home when I was a child, unsatisfactory things that provided warmth without the corresponding comfort of weight, but it is not this ancient familiarity that chimes with me. I make an instant coffee, get back into bed, feel the urge to smoke, and am briefly tempted to break the rules and smoke in the room, but there is no window to lean from, and on the ceiling next to the skylight is something that looks like a smoke alarm. When I bend to put on trousers I feel a sudden sea-swell of nausea. I decide against doing up my shoelaces.

In the hotel lobby the young Spanish-looking porter smirks at me. I smile back unconvincingly. Was he on duty when I came in last night? I don't believe so, but I sense that I know him, as if he were a distant half-forgotten school friend. I smile weakly back. His smirk intensifies.

I sit on an ivy-covered wall by the bus park to smoke. The wood pigeons are gurgling. I feel myself reviving in the cool air, shivering my way out of the gauze cocoon of last night. A driver steps from the door of his huge white tour bus, lays a scrap of carpet on the asphalt, gets down on his knees and places his forehead on the ground in the vague direction of the low thin sun. I bet Morton didn't see that in Winchester.

Monday morning feels markedly different to Sunday morning. I walk a while, recuperating, travelling slower on the
pavement than the work-bound. I was told last night that
Winchester had become a dormitory town for London, but
there's an abundance of people going to work right here in town
on foot. The clothes give clues to their lives – jacket and tie, dress
and coat, donkey jacket and jeans, briefcases, hand bag, duffle
bag – but their faces give little away. A thousand cryptic auto-
biographies pass me on the street, saying nothing. The thought
of them all going to work and of me not does my health good.

The key to my hotel room is an electronic card. I slide it into the
slot on the door and nothing happens. I turn it over, try it again,
turn it back, then give in and return to the lobby. The Spanish-
looking porter is on the desk.

'My key,' I say, waving it, 'it doesn't work.'

'Is the new one?' asks the porter.

'The new one?'

'I give you new one this morning, two o'clock.' He is smiling
with complicity. I am about to deny it, to insist that there has
been some mistake, when I sense a memory breaking the surface like a sea creature, its identity not immediately obvious,
but its presence insistent and unignorable. Then it rises fully
formed from the water and I remember.

It's happened to me before. I wake in a strange room, desperate to piss, but fuddled with booze and sleep. I am
convinced that I am elsewhere, my own house perhaps or some
dream house, and that a certain door is the door to the loo. In
Canada once I pissed on a cupboardful of newly imported
cricket bats.

Last night the delusion led me into the hotel corridor and my
door closed automatically behind me, and locked. I was naked.
In a cupboard at the end of the corridor I found a cellular blanket, and went down to reception with it wrapped around my
waist, where the same Spanish porter . . .

'Christ,' I say, 'I'm sorry. I forgot.'

'Is OK,' he says, 'you are drunk,' and he laughs openly with strong white teeth. He's a good lad. And his sight of my half-asleep and all-but-naked self stumble-drunking downstairs to get a key in the middle of the night must have afforded him a laugh. Hotel work, I suppose, offers constant similar glimpses. The majority of guests will always come and go decorously, hiding the dirty linen of themselves behind their locked doors, but every now and then the soiled imperfect self will peep out, will proffer a peek-a-boo of comic absurdity. I resolve to write a novel about working in a hotel, a startling novel full of the frailties that lie just beneath the cloak of civilized behaviour. The resolution endures all the way to breakfast and then, like a thousand others, dissolves into coffee. And anyway they did it on *Crossroads*.

On the way from Winchester to Romsey, Morton saw a car on a bridge and a pretty girl beside it. He stopped.

'Could you lend me half a pint of petrol?' said the pretty girl.

'I could not lend you half a pint of petrol,' said Morton. 'But I could and will give you two gallons.'

She protested. He insisted. What Morton wanted to say, but didn't, was: 'Lady, the essence of chivalry is the joy of performing a service for an entire sex – your sex, of course – because had you been a man I would have called you a glaring ass to travel on a dry tank and have charged you double. Also, had you worn spectacles, been spotty or possessed rabbit teeth or legs like a Norman nave, I would still with almost the same alacrity have given you two gallons of petrol. The fact that you are utterly delicious and can flicker your eyes so charmingly adds pleasure without altering the ethics of the act.'

And no, I am not about to accuse him of sexism or patronage or condescension. He was of his time. What interests me is that beneath this knight-errant pomposity there crackles a bushfire of sex. Indeed that bushfire crackles just beneath the whole text of *In Search of England*. I don't remember noticing it at sixteen. At forty-seven, I couldn't ignore it.

I don't know whether any of Morton's flirting led to anything, and if it had he certainly wouldn't have written about it, but the association between travel and sex is obvious. Travel frees the traveller from constraints, from his social mores, from his neighbours' gaze. Part of the charm of going has always been the sexual possibilities it affords, at least to the mind. The travel agencies know it. Advertisements for holidays are awash with flesh. Travel is titillatory. And yet how rarely have I read any travel writer who has said as much.

More honest was a middle-aged bricklayer I worked with on a building site in London many years ago. In the pub one lunchtime he offered to show me his holiday snaps. I submitted with the obligatory faked enthusiasm. There were no landscapes. The snaps had all been taken in a hotel room. I had to turn them round and round in my hand to work out which naked limbs belonged to whom. It helped that the bricklayer was an exceptionally hairy man.

In Romsey, Morton found a statue of Lord Palmerston, and a man crossing the square with a cow. Palmerston's still there, but if a man and cow tried to cross the square today, either he or the cow, or quite possibly both, would die. The narrow central streets are choked with cars and trucks.

The roof of each truck passes perilously close to an iron bracket protruding from the wall above the Romsey Working Men's Conservative Club. 'It is recorded', says a sign beneath, 'that in 1642 2 soldiers of Cromwell's army were hanged from the wrought iron sign bracket on this wall. This bracket is a good example of old Hampshire wrought iron work.'

Just round the corner stands Miss Moody's Tudor Tea Room, built around 1250. The window lintel is at shoulder height. The timber-framed walls buckle and bulge. The tablecloths are gingham and the customers all white-haired.

Morton came to Romsey for the surprisingly large abbey. There he met a seventy-six-year-old churchwarden who looked fifty-five and who ascribed his apple-cheeked wellbeing to the peace of mind that came with a sedate and rural English life. In the abbey Morton found impressive Norman architecture and a couple of picturesque local legends. 'In the little whisperings and creakings that go on when an old church has shut its doors', concludes Morton, 'you can fancy old memories are stirring, so that you almost expect to meet Aedgyth, pale and trembling, or holy Ethelflaeda, cloaked like Monna Vanna, going to her cold bath with a psalmbook.'

I am accosted on entry by a man and a woman in matching capes. 'We show people around and look after the place,' says the man. 'I mean you've got to these days, haven't you?'

'It's a pity,' says the woman, 'but it's the way things are, isn't it? Is there anything you're particularly interested in?'

There isn't. I don't know my architecture and I am deaf to the stirring of old memories. As I tread the cold old flagstones, stopping to note only a memorial to Mountbatten and another to Bob Ward aged twenty-four who went down with the *Titanic*, I reflect that if I follow Morton too closely I shall often find myself much at a loss like this.

But I am eager to see the subject of Morton's next chapter, the village of Buckler's Hard. I have heard mention of it nowhere else and it sounds like nothing I have ever seen. Dodging the caped informers at the door, and pretending not to see the donations box, I return to the Audi.

The route leads through the New Forest. Once or twice in my childhood we came on holiday here. It seemed then an unthinkably distant place, a different landscape, a fabled for-eign land. Forty years on, the world has shrunk. If I turned the Audi round now I could be at the door of my childhood home in time for lunch.

Alice Liddell lived much of her life in Lyndhurst and is buried there. She was Lewis Carroll's Alice. That may or may not have been good for her. Today, I suspect, it might attract the attention of the social services. But now, of course, she is celebrated by a Mad Hatter's Tea Room, and, in the hotel, by a Tweedledum Suite and a Tweedledee Suite about which I plan to say nothing for fear of becoming shrill.

Lyndhurst also has a Ferrari showroom, and too many cars in general and an abundance of hikers. They have hiking boots with fat laces and hook-around eyelets, and hiking socks and hiking sticks and they wear muted hiking colours and they carry hiking maps in plastic bags designed for hiking and have a hiking compass round the neck on camouflaged hiking string and the land that they hike through is as tame as a garden. It's just patches of scrub and gorse, boggy bits, and miles of gentle woodland that give way at intervals to unfenced pasture cropped by herds of the friendly indigenous ponies. Each pony looks as if it's swallowed a barrel.

I send a postcard to my mother, in acknowledgement of those innocent ancient holidays. A camp site welcomes 'Campers with own toilets only' and with a surge of sensory memory I recall the chemical toilet in the family caravan, the ferocious blue liquid that went into it, and how the bowl filled gradually over a week until turds floated in perilous proximity to the rim, like half-submerged seals. Then my father would sigh volcanically and with undisguised distaste would clamp a metal lid on the thing and heave it from its moorings and lug it away, striving as he walked to keep its awful weight from banging against his leg. I can remember the sound of sloshing. Ah, romance.

Buckler's Hard is a village artificially created in the eighteenth century on a bank of the Beaulieu River. It existed to build ships. According to Morton, between 1745 and 1808, over forty men-of-war were built and launched here, including ships that fought at Trafalgar. For him this was the very stuff of romance. In 1926 the British Empire was still vast and not a thing to apologize for. Despite the recent horrors of the

Great War, there was still a glory attached to conquest and dominion.

Morton found Buckler's Hard desolate and forgotten. I find it has been christened Buckler's Hard Historic Village.

I have to drive beyond the village to a gravel car park that is larger than the village, then walk back along a wheelchair-enabled path, past the gift shop and the tea rooms and a chalet where I pay a fiver for a pamphlet and a ticket, then through the museum and into the village itself. It appears uninhabited except by the heritage industry.

The place is bizarre. Two parallel terraces of sweet brick buildings stand in rural nowhere, as if airlifted in two and a half centuries ago. Between them lie thirty yards of grass and a sandy-coloured track. The track ends in the fatly tidal river. Across the river lie reed beds and beyond them forest, low, grey-green and deciduous.

Here in the space between these buildings, the skeletons of ships were clambered over by men with hammers and saws and chisels and no motive power but muscle, before being released down the slipway into this unassuming river and sent out to enforce an empire. Beautiful, wooden and intricate, they went from here to bully the world.

In short, Buckler's Hard was an armaments factory. It was also a purpose-built green-fields development, the eighteenth-century equivalent of a business park. But time has reconfigured it into something strangely sweet. The buildings have settled into the land. The slipways have rotted to their piles, like the ruined stumps of teeth. Gulls and tourism have adopted it.

One of the cottages has been returned to its supposed original state, with truckle beds beneath the stooping ceilings, and rush lights, and deeply unconvincing life-size dummies in breeches or lace or baby clothes, frozen in the act of eighteenth-century suckling or stirring an eighteenth-century pot or heading out to work with a leather bag of eighteenth-century tools, rendering the past quaint and assimilable and quite without life, an insipidity.

In the bright museum stands a predictable collection of model ships, cut away in section, faultlessly miniature, made with obsessive time-chomping dedication. Only two things seize me. One is the copy book of the eight-year-old Henry Adams, later to become the master shipbuilder of Buckler's Hard. On 19 August 1722, he wrote, in a hand so close to copperplate that it would shame almost every twenty-first-century adult:

Conceal your wants from those who cannot
Conceal your wants from those who cannot
Conceal your wants from those who cannot
Conceal your wants from those who cannot
Conceal your wants from those who cannot
Conceal your wants from those who cannot
Conceal your wants from those who cannot
Conceal your wants from those who cannot
Conceal your wants from those who cannot
Conceal your wants from those who cannot
Conceal your wants from those who cannot
Conceal your wants from those who cannot
Conceal your wants from those who cannot
Conceal your wants from those who cannot
    help you.

Which isn't a bad idea.

And on a wall nearby I read the following: '"the heron perches on the great oak pathway from which ships of the line stepped majestically into our naval history." H.V. Morton. In Search of England, 1927.' I ask an attendant whether Morton's book was the spark that lit the fire of tourism in Buckler's Hard.

'Morton who?' he says.

*

Back in the New Forest a cow steps into the path of the Audi. It's a white cow. I stop the Audi. The cow stops too. Half a ton of car stands humming while half a ton of ruminant beef makes up its tiny mind which way to go. It decides to go nowhere. I honk the horn. The cow does nothing. I am reluctant to risk Mark's low-slung paintwork. I get out and say shoo. The beast looks at me, lumbers a few slappy yards up the middle of the road then stops again. I follow it and smack the warm heft of its rump. The cow looks round without apparent emotion then trundles back into the ancient forest swishing its tail, and I return to the plush, cool and odourless leather of the Audi's twenty-first-century seat.

My first sight of Salisbury is as corny as corn. I crest a rise as the sun is setting, a muted orange ball beneath a bronze fringe of cloud. And set out before me in the hollow of the evening is the urban smudge of Salisbury, its pencil-point cathedral steeple alone distinct, fingering the sky's gold.

In the hallway of a backstreet guest house, while I wait for the landlady to return with a key, I notice a calendar from Christchurch, New Zealand. I flick through its dozen predictable images – the unimpressive cathedral, the River Avon with blossom, the Port Hills where I roam with my dogs every day. I am surprised by the strength of my feeling.

'There you are,' says the landlady, 'down the corridor on your right.' She is holding the key out as if it were soiled.

'Christchurch,' I say, gesturing towards the calendar, 'that's where I live.'

'Oh really,' she says, but it is an oh really that's as flat as cardboard, an oh really that shuts the door of conversation then locks it. As I head down the corridor I glance back. The woman is straightening the calendar. I dump my bag and head into town.

Tesco is still open. When I was young Tesco was the poor people's supermarket. I remember standing at the checkout in the Brighton Tesco some time in my teenage years, watching women trying off-the-peg wigs.

This week Tesco announced their annual results. I forget the figures, but they made an absurd quantity of money. The predictable bleats went up: Tesco was ripping the heart out of villages; family butchers were bleeding to death; the little bakeries, the corner shops were dying. In other words, Tesco was ruining Morton's England. But the truth lies in the bottom line. In the battle between a notional ideal and cheap groceries, cheap groceries win without raising a sweat.

This late in the evening the miles of aisles are almost empty. I buy digestive biscuits and a bound notebook for a price no corner store could match. Light has thickened. Out beyond Salisbury the crows have made wing to the rooky wood. Good things of day have drooped and drowsed and from the shadows emerge the drivers of the night. They are young. Their cars are cherished throatmobiles, all sleek and growling, their mag wheels polished to a lustre, the antonyms of the traditional teenage bedroom. In ancient Ox Row an aptly ox-like youth is sitting in his spoilered monster, the seat belt carving a ravine in his pudgy urban belly. His hair is gelled like a hedgehog. He isn't playing rap music so much as sitting inside rap music. The whole car pulses. As usual, the only epithet I can make out is motherfucker.

The car is poised at the kerbside, growling. Such older people as are still about step well wide of it. The whole ensemble is a throbbing penis, a mechanized testosteronic shout. I wonder whether the lad on board the penis would be interested to know that on the other side of the world, in the similarly sedate streets of Christchurch, boys his age are driving the same penises in the same way with the same accoutrements and the same simian music. On mature reflection, I doubt that he would.

I choose a near-deserted pub because it's called the Chough. My only knowledge of choughs I got from *King Lear*, and that knowledge in its entirety is that choughs wing the midway air with crows. The pub sign depicts a crow-like bird with green wings. I intend to ask the barmaid what she knows about choughs, but when I see her tongue-stud I just watch the news on the telly instead. MG Rover has collapsed. The British car industry, which spent all my youth dying, has died again. And a new pope is being chosen. It's an extraordinary business. A false floor has been built beneath the cardinals' discussion chamber to house electronic jamming gear. The cardinals are plump little barrels of crimson self-importance. The media and a hundred thousand faithful are hovering around the Vatican waiting for a puff of anointing smoke. And no one seems to find it funny.

7

Writer Way

Old Sarum was a hill fort. It was a Neolithic hill fort for a thousand years or two, then a Celtic one, then Roman, then Saxon, then Norman. Indeed the only invading mob who didn't grab it were the Vikings. They had a go in 1003, but were repelled by whoever the tenants were at the time.

A couple of hundred years later the mongrel descendants of the Neoliths, Celts, Romans, Saxons and Normans – who by

74

now surely thought of themselves as English – left. They marched down to the plain and built themselves a nice new Salisbury with plenty of parking and civic amenities. The spot they chose was supposedly the spot where an arrow fired from Old Sarum landed. If that's true, it's impressive. It took me half an hour of brisk walking to get from new Salisbury, where the arrow landed, to Old Sarum, whence it was fired.

At eight o'clock on a weekday morning the ancient fort is alive with wind and dogs. The wind flattens the grass. The dogs exult. They are polite dogs: collies, Labs, a lissom Weimaraner. All have women in tow, sturdy women with head-scarves. Some of the women carry rubber balls on ropes that they fling inexpertly for the dogs to fetch. The dogs don't mind the lack of expertise.

Round the foundations of an eleventh-century cathedral I am weakly attacked by an old brown sausage dog, like a plump and stroppy weasel. The owner calls to it, but it prefers to growl and worry at my wind-flapped trouser leg. The woman lum-bers over, out of breath. 'I'm so sorry,' she says. 'Come HERE, Felix.' Felix does not come here.

I tell her that it's fine and not to worry. She lunges for Felix. Felix evades her. The woman is embarrassed. She lunges again. Between us we seize Felix and she clips the lead on with relief.

'Lovely morning,' I say, but the woman says, 'Isn't it,' in a tone that ends not with a question mark but with an audible full stop. She strides away, still panting and red of face.

I seem to have lost the knack of middle-class English con-versation starters. Time and again in the few days I've been here, I have striven to open a conversational door only to find it politely but firmly shut in my face. Have I lived too long abroad? Or have I become an object of suspicion at forty-seven? If so, it will only get worse. I turn 48 tomorrow.

The views stretch down to Salisbury in the hollow, and across the standard-issue quilt of villages and fields to the vague grey remoteness of the plain beyond. I circle the steep

dry moat and the grassed ramparts of Old Sarum, peer duti-
fully at the stubs of fat flint walls, but I take more pleasure
from the wind and the dogs. So do the dogs.

Back in Salisbury an hour later it's market day. In 1926,
Morton found 'the cattle market . . . loud with mooing and
bleating. Country gigs stood in the square and over the pens
leaned the burly, red-faced Wiltshire farmers. Many a Tess went
off with a basket over her arm . . .'

Seventy-nine years on, the market is a tawdry affair: Chinese
tea towels at Chinese-tea-towel prices, paintbrushes, strawberries from Egypt, pet supplies, coconut halves crammed with fat
and seeds, a rack of quilted anoraks. One open-sided van offers
the grey carcasses of wood pigeons for one pound fifty a bird,
and tempting bags of duck giblets for six quid a pop, but most
of this local market is as local as Tesco. There's a stall of bling
jewellery, a fad that has yet to reach New Zealand, and that,
with any luck, won't. The stuff is encrusted with ostentation,
like the chest medallions of the seventies.

I buy a non-bling watch, partly because my own has died,
and partly because it's only a fiver, but mainly because of
Laurie Lee. I'm a sucker for Laurie Lee.

At least twice a year I reread *As I Walked Out One Midsummer
Morning*, Lee's account of walking through Spain in the thirties.
I shouldn't. The prose is close to bling. Lee winds the sensual
experience of travel to a false romantic pitch. His despairs are
too desperate, his joys too joyous, his images too rich. And yet
I love it. I roll in every word, like a dog in dung.

It was the influence of Lee, I suspect, that made me accept a
job in Spain after I left university. I pictured myself in the front
cover of *As I Walked Out*, striding a white road through heat
towards a grove of oranges on a hill. The road never material-
ized, of course, but for the next ten years I kept walking it in my
mind. It was only in New Zealand that I contracted middle age
and stopped.

The passage that comes to mind now is one of many I can

quote by heart. A smuggler gives Lee a watch. It 'ticks madly for an hour and then explodes in a shower of wheels'. And there in those few sparkling words, that tiny unconsidered image, I find the sort of bright unpredictability, the strangeness that I still half hope to get from travel, while suspecting that I won't. All of us live by some form of delusion. To acknowledge it is not to cure it.

I keep glancing at my new watch. It keeps irritatingly good time.

On a bench on Choristers Green two lesbians sit snogging. Above them rise three hundred feet of stone that are the cathedral spire, its zenith capped with a cross and an anemometer. The spire is carved with magnificent pointlessness, its flanks heaped with spirelet piled on spirelet. It's thirteenth-century bling.

Cathedrals strive so hard to deny that they've become theme parks. Salisbury Cathedral is typical, in refusing to charge an entry fee. Instead you pay a four-quid 'donation'. The dean and chapter appease their God and assuage their guilt by waiving the donation on Sundays. But it isn't a donation, of course. If it were, I wouldn't have paid it.

The people inside do not pretend to be anything but tourists. Like me, they finger and gape and read inscriptions and lean back to take in the roof. Guides in sashes abound, all middle-aged or older, their children gone, their walking of the white road almost done. I watch an agitated elderly female guide explain to three equally elderly male guides that a party of French kids are larking around near the altar. The men listen, set their chins and march down the nave as one, a little English army setting forth to subdue the foreigners.

Morton found this cathedral to be 'chastely dignified'. To me, it's just another cathedral. In a room off the main building I gawp at one of only four original copies of the Magna Carta. Minutely hand-written, it's as neat as any typeface. If nothing else, the ancient monks who copied texts, and the ancient masons who built the spire, and the ancient city fathers who planned this building that took I don't know how many years to complete, knew singleness of purpose.

Back outside in the precinct I come across a plaque informing me that here, at Bishop Wordsworth's School, from 1945 to '62, one of the members of staff was William Golding. I didn't know he'd been a teacher, but it now seems obvious. He did seventeen years of anonymous research, then wrote *Lord of the Flies*, said bye-bye to the classroom and hello to the Nobel Prize.

I don't know why it pleases me to know that Golding lived and worked here, that he must have trodden this close-cropped grass a thousand times, but it does. He was, I'm sure, a man like all of us with bowels and a liking for chocolate or smoke or heavy woollen sweaters, as frail a man as the monk who bent shivering over the vellum of the Magna Carta, or as the mason on the spire with his warts and chisels. And yet, because Golding wrote words that have meshed with my head, words that affect the way I see the world, words that please me, to know that this was where he lived adds a lustre to this spot, a resonance. From this soil sprang that flower. It's just tourism by another name, I suppose, the desperate search for significance, no different from the urge impelling those inside the cathedral now to stare at the oldest working clock in the world (1386) or to read the inscription above some martyr's bones. Salisbury was not changed by housing Golding for a while. Only my attitude to Salisbury is. What I see and feel of Salisbury is what I choose to see. We make our own ghosts and mine are different from Morton's.

It's the same a couple of hours later as I nose the Audi through the clogging traffic and out to the north-west. Suddenly, there to my right is Stonehenge, romantically positioned between the A303 and the A360.

Doomish clouds are sprinting across the sky, dragging their

shadows across the big bleak land. Here are stones so huge
that five thousand years of wind have failed to rattle them. But
it isn't the unthinkably ancient builders that come to mind for
me, nor prehistoric astronomers, nor druids. I see Tess of the
d'Urbervilles, Thomas Hardy's Tess, laid out on the sacrificial
altar, sleeping, the fated victim of circumstance and men.

There are few parts of this cramped country that have not
been written about. It's going to be hard to escape literature on
this trip. I don't think I'll bother to try.

I stop at a layby and unfurl from the Audi. The wind's a
door-slammer. I make to light a cigarette but the wind snatches
it from my fingers, tosses it into the traffic. Crows wheel in the
distance like scraps of black paper. I stare across barbed wire
and an empty field to the big old stones. I've no desire to go
closer. I visited this pile some years ago. I remember a car park,
an ice-cream van, informative historical displays and a tunnel
that took me under the road to the ancient stones. A path and
fence and warning notices kept me always twenty yards from
doing what I wanted to do, which was to slap those stones, to
clamber on them, to lie where Tess lay.

From where I stand now I can see a scattering of tiny people
doing the same circuit in the wind, not slapping the stones,
nor clambering on them, nor lying where Tess lay, but stopping
to stare as I did, thinking their thoughts, seeing this place as
only they see it, then obediently moving on.

My eyes are watering in the wind, my fingers numb. I get
back into the car. The Audi's cabin is a relief of windlessness. I
fumble at my packet of Tesco digestive biscuits, despair of
opening it and slit the tissue-thin plastic with the car key. The
snake of biscuits droops in my hand, the plastic splits along its
length, and the fragile wheaty salty discs spill out across the
passenger seat and into the foot well. I eat the broken ones,
gather the rest into a pile like gamblers' chips and try to refit
them in the plastic wrapper. No good. I lay them loose in the
Tesco bag where they will soften. The forest-green leather of the

passenger seat is sullied with a million crumbs. As I drive west, the crumbs settle into the stitched seams like drifting sand.

On my map, Salisbury Plain is the nearest thing to a blank for several counties. A couple of roads traverse it. Between them stand only the words 'Danger Area' in red.

Twice I see a fighter plane absurdly low to the ground, absurdly swift, outstripping its own stupendous noise. I overtake a convoy of dun-coloured army trucks, the squaddies on the benches in the back looking disconsolate and quite ridiculously young.

I turn south and the road sinks into the land and becomes a lane. The names on the fingerposts become Hardyesque: Fontwell Magna, Compton Abbas. A sign to Iwerne Minster brings a sudden jolt of recognition. It takes a couple of seconds to disinter the memory. I'm surprised how vivid it is.

In what must have been about 1982, I went there to be interviewed for a teaching job. I was there only a few hours but I retain an almost tactile image of the place. School and village seemed buried in a valley, a valley like an embrace, all deep and green and over-intimate, oppressive. The headmaster exuded youth and ambition. The deputy head didn't. In the tradition of deputy heads, he had been there since Napoleonic times. He didn't like the new head and he even more clearly didn't like me. Perhaps to spite his deputy, the head offered me the job. I turned it down and followed the white road to Canada.

The valley in which Iwerne Minster sits is not as deep or richly cloying as I remember it, but there's a silence here like a rural blanket. I stop the Audi in the staff car park, and watch a groundsman mowing the first cricket pitch of the summer, carving through the lushness. This field could easily have become the one where I stood on the boundary and suffered hope and fear, delight and disappointment for the kids I coached. That it didn't, well, all there is to say is that it didn't. The road you take becomes the road you took.

I am leaning on the Audi smoking. A passing teacher looks at me for a little too long, as if assessing the precise extent of, and the likelihood of my indulging, my obvious paedophilia. I drive on.

I am following Morton towards Weymouth but when I see a sign for Dorchester I make a last-second decision to turn. In doing so I cause huge delight to the driver of a Morrison's truck, a delight that he expresses with a scream of the brakes and a tune on the horn.

Halfway up the main street in Dorchester stands the Casterbridge Hotel. I stop the car and take a room. It's sixty quid for the night, but I don't care. I am an unashamed literary tourist now. I haven't come for Dorchester. I've come for Hardy's Casterbridge. And Dorchester is keen to give it me.

The little museum devotes a whole floor to Hardy. Here is the lace cap he wore as an infant, and over there's his coffin plate, next to a lousy drawing he made of a rabbit called Juno the I, when he was sixteen and the rabbit six months. Here's a photo of the terrier Wessex jumping against Hardy's thigh. Hardy wrote a poem on Wessex's death and erected a tombstone. Here are letters to Hardy from Sassoon, R. L. Stevenson, T. E. Lawrence. And over there beyond the glass is Hardy's study, set out precisely as it had been in his house. On the desk is a tray of pens, and into the bone handle of each is carved the name of the book that Hardy wrote with it. There's the nib that laid Tess on the Stonehenge altar. Beside it the desk calendar stands at Monday 7th March, 1870, the day Hardy met Emma Gifford. I am pressing against the glass like a lecher at a peep show. The glass grows misty with my breath. I am rapt.

All books are infused with the author, Hardy's most emphatically so, but here is the author as more than author, as dog-lover, rabbit-drawer, friend and failure, child and ancient. Here is Hardy, in other words, as a frail and fallible man, a man who hated to be touched on arm or shoulder, a man whose best friend, Horace Moule, cut his own throat at the age of forty-one.

I find it hard to justify my rapture, but I note with something similar to relief that Hardy was subject to the same sort of sentimentality. For there on his desk is a pillbox of violets that he picked from Keats's grave in Rome in April 1887.

Hardy died in 1928. It comes as a slight shock to realize that Morton could have met him. But though they shared an interest in history, and though both heard the whispers of yesterday in the streets of today, something tells me that the two might not have got on. Hardy was not big on idylls. And Morton shows no sign of having read him.

Hardy called Dorchester 'compact as a box of dominoes' and it still feels that way. There's too much traffic, of course, but on the steep little main street the clustered buildings of stone or timber or brick, no two the same, form a compressed sweetness. Behind them run lanes and alleyways. The building in which Hardy's fictional mayor, Michael Henchard, lived stands opposite a branch of Marks & Spencer. The ground floor of the building is now a Barclay's bank. I head down the hill past the King's Arms Hotel, where Henchard held a fictional banquet, in search of the bridge that Henchard came to when his fortunes fell. He would spend hours and days just staring into the water.

Grey's Bridge at the foot of the main street fits the bill: three arches over a gentle peat-coloured swirl of a river. The coping stone of the bridge's wall is covered with a yellow lichen like a skin disease. I lean my elbows on it and play Henchard, but it's hard to do moodiness justice with BMWs skimming inches from my backside.

'Any person', says a suspiciously well-preserved sign, 'wilfully injuring any part of this county bridge will be guilty of felony and upon conviction liable to be transported for life by the court. T. Fooks.' Below me two Labradors, one yellow, one black, frolic in the shallows. Beyond them lie water meadows, knee-deep or more in grass and buttercups.

A hundred yards along King Street I find another bridge; two arches only, but every bit as good for moodiness. Perhaps Henchard used both.

I climb a hill through silent early-evening suburbs, the cars in the driveways like hunched immobile cats, then over a bridge that spans a deep-cut roaring bypass and I reach the house that Hardy built, Max Gate. It's closed to the public and barely visible behind a veil of thick tall trees, some of which Hardy must have planted or had planted, or noticed the planting of.

I tiptoe, crane, secure brief toeholds in a wall and heave myself up like a paparazzo to snatch a glimpse of the house. It's nothing much: plain brick, plain tile, an ugly conservatory and a smothering of vegetation. Hardy didn't think much of it either. He wrote a poem about how cold it was.

The setting sun turns the leaves translucent yellow. Two men in suits emerge from the house and drive off in an Audi just like mine. A schoolgirl click-clacks past on toppling heels, her skirt a clinging buttock-wrap, her eyes intent on a mobile phone that glows Doctor-Who purple in her palm. She teeters down the hill towards an acreage of bungalows.

Behind the house a scrubby paddock, gorse, holly and a fat little pony that I feed with handfuls of Dorset grass. Beyond the paddock lies the view from Hardy's study, a view of fields and hills and unremarkability.

The pub along the road is inevitably 'The Thomas Hardy'. It has the obligatory stuffed trout on the wall, reproduction Spy cartoons, warming pans like brass banjos (when did anyone last use a warming pan, and how come there are so many? Is there a factory still making them for pubs, along with horse brasses?) and a sign over the food hatch advertising 'Thrilling Grillings'. In short, it's about as Hardyesque as Montana.

'England is in moral decline,' says Robert cheerfully. 'Has

been for years now.' He's another former soldier, but in his sixties, bald as a plate, dressed in clothes so muted that to look away is to forget them completely. Five minutes ago he took a seat at a bar stool two along from me and ordered a half of 6X. I like half-drinkers. They are ex-pint-drinkers with prostates. They don't need the booze, but they refuse to relinquish the pub.

I cultivated Robert carefully, wary of the conversation blocks I have met so often. We did the weather first, agreed it was cool and that it had been a dry spring, while assessing each other's accents, vocabulary, linguistic class. Politeness is wary of diving into conversation for the excellent reason that politeness forbids abruptly ceasing conversation. Get talking to a bore and escape's impossible.

When I mentioned Morton, Robert smiled. 'Ah,' he said, 'such light and lovely prose,' and we were away. Robert spent much of his army life in hotspots like Cyprus and the Middle East. In Malaya he'd had to shift villagers from the jungle. 'Terrible business,' he says. I nod. I don't admit that I've never quite known what the Malayan war was about, or indeed, exactly where Malaya is.

The army shrank and Robert retrained as a land agent. He brought his family to Dorset for a job and settled. 'It's an oasis,' he says. 'The schools are still all right. No cities. No immigrant underclass. An oasis.'

I ask him to explain what he meant by moral decline. He thinks a bit, sips at his beer. 'Parents,' he says eventually. 'Parents of boys in particular. Boys need a bit of discipline. Too many don't get it. It's a classic symptom of decadence.'

'Do you mind if I smoke?'

Robert laughs. 'I used to smoke a pipe myself. I still miss it. I had dinner in London the other week and was sat next to the President of ASH, you know, the anti-smoking brigade. God, he was a twit.'

I manage to persuade Robert to take a second half. As the

barmaid pours it, she announces that they've appointed a Pope. 'Ratzinger got it,' she says, 'and he's decided to be called Benedict. Any name's better than Ratzinger, though, isn't it?'

Robert says that he knew a trainee Catholic priest called Christmas, who changed his name before he was ordained. I don't get it, but the barmaid does. She snorts with pleasure. 'What a pity, though,' she says. 'Father Christmas would be rather sweet.'

'But not very doctrinal,' says Robert.

The pub slowly fills. Three young men with earrings order lager. All three have bleached hair and are wearing sweatshirts bearing the legend 'Weymouth F.C. – The Terrors'.

Robert leaves and Richard takes his stool. He's a builder, has lived here all his life. His burr is as gentle as a bee's buzz. 'Dorset's a backwater these days,' he says, 'it's turning into an old-people's home. There's thousands of them. They find themselves stuck in a house in London that's too big for them, sell up for seven hundred and fifty thousand, buy a place round here, stick half a million in the bank and clog up the health system. There's no industry round here, nothing. Just a bit of farming and tourism. And industry's not going to come here either, 'cause we haven't got the motorways. So there's nothing for the young, and anyway they can't afford to live round here. So off they go.'

He has two kids himself, one working in Cambridge, the other in Portsmouth.

'It's all right for us older folk, but what's it going to be like twenty years from now? A rural desert, that's what, a rural desert full of old people.'

On my walk back into town, I note the number of old-people's homes, all tucked up warm for the night. And I recall a line from, I think, *The Mayor of Casterbridge* in which Hardy compares the migration of people from country to the city, to 'the natural tendency of water to flow uphill when forced by machinery'.

I dine on noodles. The Asian lad who takes my order and the other who cooks it don't look as though they have read much Hardy. They pay less attention to fulfilling my order than they do to a television that shows two bearded sages talking energetically to each other in an Asian language, subtitled, in, as far as I can determine, two other Asian languages.

The only reading material in the waiting area is a three-day-old copy of the *Star*. It is mainly tits and television. Its banner headline is devoted to tits on television.

I take my noodles to a churchyard off Church Street and eat with a grave for a seat. The stone numbs my buttocks, the yew tree is throttled by ivy, the noodles are mainly sauce, and the sauce is awful. But this is Hardy's town, and it is whispery with good ghosts.

8

Hoe Hoe

When I wake I discover that this is my second bite at my forty-eighth birthday. The first one must have been in the small hours. Evidence abounds. The bathroom light is on, the cold tap is running in the sink and the wardrobe door is open. I lay my palm on the wardrobe floor. It's dry. I am relieved, too, that the door key is still behind the television where I hid it to thwart my somnambulist self.

In the cold half-light and silence of early morning, Dorchester feels as sweet as old honey. I amble along lanes behind the main street, peering into windows and down alley-ways. The terraced cottages seem too small for today's lumbering people. I turn a corner and find myself in sudden low sun. My skin drinks in the warmth.

At the top of the main street a statue of Hardy sits in knee breeches, looking pinch-faced and peevish. At his feet a black-bird darts a dozen steps across the dew-bright grass, stops, listens, darts again and commits a swift and gulping murder. Shreds of mist loiter in hollows like wisps of gauze on a Rubens crotch.

Hardy is sitting on the remains of a Roman rampart. Nearby are the flint foundations of a Roman townhouse. Standing among them I can see the edge of town. Only a car park and a roof of thatch between me and the open fields, almost colour-less in the thick air. The place reminds me oddly of Salamanca, where I spent New Year's Eve in 1979. Even now, with full sen-sory recall, I can remember walking out past the last house of Salamanca and being suddenly among fields. Since then Salamanca has sat in my mind as a template of how a small town should be.

Up the road a bit is Poundbury, Prince Charles's model vil-lage. I am suspicious of it. Charles has always seemed to me a little precious, pushing towards quaint. I don't trust quaint.

In Poundbury, the new roads curve like old roads and the new buildings are as various as old buildings. Most of the buildings are in stone. There are gravel footpaths, little parks and public spaces. Pommery Square has a twentieth-century version of a covered market cross, tastefully done in sandstone. Across the road is a mini-supermarket, its acreage of windows deliberately smaller than normal to suggest a more Blytonesque shop. On a corner of the square stands the pub.

Poundbury is not yet complete but the intention is clear. They've tried to create a village. They've tried to distil

Englishness. With the mix of house sizes and prices, they also seem to have tried to reproduce the English class system. Whether it will work or not, time has yet to decide, but there are ominous signs.

Though the place was clearly built to encourage pedestrians, the number of Volvos parked halfway up the pavement suggests that the marriage between the English and the motorcar will not be easily dissolved. And the shops that have been established are firmly middle class, the sort of shops that accept only discretionary spending – a delicatessen with a window full of olives and pastrami, a kitchen shop offering pasta tongs like horse-combs and gleaming food machines in stainless steel whose purpose I can only guess at, a knick-knack shop offering decorative stuff whose spiritual home is the pages of the heavier magazines. And the pub is called the Poet Laureate. I fear that Poundbury will become a middle-classness, a posh suburb, a niceness.

But I hope I'm wrong. If a way can be found to create a modern village, something that works in the twenty-first century, then I am for it. It has to be better than Slough.

The morning is under way. Dorchester has woken. In a gym near Hardy's statue, weights rise and fall. A Waitrose truck the size of two cottages struggles to make a turn. Its chest-high wheels mount the kerb while pedestrians flatten themselves against old stone walls.

Treefrogvillas.com is opening. Its sash windows offer apartments for sale in Florida, the Algarve, Brazil. They come with sunshine, beaches, an abundance of parking and no burden of yesterdays. Nor will they know many tomorrows. The photos show the sort of tilt-slab buildings that won't last fifty years.

To drive the ten miles between Dorchester and Weymouth is to understand the appeal of Brazil. Several million pounds' worth of cars are stuck bumper to bumper, crawling. And yet when I reach Weymouth the traffic-management system sweeps me through the town, offering little chance to stop.

Morton described Weymouth as having 'not yet recovered from the surprise that George III discovered it as a health resort'. I see women with pushchairs, men with briefcases, a jogger wearing a mask. The women look glum, the men serious and the jogger absurd, but none of them surprised. I drive on to the Bill of Portland, a peninsula shaped like South America. At its southern tip, its Tierra del Fuego, I ease the Audi into a vast and almost empty car park.

A lighthouse stands like a great white dalek. Beyond it a dribble of rocks descends to the sea. On the furthest exposed rock stands an obelisk, marking, I presume, the end of land, the decisive final moment of the dissolution of England. There are few visitors about, but those few all rock-hop to the obelisk, to stand a while at their terrestrial limit, as if contemplating a return to amphibiousness. The rock that I am sitting on is packed with fossil shells.

A dozen Philip Larkins tread softly past me, all carrying tripods and cameras, or binoculars the size of twin bazookas. I say good morning to the first of them, and each as he passes says a good morning of his own. They're here for the birds, I presume, though apart from the obvious wheeling and mewing gulls I note only a pair of starlings nesting noisily in the gutter of the Lighthouse Visitor Centre. Behind me a stark Ministry of Defence establishment is ringed with razor wire and notices that cheerily invite you to fuck off or die.

To the east stand the remains of what I take to be primitive cranes, the legacy of quarrying, for it is from here, as Morton delighted in discovering, that they cut the stone that built London. St Paul's came from here, Whitehall, Somerset House and all those other monumental buildings that so enshrine the visual tone of imposing imperial London. Buildings that express nothing but solidity and confidence, buildings without flounces, built four-square and ageless from stone and certainty, beginning life as the greyish innocence of this lime-stone I am sitting on, weathering to a stately silver then slowly gathering grime for half a century until up goes the scaffolding and out come the water blasters.

I can't find a working quarry. Perhaps Portland has stopped digging out its own flesh and selling it. I find only a couple of stone-built villages and a view of the long curve of the Chesil Bank, a twenty-mile barrier of pebbles stretching west to a smudge and flanked the whole way by a white feather of surf. Even from up here, the surf on those pebbles is audible, a cease-less, slow-drawn sigh and hiss. The gleaming roof tiles of the terraced village below step down to the sea like ladders.

I head west, towards accents. I have always thought of Dorset as a barrier county. On this side of it lie the Home Counties, all smug and money-making. On the other side lies the south-west, which I imagine to be deeper-rooted, in some way vegetative, its movements slower and richer. But maybe I delude myself.

The road west carves through villages where to step from your front door is to step into traffic. On the road-front side of the cottages, the curtains are perpetually drawn.

Abbotsbury is all thatch and sandstone and hollyhock-quaintness, and there are road signs to Loders, Uploders, Wootton Fitzpaine and Whitchurch Canonicorum. They sound like a Betjeman poem. Used as I am to the South Island of New Zealand, I continue to be struck by the sheer density of settle-ments, the very usedness of the land, the unavoidability of its human imprint and the absence of the truly wild, to such an extent that I have to wrench the wheel of the Audi to avoid a wagon-train of abstract nouns.

I stop only in Ashburton for a cup of coffee because there is an Ashburton in New Zealand. The difference is stark. This Ashburton sits clamped in a valley. That Ashburton sprawls like a spilled drink. There the houses are built of wood and set apart with gardens, and the streets are as straight as the All Blacks and almost as wide. Here the little stone houses stand in gardenless terraces, and the streets twist like intestines. Behind this Ashburton the hills rise steep and rich to Dartmoor, divided into tiny parcels by hedges, fences and walls of stone. Behind that Ashburton the paddocks stretch for fifty miles, wire-fenced and rectilinear.

'Every boy in England', wrote Morton, 'should be taken at least once to Plymouth.' I was. I went there on a school football tour, aged perhaps sixteen. I remember nothing of the town. What I do remember is a pair of images each of which is as clear as a lark's song.

All my contemporaries were shaving. Keen to seem equally adult I went out and bought a pack of disposable razors. Having made sure there were people around to be impressed, I lathered my face at the sink and scraped at my peach-rind cheeks with the casual aplomb of the most ancient grizzle-chops. But it felt wrong. The razor smeared the foam instead of removing it. It was Brian Coverdale, the centre forward, who pointed out that I was supposed to remove the plastic cover. I am sure good things happened on the tour, but embarrassment has outlasted them all, seared into the skull as if by a hot wire.

The other memory's a photograph. I've got it still. I am posing in a hotel bedroom wearing only a towel around my waist and hair to my shoulders. I've raised and bent my arms like a boxer at a weigh-in. I am grinning because, although puberty has not yet got round to sowing bristles on my chin, it has given me biceps and pectorals. The photo oozes a primitive pride.

But these are not quite the experiences of Plymouth that Morton had in mind. Morton wanted his English schoolboy to be taken round the naval dockyard and 'most importantly of all, his imagination should be kindled by tales of Hawkins and Drake on high, green Plymouth Hoe, the finest promenade in Europe'.

I take the wrong turn off the motorway, and find myself attacking Plymouth from the rear. I can't find the Hoe or the city centre or anywhere to park. Urged from behind by ceaseless traffic I follow three-lane one-way streets that render me baffled and impotent. When I recognize a street and realize I've described a giant circle, I start to grow distraught. I feel something close to panic swelling like a vegetable in my chest and skull. I turn at random up a side street, park in a residents-only space and sit a while at the wheel to come off the boil. I want out. It's my birthday. I want to find a village, and a pub, and to get drunk with slow-talking locals who make me laugh. But the thought of trying to drive out of Plymouth is too much. I stop a man in a British Legion blazer complete with badge and food stains.

'Excuse me,' I say, 'where's the Hoe?' The words sound absurd.

'The what?' he says.

'Plymouth Hoe. You know, Drake and bowls,' and I astound myself by miming the act of bowling.

'Oh, the Hoe,' he exclaims. This is turning into Gilbert and Sullivan. But it seems that the Hoe is just up there a bit beyond a terraced street of guest houses. In the first of the guest houses I find a landlord of such determined surliness it's almost an art.

'Thirty quid,' he says when I ask if he's got a room. 'How many nights?'

'One, maybe two.'

'One or two? Which?'

'One,' I say. It's the wrong answer. The right answer is none. But I am English, and the fear of giving offence to a man who deserves offence given to him repeatedly and in substantial quantities, condemns me to spend the night of my forty-eighth birthday in a room that smells of rot. Where a light should be at the head of the bed, two wires protrude like the antennae of some wall-burrowing insect. They terminate in warts of insulation tape.

I fetch the Audi, mercifully unclamped or ticketed, and park it with difficulty in the walled back yard of the guest house. The proprietor appears at the back door. 'Nice,' he says. I imagine for a moment that he is scoffing at my seven-point turn. But no, he's liking the Audi. And as a result he's liking me. He becomes, as far as he is capable of becoming, which isn't far, Mr Nice from Niceville. He gives me a map of the town, directions to the Hoe, and the name of a pub where he's a regular and which I make a mental note, underlined in red, to avoid.

The Hoe's a cliff-top park, a stretch of wind-blown civic grass with a fine view of the outer harbour and a statue of Drake. The inscription on the plinth says merely 'Drake'.

'I am sorry', wrote Morton, 'for the man who can stand for the first time on Plymouth Hoe without a tingling of the blood.' Well, here he is. And here, too, is the widest gulf between Morton and me. He was a child of empire. I was not. When he was born the map was red. When I was born it had only a few red blotches. And by the time I was twenty even those had gone.

As a child, Morton would have been surrounded by unquestioning patriotic fervour. I was not. I was pleased when England won the World Cup or a test match, but that was about it, although I do remember a brief and ineffectual 'I'm Backing Britain' campaign in the sixties supported by little Union Jack stickers. In Morton's childhood such a campaign would have seemed both redundant and squalid.

In other words, and even though Drake set sail against the Spanish Armada three hundred and thirty-nine years before Morton wrote *In Search of England*, Morton is closer to Drake than he is to me. In the interlude between Morton's birth and mine, something snapped.

Drake stands with one hand on a globe. His puffy pantaloons remind me of the frilled knickers that Virginia Wade wore at Wimbledon. Not far away is a bowling green. No one is playing. A giant cenotaph stands in memory of those 'who have no other grave than the sea'. Its flanks are set with imposing panels of bronze on which are moulded the names of the naval dead. A workman finishes water-blasting the steps, lugs his gear up to the bronze panels and unclips one. It swings on hinges to reveal a storage cupboard where he neatly stashes his gear.

I amble down the hill towards the port, passing under the artificial cliffs that are the walls of the Royal Citadel. A mile or so out to sea sits a warship, grey as a shark and stationary. All along the waterfront the promenaders demonstrate the remarkable ability of the English to eat ice cream in chilly weather. Down by a groyne a youngish man and woman are actually sunbathing. Both are lying with a hand laid across the eyes to protect them from the blinding glare of the other's flesh.

The wall of the inner harbour is a mass of plaques: to the *Mayflower* (1620), Convicts to Australia (1787), Tolpuddle Martyrs (1838), the founders of New Plymouth, New Zealand (1840). A chubby youth in Reebok trainers and a lurid Adidas tracksuit lowers a nylon crab pot into the thick, oily, olive-green and detritus-strewn water of the inner harbour. He smokes a cigarette, adds it to the detritus, then hauls up five dwarf crabs and one prawn. He throws the crabs back and puts the prawn in a screw-top plastic jar and I go looking for No. 9, The Barbican, where the passengers on the *Mayflower* are supposed to have spent their last night in England and where Morton found an old woman peeling spuds. I can't find it. I explain my quest to the merry woman in the tourist information office, who hasn't heard of H. V. Morton but is keen to help.

'It may have gone,' she says.

'Gone?'

She fetches a book, opens it to a road map of Plymouth. The map is all but obliterated by black dots. 'Every dot was a German bomb,' she says.

Most of the bombs hit the city centre. I walk three blocks and

find myself in Armada Way. It could be Bucharest or Beijing.
It's the town planner's notion of civic living. Vast spaces lie
between buildings of unremitting hideousness. The concrete
boxes that house the usual department stores are hideous. The
county court is hideous. The council building is super-hideous.
The materials are wrong. The roofs are wrong. The metal
window frames are super-wrong. Above all, the scale is wrong.
It's inhuman, austere, dwarfing, suited only to May Day
parades of missiles and goose-steppers. The wind knifes round
the corners and stabs the shoppers. Only the skateboarders
seem happy, roaring across the sterile wilderness like insects.

Here's the post-war utopia that rose to replace what Hitler
had flattened. It sprang from a dream of a modern Britain. It
came with straight suburban roads of pebble-dash semis and a
belief in progress. It built the awful festival buildings on the
south bank of the Thames. And nothing in the history of
English architecture was more disastrous.

And here, I think, is the dividing point between Morton and
me. Post-war England was different from pre-war England.
The First World War was a bloodbath, but after it was over not
a lot changed. The Second World War produced Churchill, the
final incarnation of Sir Francis Drake. And as soon as the war
was over, they threw him out. They then set about building a
better Plymouth.

Near the top end of the dismal open-air shopping plaza, on
the benches where mothers were meant to sit with winsome
infants, or office workers with sandwiches, a mob of winos has
gathered, loudly bearded, bottles in bags, switching from jollity
to rage and back again in seconds, roughing each other up,
roaring like stags and oblivious to all but internal urges. I don't
blame them. Behind them stands the Copthorne Hotel, a thing
in corrugated concrete that Stalin would have considered just a
little grim. I scurry back to the harbour and spend the last of the
afternoon sunshine with a birthday beer on the quayside.
When the air cools I retreat into the pub where I find the

obligatory football match on a wide screen TV and a pair of sailors.

The sailors are not real sailors. They're naval inspectors and they're both drunk. Pete's repetitive and John confesses to having recently attended a Kylie Minogue concert. It was his birthday present to his wife. She didn't enjoy it much but 'I thought what the fuck and just got up and danced. It was great.'

He asks me what I do for a living, then apologizes for not reading much. 'But this bloke at work gave me a book called *Animal Farm*. Have you heard of it? I couldn't put it down.'

I leave the sailors to their football and take a seafood pizza up to the Hoe. The seafood is canned tuna. The Hoe's deserted. The wind has died. I sit beside Drake. Far out a lighthouse winks and as my eyes adjust to the gloom I make out the warship I saw this afternoon, rocking on the ink, ready to defend the island on which I was born forty-eight years ago today.

9

Nice Place

When I become President of the World I shall hire someone to invent a shower control that a baboon could understand. It will have a single dial. That dial will say warm on one side and hot on the other and the distance between warm and hot will be substantial. There will be no 'cold' because no one takes cold showers except Mormons and I am happy to annoy

Mormons. I shall have this shower control installed in every rentable room in the world.

But I doubt that even this would fix the shower in Mr Surly's guest house. When I turn it on in the morning it delivers cold water in pulses. Between pulses the showerhead droops. During pulses it swings around on its armature like an alien seeking prey. When the stream of water finally steadies itself the whole thing vibrates as if striving to wrench itself from the wall. It looks close to succeeding. Naked, I reach through the water to adjust the temperature control. I try it on the red end and the blue end. The water remains cold and I remain unshowered.

The landlord is wearing the same shirt he wore yesterday. I recognize the armpits. Perhaps the plumbing is shot throughout the building. He interrupts my breakfast order to answer the phone.

'A double room for tonight, yes, that's forty-five pounds including full English breakfast . . . I beg your pardon?' The tone in which he delivers this last phrase causes me and the two other guests to perk up and listen intently. We are well rewarded. Mr Surly rises from a slouching lean to a standing position to deliver his next line. 'What do you mean, "It wouldn't be a very nice room for that price"? Anyway we're full.' He smacks the phone down on the word 'full' and returns fuming. 'The cheek of it,' he says, and then, in a parody la-di-da accent, '"It wouldn't be a very nice room for that price." The rude bitch.'

I don't mention that the rude bitch was bang right. Nor do I say that I wish I had the forthright honesty of the rude bitch. I say, 'I'd like the full English breakfast, please.'

The landlord writes F/E on a scrap of paper.

'Don't know what the world's coming to,' he says.

Morton called Cornwall fairyland. I wouldn't go quite that far. But still Cornwall has a whiff of romance to it, removed way down there to the west where the daffs come early and the smugglers roam.

At first sight it seems like a compressed and bumpy Sussex, with sharp hills, stone villages and roads like worms. The place names are spectacularly alien, many of them devoted to saints the rest of the country hasn't got.

The tourist information centre for St Austell is a Portakabin behind a newsagent's, staffed by a gentle man with an educated burr and a refreshing approach to his job. I ask if he can give me two good reasons to stop and poke around St Austell for a bit. He pauses a moment to sieve the many and varied delights of St Austell for the two most likely to suit a middle-aged male in a posh car, then he says, and I am quoting, 'No.'

'No?'

'No.' The woman next to him behind the counter looks sharply across, but he persists. 'The place is a bombsite,' he says. 'They've knocked half of it down but they haven't got planning permission to put anything back up. There's only two pubs and I wouldn't go into either of them. I shouldn't be saying this, but . . .'

To his evident surprise I burst out laughing. To his even more evident surprise I tell him he's made my day and I offer him my hand. He shakes it with only a little uncertainty. His colleague cracks a smile.

He has indeed made my day. For amid the hype and the bluster, the constant lies about travel and places other than the ones we live in, the hyperbole of it all, the faux glamour, the dishonest guidebooks, the gross and culpable commercial delusion that is the travel business, this gentleman's sharp burst of anti-puffery strikes like a volley of well-aimed machine-gun fire against a bank of balloons.

By rights of course I should now stop and find an abundance of quiet delights in St Austell, but I drive on. At Tresillian I catch a glimpse of an egret, and a sniff of the exotic. And just beyond Truro I turn off the main road in search of St Anthony in Roseland. I'm keen to see it. Morton compared it favourably with paradise.

Like Morton I take King Harry's Ferry, a sort of barge on cables across the widening River Fal. A faded news clipping, pinned behind Perspex, announces that this has been judged one of the ten greatest ferry trips in the world. The list includes the Staten Island ferry and one across the Creek in Dubai. I mentally compile another list of the ten most meaningless activities in the world. Number one on that list is compiling a list of the ten greatest ferry trips.

Nevertheless this is a pretty place. The ferry chugs across a couple of hundred yards of slow dark water, between steep and wooded banks just flushed with the lightest green of spring. It then releases us into sunken lanes that are precisely the width of the Audi. The other cars soon turn off down equally narrow lanes and I creep in second gear between banks the height of two men, sucked ever deeper into a vegetative luxuriance. In places, the trees join above the lane to form a roof.

At every rise I hold my breath. Twice I meet oncoming cars and each time I reverse to a passing bay. Once while reversing I collect another car behind me and he too reverses, so the oncoming vehicle appears to be shunting the pair of us backwards. At the passing bay we do a little three-car jig.

The whole region is known as Roseland. The name owes nothing to roses, apparently, but derives from the Cornish word 'ros' meaning promontory. The lanes are not shown on my road atlas. I follow fingerposts to St Anthony, but a vital fingerpost has fallen or, more likely, been swallowed by the vegetation. Either way I get lost, but keep driving. I descend a little hill and stop. I have to. The road ends in water. And I find myself in a place called, as far as I can tell, Place.

There's a view across to another bay with a beach and a row of cottages, and beyond the estuary, St Mawes. The silence is like a thrown green blanket. I sit on an ancient stone and breathe. The water at my feet is like smoked glass. Tiny fishes flick. At the head of the bay to my left among trees there's a huge lawn like a shallow dish and behind it stands Place House. It's big. It's got turrets. It abuts a little church. It's painted butter yellow. And I want it. I want to sleep in one of the turrets. I want my dogs to race about the lawn. I want to push a rowboat out from this little quay and fish a sleepy afternoon. Above all I want to imbibe the long-brewed peace of the place, the deep green seclusion. But Place House is not for sale, and even if it were I'm confident that my amassed wealth would fall short of what was required by a couple of million or so.

I follow a little path that swings through the overgrown remains of a graveyard. Flowers abound: red campion, bluebells, primroses, violets, celandine and a creeper I can't name that's snaking over the stone rim of an open medieval coffin to peep inside. The quaint church is open and offers a pile of photocopied pamphlets telling, I presume, its history.

I climb past the back of Place House through dark woods, all bird-strewn and ivy-choked, and emerge on to a hillside of calf-deep grass where sated cattle laze like great brown sacks of flesh with eyelashes. Full of zest I vault a hill-top stile. I see the sea and hear, 'Good afternoon,' at the same time. In the lee of a hedge a couple are sitting on a bench. 'Lovely day,' says the man. He has a muted northern accent. He's keen to talk. His wife is smoking.

They live in Manchester but come here several times a year because they 'just love it'. They'd like to be able to live here.

'Yes,' I say, and tell them how I'm smitten with Place House.

'The old boy there died last September. Spry his name was, he's buried in the churchyard. Naval type. His descendants fought with Nelson at Trafalgar.'

Ever the schoolteacher, I sense myself wanting to correct 'descendants', but bite the words back. I ask if he's heard of *In Search of England*.

'Oh, Morton, yes. Lovely writer. We met his nephew, once, or it may have been his cousin. I don't remember. He was following the old boy's route round the country. We told him how to get to Bohortha – that's where Morton stayed, you know, at the old school house.'

'No,' says his wife, speaking for the first time and looking pointedly at her husband. 'It was the cottage next door.'

'I've been corrected,' says the husband. And he has been. A wealth of emotional undercurrents twitched and tugged beneath her remark and his reply, the long-distilled complexity of marriage.

There's a brief, fraught pause. The husband snaps the tension.

'The water in that port,' he says, pointing across the sea to Falmouth, 'is deeper than in any port in the world except Sydney and Honolulu.'

I don't know what to say to that. His wife lights another cigarette.

'See that castle, and that one over there,' the husband continues, waving at a pair of massive smudges either side of the channel, 'Henry VIII built those, to protect the harbour.'

I'm not exactly full of ideas of what to say to that either, so, like Morton's nephew or cousin, I ask for directions to Bohortha, and then head away across a springy cliff-top field. Fifty yards on, I turn to see the pair of them still sitting, unmoving, apparently silent, married. The husband waves. I wave back, then bound along feeling pleased to be alone.

The cliff top is thumped by wind that smells of grass and salt. I reach a set of steps through rocks to a lighthouse and then I turn as directed along a lane leading to another lane and down then up a hill and round a bend and here's Bohortha. The clouds have rumbled in from the west. The light has thickened. I unwrap the sweater from my waist.

Bohortha is a scattering of cottages, a farm, a barn, no shops, no bus stop and nobody. If this is indeed where Morton stayed the night with an elderly couple, where he dined on eggs and cream, and listened to a crackling radio and thought that he had stumbled into paradise, then here's the former schoolroom that he wrote about, and that, right there, must be the thatched and whitewashed cottage where he climbed the wooden stairs by candlelight to sleep beneath the rafters in 1926.

I see no sign of life. No dogs bark in Crotchet Cottage or Manor Farm. I poke around a bit, feel intrusive, reflect that Morton may have laid it on a little thick, and am about to head back down the hill to Place when a battered blue hatchback turns the corner, its boot wide open, a wooden door protruding. It stops.

The driver is from Cheshire. Sparely built and gently spoken, he used to come here as a boy to stay with his Auntie Kitty. When Kitty died ten years ago he bought the cottage, and he and his wife moved down.

'Oh yes,' he says, when I explain what I'm here for, 'of course I've read Morton. He's very popular.'

'He thought he'd found paradise.'

'Well, it is quiet here,' he says, 'even in the holiday season. Effectively we've got our own private beach,' and he waves an arm to indicate the beach's presence unseen in the dusk to the west. 'If you've got a boat you barely need a car. And it's certainly no good having a nice car.' He gestures at the hatchback's many dents. I'm pleased the Audi is half a mile away.

The man has time to chat, is keen to tell me things. Apparently, Bohortha means 'the place where a donkey fell down the well and poisoned it' (and if that's an example of Cornish, it's a remarkably concise language). There used to be five farms here, but now there's only the one, growing daffodil bulbs and broad beans. The beans go to the Middle East where they are made into a spicy snack. The farm's owner lives in Somerset. And the little bay at Place is supposed to be where Joseph of Arimathea first landed in England, bringing with him a precocious nephew who went by the name of Jesus.

I am most surprised that Morton didn't unearth that little nugget.

I help the man wrestle the door out of his car and then I toddle down the hill to find the Audi. Before driving off to find somewhere to stay, I sit awhile on the rocks, watching the last light fade among the hills and water. The birds fall silent. No lights come on in Place House. The peace is tangible. But it is far from wilderness. For all its beauty the land feels warmly domesticated. The house has settled among the gentleness and become a part of it. It feels like what it is, a haven, beyond the swing of the world. I'd probably be bored here. But it is sweet. And the dogs would love it.

10

Banging in the Rain

It is raining. Hard. A tall woman is hastening through Truro wearing a plastic headscarf and one of the thin and shapeless plastic macintoshes that are, I think, unique to England. She is towing a basket on wheels past a branch of the Body Shop. She is not the sort of woman who shops at the Body Shop.

An example of the sort of woman who shops at the Body Shop is emerging from it. She has plenty of body but it is wide rather than tall. She is wearing clothes to a value of perhaps seven hundred and fifty pounds but no protection against the rain. She too is moving at speed. A taxi is waiting for her across the street. She swings round the corner of the plate-glass window and meets the woman in the plastic mac with such drastic accuracy that neither has the time to raise an arm. They clash so thoroughly that body strikes body full on. The Body Shop woman's face sinks into the chest of the plastic mac.

Even in the rain their clash and gasps are audible for twenty feet. A dozen shoppers stop and turn their heads or raise umbrellas to stare.

Neither woman has fallen, but both are deeply shocked. The encounter is just so intrusive, such an appalling clash of flesh on flesh, so great an offence against the rules of decency and privacy. A clash of class too, a clash marginally won by Mrs Body Shop, who had the advantages of greater bulk and a lower centre of gravity. The taller woman staggered several paces backwards.

But it is she who is the first to regain the power of speech. 'Are you all right, dear?' she says. She makes to lay a hand on the other's arm but then retracts it. The other is patting desperately at her clothing. 'Thank you,' she says and it is all she says and it doesn't mean thank you. She goes to her taxi. The taller woman moves on too. The incident is over. Truro resumes being wet.

Rain is England's international signature note. Though England is no wetter, I suspect, than Normandy, say, or northern Germany or Patagonia, none of these places has become synonymous with rain as England has. Picture a test match in Australia and you see a shirts-off crowd with hats and sunglasses, and the players so brightly sunlit that you have to squint. Picture an English test match and you see players in sweaters beneath a louring sky, and then the crowd suddenly sprouting umbrellas, like speeded-up film of a mushroom farm, as the players dash from the field and the ground staff dash onto it with covers.

The English don't celebrate their rain. There are no post-cards available of Truro wet, or of a drenched Big Ben. The postcards are all sparkly with sunshine, just as they are, with greater honesty, elsewhere in the world. Meanwhile the English delight in bemoaning their climate, stressing its dampness. It suits the national trait of self-deprecation, and of muddling along somehow despite mild adversity. It's the attitude expressed in that defining phrase, 'mustn't grumble', striking a uniquely English note of making do, getting by, being grateful for small mercies, and knowing that there's others worse off.

I sometimes wonder whether I am alone in liking the English climate. It provides the occasional exciting extreme, the phew-what-a-scorcher heat wave, the nation-stopping dump of snow, but generally it provides a temperature you can do things in, a soft light and the ceaseless swing of the seasons. Put me in the endless sun of California or Brisbane and I'd soon be screaming for drizzle.

The Body Shop incident isn't the first collision I have seen this morning, though it is by far the most enjoyable. The cars are doing fine, headlights on, wipers sweeping, the road rules dictating their path. Not so the pedestrians, who are like an inferior species with less developed senses. On narrow pave-ments they hold umbrellas up and forward like medieval shields against a shower of arrows. Umbrellas are wider than people. Umbrella rim strikes umbrella rim and there is an instant simultaneous susurration of 'sorry, sorry' before the brollies straighten and move on. It's fun to watch in a low-key way, or it would be if it wasn't raining, although if it wasn't raining it wouldn't be there to watch. I take refuge in the public library. The place steams. Coats hang dripping from the backs of chairs.

A library is a church with books. It smells musty, fusty. Like a church it holds a hushed approximation to reverence and like a church it accepts all types – the shy, the serious, the desperate, the lonely, the scholarly and the drunk. Almost all are just off the main stream, partial outsiders, in some way odd. I too am one, a rootless passer-through. The rooted are at home, or at work, or battling through the rain.

I want to look up Joseph of Arimathea on the Internet but the bank of computers is fully occupied and others are waiting to get on. They'll have to wait a while. Few of the keyboard-users are prepared to risk a second finger. I find the books of local history, but am not bothered enough by Joseph of Arimathea to do more than skim unprofitably through a couple of indexes.

The table of newspapers is unoccupied except by a bearded man who appears to be asleep. 'Pet parrot dies after 39 years,' says the headline of the *West Briton*. 'Pet cat stabbed in eye,' says the *Cornish Gazette*. There are pictures of both parrot and cat. The *Daily Mail*, as befits a national paper, is more ambitious. Its lengthy headline demonstrates the *Mail*'s customary respect for the rules of reasoning: 'Crime is falling, says Blair, as a young mother in the safest part of England lies stabbed and paralysed.' There is a picture of the woman.

The queue for the computers continues to grow and the condensation on the library windows thickens. I leave, intent on making a tour of Truro regardless of the rain. But that rain is drillingly vertical, each drop a shell that hits a puddle with force enough to blast a momentary crater and spout. By stepping off the pavement to avoid the metre-wide umbrellas my feet are soaked in seconds. I take shelter in the museum. Another sanctuary. Another public collection of yesterday.

I'm not alone. A pair of harassed teachers has brought a class of excited kids. The kids are not excited by the museum. They are excited by being kids, and by being with other kids, and by not being in the classroom.

The museum knows about kids. It pretends to want them. It has set up exhibits with things that the kids can touch and move. I suspect they call it discovery learning. The kids discover that they can make a lot of noise and get away with it. The teachers try to keep some sort of lid on the noise, conscious of the infraction of the law of adult seriousness, but fail. The kids start doing something deeply educational with wooden fish and I flee to the minerals room. I know nothing of minerals. I spend half an hour among the glass cases, staring at crystals that look like dinosaur teeth, inspecting samples of ore that look like rubble, and reading about the multiple compounds of multiple metals. If you tested me tomorrow I would still know nothing about minerals.

But I do absorb something of Cornwall's past: the industrial slavery of the mines, the women who broke ore for a living, the gradual depletion of the lodes, the mass emigration to Australia, South Africa, anywhere in the new-found world where there were holes to be dug and minerals extracted. So much for fairyland. It's a harsh story and a typically Celtic one, the hardship of a peripheral breed. They worked all they'd got, which was the land, worked it until it had no more to give, and then they left its exhaustion behind.

When the kids come to minerals, I go to fish. I read of the massive harvests of pilchards, the vast industry that grew around this single fish followed by the inevitable decline of the stocks, the poverty that ensued, and more emigration.

I lunch on a pasty, which I eat in the porch of a church. If this were the nineteenth century, and I were a Cornishman weighing up whether to emigrate or not, a traditional pasty like this might just tip the scales in favour of going. It is thirty-five per cent pastry, sixty-four per cent potato and one per cent nostril.

I pull the blue plastic hood of my rain jacket over my head and set out to try to get a grip on Truro's present. I'm never sure how to go about it. Countless travel writers tell me that such and such a town is down at heel, or long in the tooth, or jaunty with optimism, or surprised to have been discovered by George III, but I am rarely convinced. Take, for instance, swinging London of the sixties. It's an accepted fact that it swung. But in truth only a few streets swung, or believed that they swung, or wanted other people to believe that they swung, which are all more or less the same thing. Meanwhile a hundred thousand Acacia Avenues didn't swing an inch. Something was happening in Acacia Avenue, of course, because something is always happening, but that something is the aggregate of a million impulses, a multiplicity of people making their own decisions. And to see the grand sweep in this, to see how the herd is moving, the mood developing, is something I find hard.

The past you can grasp. It has been moulded into stories: Joseph of Arimathea, the decline of tin, the demise of the pilchard. You can hold these things in your hand like a box of eggs, all neatly parcelled and recognizable. But the present is smashed egg. It drips between your fingers. It's a mere mess. What can I say of Truro now, on this wet Wednesday, that is true of Truro and Truro alone, that is definitive? What I seek, I suppose, is that tyrant the story, the falsely neat narrative, our way of filing and ordering the apparently random.

The rain has shrunk to drizzle and I set off around the random with eyes, ears and a damp notebook. Rows of terraced houses line the steep street. Little front rooms house huge plasma screens, and on the wet Victorian walls outside, satellite dishes sprout like fungi. The front yards are a couple of metres square. One is cultivated with a single shrub, a pair of terracotta pots and a faultless shred of lawn with room for a single chair. It's a Lilliputian country estate. In its neighbour, a mattress sags and weeps beside a pair of rubbish bags and a dead bike.

The few people about are scurrying against the persistent drizzle. At the top of the hill, the railway station and more suburbs have climbed beyond Truro's natural declivity and peep at the rest of Cornwall. Occasional cabbage trees, which the locals call palms, suggest a cheerier climate than the one I'm getting. A railway viaduct highsteps across a valley on magnificent brick stilts.

I wind around the city limits, through streets devoid of interest to a visitor, circling the city centre but being slowly sucked back down towards it like water towards a plughole. Up top, the newsagents and corner stores are sorry, fly-blown, seedy places. The further down I go, the brighter the window displays, the greater the commercial optimism, the more populous the pavements, the denser the traffic. The window of a burger bar is vivid with images of burgers standing impossibly tall with promise, each ingredient distinct, a triple-decker stack of indulgence. The disparity between the sagging burger you get in its little cardboard box and the burger you see in the window is the same disparity as between the dank small houses that line the street and the pics in the travel agent's of beaches in Barbados and Gran Canarias and Lanzarote (direct flight from Exeter). There are no pictures in the travel agent's of the Roseland beaches twenty miles away, no pictures of the sweet serenity of Place.

Fantasy has always been the stuff of commerce, and the National Trust shop sells a distinctively English fantasy. Its shelves are crammed with honey and beeswax soap, scented drawer-liners, jams with lids of chequered cloth, aprons with flowers on them, mugs with flowers on them, place mats with flowers on them and a CD rack of 'music for tired gardeners'. It's a nicely-nicely, middle-class Englishness, born of the same impulse, the same ideal, as the Lilliput Lane ceramics and the tended prettiness of, say, Faccombe. The natural world it celebrates is a domesticated, governed one, fragrant and threatless. Such animals as inhabit it are Beatrix Potter animals, half-tame and utterly endearing.

The National Trust sells a range of winsome wooden ducks. A sticker on each duck says, 'If you want to put me outside I need a coat of varnish to protect my joints.' You can smell Beatrix Potter in that first-person pronoun.

I pick a duck up. In doing so I knock another down.

'Sorry,' I say, as a woman comes across. She is dressed

precisely as one would expect. Her skirt, her blouse and her cardigan would all vote Tory.

'We have a full list of the names,' she says, picking the duck up and stroking its smooth wooden head. 'To save you going through them.'

'Sorry?' I say again. It's an invaluable word in England.

'They're all individually named,' says the woman, 'the ducks.' Her accent is not Cornish.

I upturn the duck in my hand. It's called Elvis. I show the name to the woman. She grins. I tell her that if she can find me one called Elton John, I'll buy it.

'Really?' she says.

'Yes, really. I'd like to wring its neck.'

The woman hoots with laughter. 'Oh,' she says when she recovers herself, 'we have enormous fun with these ducks.'

Round the back of the nineteenth-century cathedral runs a rain-swollen little river. There's a weir and a paved seating area and a pair of real ducks, mallards, who come rocking towards me like portly comics on stumpy orange legs. I have nothing for them but cigarette ash, which they inspect then reject. I stare a while at the shifting iridescence of the male's head, the precisely-defined collar of white, the pearls of water on the duck's back. In the window of a bungalow an old man sits immobile in an armchair, suspiciously watching me watch his ducks. I wave to him and he does not wave back.

The Old Chapel House doesn't do chapel any more. It's moved on to alternative fantasies these days, offering Yoga Ltd, Pilates in the City, Mandarin Holistic Health, and a Beauty Retreat, to the damp and disbelieving streets of Truro.

In the twenty-four-hour Tesco you can find the village that Truro isn't any more. The bakers wear bakers' hats, the butchers striped aprons. You can eat there too, and buy insurance, and do your banking. In short you could live there. One bearded drunk is trying to do just that, sitting in the foyer grumbling at nothing. The patient security guard, acting as village policeman, ushers him slowly out of the air-conditioning and into the low grey afternoon.

In Marks & Spencer the food seems posher than in Tesco. The labels offer luxuriant descriptions of what the plastic boxes hold. Most hold prepared meals.

Forty years ago, Raymond Baxter on *Tomorrow's World* promised us a society of leisure. It was due, if I recall, about now, but to judge by the array of prepared meals, the society of leisure hasn't arrived. Or else it has, but people choose not to spend their increased leisure time cooking. Instead they read the ever-proliferating numbers of cookbooks or watch celebrity chefs on television. What was once a daily necessity is increasingly a spectator sport.

In search of a pork pie, I seek help from an assistant, who seeks help from another assistant. Between them they find a three-pack of mini pork pies and a two-pack of proper-sized pork pies. I want one pork pie.

Apart from the food, Marks & Spencer still looks and feels as Raymond Baxter would have known it. The corporate blue and green remains the same, the air-conditioning dial is still set half a degree below that of rival stores, and there are still abundant racks of women's underwear. But that underwear does seem to have got more skimpy. There are fewer of those traditional white knickers the size of trawler nets.

I check some labels. It used to be a boast of M&S that almost all their clothes were British-made. They aren't now. But women still browse them in the same way, rubbing material between finger and thumb, holding hangered tops against their chests, turning once, twice in the mirror, then returning the clothes to the racks less neatly than I would. I feel as alien here as I did aged six.

I take a seat on a bench in the town centre and try to resolve what makes this place distinctively Cornish. I can find nothing. And when I try to define what makes it distinctively English, rather than, say, French or German, I find that hard too. Apart from the obvious – language, street signs, architecture, weather – to my insensitive eye this could be downtown Anywhereville in the prosperous West.

The evening rush hour has started. The little streets grow clogged with swishing vehicles. The clouds stay low and the bus interiors shine bright, holding a cast of silent people staring out of the half-misted windows, like a moving theatre showing one of the duller plays by Chekhov. 'One of the duller plays by Chekhov', by the way, is a text-book example of redundancy.

The pub, at least, is incontrovertibly English – low, bottle-lined, the ceiling browned with smoke, the bar ringed with sticky stuff, and the barman aged and grizzled. In front of him stands a row of hand-pull beer taps like stretched pepper mills. I ask for a pint of bitter. The barman says nothing. He places a glass under one of the electric pumps.

'No, no,' I say, and tap the nearest peppermill.

'Ain't got none on,' says the barman and carries on pouring. I meekly buy what he puts in front of me.

It's too cold to taste, and too sweet to be called beer. It's alcoholic lolly-water, Orwellian beer, fuel for loutishness, bad brown lager, a travesty of English beer. It's the sort of beer, in fact, that the rest of the world drinks.

11

The Bloody End

I suspect that people have always travelled to places of significance. I bet, for example, that Stonehenge has been catering to visitors from the day the first stone went up. Whether these visitors are referred to as pilgrims or tourists depends only on the century they travelled in. The urge remains the same: to see somewhere that is distinct or pleasing, in some way remarkable, somewhere that matters.

There are few truly remarkable places. Most are more significant when imagined than when visited. But with the growth of affluence and the ease of modern travel, remarkable places are greatly in demand. When I was born, most Brits took holidays on the English coast. These days they go anywhere in the world – the Seychelles, Dubai, Bali. Increasingly I meet them in New Zealand.

What draws people to New Zealand is the scenery. They've seen brochures and *The Lord of the Rings*, and they want to see wilderness and mountains and sheep and, astonishingly, the paddock round the back of Ashburton where Gollum slithered or Gandalf walloped an Orc. (I am not making this up. In 2005 the best-selling book in New Zealand was the *Location Guide* to *The Lord of the Rings*.)

When the tourist arrives at the significant place, he finds enough to look at to last him an hour or so. He's then faced with finding something else to fill his time. And an industry has arisen to provide that something. Attractions sprout from the soil, and gradually a parallel world is created, a world that exists, not for the people who live in a place, but for the people who visit that place. In Dubai, for example, there is a water-based theme park called Wadi World. What the Bedouins would have made of it is hard to guess. And in New Zealand there are now abundant outfits where visitors can get 'the authentic Kiwi farming experience'. They can watch a shepherd mustering with dogs, or a sheep being shorn. It's done purely to entertain the visitors. Were those visitors not there, the sheep would be in the paddock and the shepherd down the pub. It's a form of parodic culture-packaging and it is mostly gruesome.

Mass tourism is a twentieth-century invention and Morton was at its forefront. He was one of the first to exploit the unprecedented liberty of the private car. He went where he pleased and as often as not what pleased him was the remoteness of places like St Anthony in Roseland. But he also visited places of significance, places that already drew visitors. One of these was Land's End. And I'm as keen as he was to see it. If nothing else, it's a brilliant place name. It oozes an ominous romance and a primal sense of isolation and vulnerability, though on reflection it's a name that could be legitimately applied to any bit of coast.

When Morton went, there were already guides touting for business, but he found a thrill all the same. The place was thick with fog, 'drenching the body and drenching the mind in melancholy; Land's End seemed like the end of all things'.

I get no fog. Beyond Penzance the land slides like a tilted table towards its own extinction. Hedges, gorse and outcrops of rock lie spread beneath a sky of old-man-underpant grey that presses like a weight. I follow a Vauxhall Agila with a fish-sticker in the back window. 'Caution:' says the sticker, 'never drive faster than your angel can fly.' The driver of the Agila has a seriously slow angel.

You have to pay three pounds to park at Land's End. For that you get a brochure and the chance to choose your own spot in a car park the size of Hampshire. This early in the morning it holds perhaps fifty cars. The brochure promises me 'over 20,000 square feet of Undercover Attractions'. I leave the car, and head down towards the end of England, skirting, as I do so, the walled Undercover Attraction area.

I have the place almost to myself. I scramble down a track. Rocks poke through the thin grass like blisters. Far out, the sea looks muscled and appropriately forbidding. Below my feet it froths and sucks, eroding the rocks along their fault lines, so the shoreline resembles a tumble of building blocks. The final smidgeon of land is a turret of brown stone with a seaweed hat. Gulls mew. Under the louring cloud it all feels suitably eerie. But other than the significance we've chosen to invest in it, there's nothing to distinguish Land's End from the rest of Cornwall's coast. I sit a while. Two couples come down the track. They film themselves with a palm-sized video camera.

'How do I get black and white?'

'Turn the dial, the one on the side. No, the little one.'

'No, I don't want black and white. I want that brown one, you know, what's it called, that old brown stuff. Has it got that?'

'Sepia.'

'Yeah, sepia. Has it got sepia?

'Dunno.'

'I like sepia.'

I follow a track that leads to the attractions, buy an ice cream and sit to study the brochure. Its author predictably found the lure of the pun irresistible. 'You can't go further than a day at Land's End', it says, and in a starburst on the cover, 'Legendary Land's End. The Ultimate Destination'.

'Your personal guide to endless hours of fun' details the joys available. They include 'The Relentless Sea'. 'This hands on, thought-provoking exhibition tells the heroic – and sometimes tragic – story of Mankind's struggle to win a living from the bountiful but unforgiving sea.'

'Return to the last Labyrinth' offers 'a whole new journey into wonder. Amazing tales of heroism, skulduggery and adventure told anew. An enthralling world with monsters, pirates, smugglers and wreckers, Arthur and the Age of Knights brought to life with images, sound and stunning special effects.'

Am I alone in finding this stuff repellent? No, more than repellent. I find it simultaneously absurd, hateful and terminally saddening. It's a distillation of pap, a Disneyland of verbal dishonesty. 'Heroism, skulduggery and adventure' mean sanitized glorifications of fighting and illegality. 'Monsters' is a bald lie. 'Pirates' were thieves. 'Smugglers' were tax-dodgers. 'Wreckers' were vultures. 'Arthur and the Age of Knights' were more or less mythical.

I could go on, and I shall. The Land's End Hotel is described as 'a magical place to stay'. Go on, show me the magic. Is it in the wind, the neutral grey-green sea, or somewhere in the space between the coarse turf and the mewing gulls?

Shall we move on? Let's visit 'Land's End's very own traditional Cornish Sweet [oh my God] Manufactory', or Greeb Farm, 'a restored 200 year old Cornish farmstead' (you've got to admire the 'stead') 'on land worked for centuries against the odds' (which won), 'in a spectacular setting at the World's edge'. Here you can 'meet the animals'. With sickening predictability the text is accompanied by a picture of blond-haired children feeding a bottle to a pink-eyed diddumsy piglet in a nice warm barn, just like those quaint bewhiskered Cornish farmers did.

Had enough of indoors? Spent enough money? Eaten enough sweets from the manufactory? Handled enough hands-on exhibits? Then 'take a walk on the wild side' (do they have to?) and follow 'Charlie the Chough's Nature Trail'. 'You might see wild flowers.'

This is not plain trippersville. I don't mind trippersville. I was brought up near Brighton. I like the kiss-me-quick hats, the sticks of rock, the naughty-naughty Tommy Trinder comedy on the end of the pier, the whelks and beer, the shop selling fried eggs made of dyed sugar. None of those things pretend to be anything but froth. But this stuff purports to have some bearing on reality. It is a travesty of the past and of the present. It represents the divorce of language from meaning and the divorce of cosseted urban contemporary man from any sense of the actual world he lives in. 'You may see wild flowers.' Fuck it. The place deserves bombing.

Back up the road a bit, the hamlet of Sennen sits low to the ground, skulking under the wind. Though a weak sun has emerged, the stone of the buildings is as dark as misery. All windows are small. Here's a harsh and honest bleakness that scoffs at the attractions down the road more emphatically than I do.

In Sennen, Morton drank at the pub and poked around the little church next door, where he found what he described as 'the last touch of real poetry in England' on the headstone of Dionysius Williams. It's still there but it takes a while to find, set into the low church wall, masked by nettles and guarded by a spiked and rusted railing.

> Life speeds away
> From point to point, though seeming to stand still
> The cunning fugitive is swift by stealth;
> Too subtle is the movement to be seen,
> Yet soon man's hour is up and we are gone.

Morton says the words gave him 'a cold thrill'. I get more of a buzz from knowing that I am standing precisely where Morton stood seventy-nine years ago in his tweed jacket, while his bull-nosed Morris waited on the grass beside this little church. There's a sundial on the church wall. The pale shadow on its face says eleven o'clock precisely. It's twenty past twelve.

In the pub four morose men are watching motor racing on a wide flat television. A fat man at the bar talks loudly into a gleaming cellphone in a Home Counties accent. A fat girl is sitting underneath the television looking away from it, her chin in her hands. The barmaid is vinegar-sour and she can't work the electronic till.

In Morton's day there was an innkeeper. He told Morton that there was supposed to be a vault beneath the inn where smugglers, inevitably, hid brandy, but that he'd never found the time to look for it. Morton claimed to believe the story. Ever the romantic, he believed this inn to be 'sitting on a secret'.

And it looks like the old romantic was right. Some floorboards have been replaced with thick glass to reveal the electrically lit depth of 'Annie's Well'.

A plaque explains: 'Ann Treeve presided with the local parson over local smuggling, but then turned Queen's evidence against a Sennen farmer who went to prison. Annie was staked out on Sennen beach and drowned by the incoming tide. Her body was laid out upstairs here then buried in an unmarked grave.'

All of which sounds a suitable story for a pub on a tourist route to propagate. I have no reason to believe or disbelieve it. Indeed I wouldn't mention it, were it not for the name of the imprisoned Sennen farmer. He was Dionysius Williams. Morton would have enjoyed knowing that.

The coast road that winds north and east from Land's End is a spectacular bleakness. The view of gorse and drystone walls is interrupted by sudden remarkable snatches of coastal bays and headlands. What I take to be derelict tin mines litter the landscape, their chimneys or engine towers crumbling picturesquely. Entropy's got a grip here.

The little town of St Just is stone-built and darkly quaint, its central square a prettiness with a hard hewn edge. It may depend on tourists now, but time was when life here was an endurance test.

Early afternoon and there are few people about. Just off the central square is a walled amphitheatre like a shallow pie dish, perhaps thirty yards across. Five old stones stand irregularly off centre. On one of the stones sits a boy of perhaps fifteen. At his feet a terrier. In his hand an ice cream. On his lap a girl. Over the girl's chest a pink T-shirt two sizes too small. Until the early seventeenth century mystery plays were performed in this circle. The show that's going on now is older, but less mysterious.

St Ives is full. It won't let the Audi stop. I tour a couple of scenic car parks, perform several pas-de-deux with other would-be parkers, become frustrated and drive on. I read in *The Times* the other day that there are over thirty million registered cars in the UK, twice what there were when I left school. Nose to tail those cars would stretch from London to Auckland.

And back. And then from London to Auckland again. And back again.

At Bodmin they're playing football. I have seen football on every television in every pub. The professional players wear shirts and shorts made from a synthetic material that shines like silk and ripples like water. It's a sort of sexy lingerie. The turf on television looks like an emerald carpet, and the ball is stroked across it, the players ambling with the ease of skill. But here in Bodmin is the real thing, a thing of mud and shouting. The two teams are hard to distinguish. The players wear the same synthetic shirts and shorts as the pros, but the drizzle and mud have sullied them. The goalkeeper at the less busy end wears gloves the size of hedgehogs and beats them together to generate warmth and noise. The goalie at the busy end, the losing end, wears a second uniform of mud. His eyes stare out of it. When he shouts, which is often, his tongue and teeth are a pink and white surprise. There's a small covered stand and it's empty.

The two dozen or so spectators on the sideline are all associated in some direct way with the teams. Spectators and players alike strive to imitate the fabled game of television, but they live a lot further down the slopes that culminate in the snowy faultless peak of the premiership (which used to be the First Division until the authorities renamed it in French in order to make it sound even more exalted. They then had the brilliant idea of renaming the second division 'first').

The shouts of the players are the same as when I was a boy on tour in Plymouth, a sort of footballing liturgy, as meaningless and repetitive as a Latin mass. 'Knock it square, son. Far canal. Lay it off. Man on, John, man on. Compete, lads, compete. Pressure, pressure. Keeper. Far canal, ref, far canal.' All delivered with an accent that seems to come from London.

It's a raw game of blood and crunch. Hard nylon studs crash into shins. Players fall in tangles of testosterone. The ball bounces irregularly off ridges of mud. Neither side keeps

possession for long. Shots bobble weakly wide of the goal. The
nets sag with wet. And when anyone heads the ball I wince. I
could never head the ball. I wanted to head it, and I knew how
to head it, and I would get into a position to head it, and yet
always, at the last possible moment, I would retract my head
like a turtle. I hugely admired the centre backs who would
meet a goalkeeper's punt on the full, taking the gravity-driven
descent of wet leather on their foreheads, yet seeming to feel no
pain, no dizzying after-effects, nothing.

Years later I read an article saying that heading damaged
the brain. I can't remember what evidence was put forward,
but they might have considered the television commentary of
some former centre-backs.

The bedraggled football ends with a score line I shall never
know and a tune on the whistle whose rhythm hasn't changed
since my childhood. I drift away and find a little drinking
basin set low against a wall. 'Presented by His Royal Highness
Prince Chula of Siam,' says a plaque, 'in memory of his friend
Joan, a wire-haired terrier, who died in 1945 in his 17th year.'
What Prince Chula was doing in Bodmin I don't know.
Perhaps he was kicked out of Siam for being unable to sex
dogs.

The barman at the White Hart is a Geordie. He's wearing an
England football shirt that bears the royal standard above the
legend 'Official Beer – Carlsberg'. The Geordie seems a nice
guy in the way a Siamese street trader can seem a nice guy. In
other words, he smiles and natters, but I don't understand a
word.

Nevertheless I manage to rent a room with a sash window
out of which I can lean and touch the swinging pub sign. Grass
is growing by the chimney pot. Inside, the walls of the room are
hung with three small gilt-framed pictures. Each depicts a
thatched cottage. The first two are called *Summertime* and
Feeding the Doves, but inspiration then ran dry. The third is
called *A Thatched Cottage*.

Bodmin climbs up a hill to Bodmin Beacon and so do I, past small terraced houses with notices proclaiming that the occupant won't buy anything from door-to-door salesmen. It's easier for the English than having to say no thank you. In the street where I was raised I knew a woman who hid from Jehovah's Witnesses. She'd crouch below her sink until they went away. Sometimes, she said, they would go round the back of the house to try to ferret her out. They terrified her. It's hard to imagine a Frenchwoman being similarly frightened.

Bodmin High Street is losing the struggle. Its foe is the supermarket. 'Chic Style Clothes' is dead. The delicatessen is dead. Estate agents survive for now, but surely it's only a matter of time before Tesco sells houses. And everywhere the charity shops are sneaking in, like a fungus spreading over a corpse before decomposition. A sign in the YMCA window says 'Charity shops are the new chic'.

I climb to the upper limit of Bodmin, up a muddy track lined with bright bluebells and brighter litter, then out onto the boggy summit of the beacon. Up here are wind and dog-walkers and a hundred-and-forty-four-foot tall granite monument to a forgotten Lieutenant General.

Away to the east lies Bodmin Moor, where the fabled Beast of Bodmin roams and offers only smudgy photos of itself to titillate readers of the *Daily Express*. Though I have to say that, from here, the nearer bits of Bodmin Moor look about as forbidding as Bambi's paddock, and the only substantial beast about is a prodigiously fat Lab. Its owner is built like a whippet.

A couple of hours and a few Bodmin beers later I'm eating noodles with a plastic fork from a plastic container on the cold stone steps of the county court. Across the road two thirteen-year-old girls are lounging on the street corner like prostitutes. They are appropriately dressed. They notice me, then confer. 'Excuse me,' says one, 'do you like lesbians?'

I'm not quite sure what to reply, but it doesn't matter.

Without my saying anything they launch into an elaborate pashing routine, wrapping their legs around each other like the tendrils on vines. Then their taxi arrives and they get into it giggling.

There was a certain Englishness about the 'excuse me'.

12

Dead Poet with Golf

The beach at Trebetherick is wide and sandy, and deserted but for a woman kicking a tennis ball for a mongrel. A sign says 'Dogs Welcome'. The dog brings me the tennis ball.

The woman has just this week returned from visiting a psychic surgeon in Brazil.

'You had an operation?'

'Oh no,' she says, 'I'm a healer and psychic myself. I just wanted to see if he'd got anything I hadn't got.'

'And had he?'

'Oh yes, he's got a great gift. I followed him around for fourteen weeks. Brazil's brilliant. If anyone has an idea, they just open a church. There's this one place where two thousand mediums dress up and commune together at the same time. It makes for a very sensible way of life.'

The woman's tone is impressively matter-of-fact. She discusses spiritual nonsense in the way others might discuss gardening.

When she asks me what I'm doing in Trebetherick, I say, 'Betjeman, I'm afraid.' For I have been sideswiped once again by literature. I was following Morton's tyre tracks to Tintagel when I saw Trebetherick on a signpost, felt a frisson of recognition, riffled through the mental filing cabinet, came up with Betjeman and turned down a lane.

(The signpost also mentioned a place called Pityme. I was keen to discover how to pronounce Pityme – both versions that came to mind were pleasing – and would have stopped to ask a local if I could have found one. Or indeed if I could have found Pityme.)

'Oh, Betjeman, yes,' says the woman. 'He had a house in the lane you've just come down, and he's buried over there at St Enodoc.' She waves a hand vaguely towards trees that back the beach. 'On the golf course. You can't miss it.'

The name St Enodoc chimes in my head, and the golf brings a single line of Betjeman to mind. He wrote of a drive, a chip and a putt that he played on some seaside course, resulting in 'a quite unprecedented three'. It is a line so typical of him.

Betjeman is easy to mock, to see as a sort of rhyming Morton, an utterly English lover of the old and the quaint, hater of Slough. But that's to do him an injustice. His poetry is not a metrical rendition of *Majesty* magazine. It is riddled with doubt, sex and fear, crammed with suburban detail, and his tastes are idiosyncratic. Name one other poet who would be willing to celebrate in serious verse his sheer and abundant delight in scoring a birdie. Tennyson on the ninth green? Ted Hughes in the bunker? No, Betjeman was refreshingly honest to his own truth. I can think of no higher praise.

I follow a path between houses and shrubs, its lank margins still damp with morning, and packed with the thrusting creamy-green heads of cow parsley on the point of bursting into summer white. Over a fence and I'm on the edge of a fairway, a green to my left, a tee to my right. Behind the tee stands a neat little hill that begs to be climbed, bathed in a sunshine like weak Lucozade. The golf course sits snug in a valley whose walls are grassed dunes. Nobody is playing. The fairways are hummocked like a box of eggs. The whole valley is shaped like a bath, and at the point where the plughole would be, a church tower pokes above a hedge. The tower is crooked. It looks like a bad illustration from a children's book of gnomes. A big gull sits on the spire's tip.

The turf underfoot has a wiry seaside resilience. I bounce across it, strangely eager.

The church is sunken. At the eastern end you could jump from the gravestones onto the roof. Around the graveyard stands a thick and layered hedge. I duck through the wooden lychgate and there, immediately, on my right, set into the turf, stands a black slate headstone polished like a mirror. Chiselled into the slate, amid a bird's nest of scrolls and curlicues, 'John Betjeman 1906–1984'. Nothing else. No Sir. No Poet Laureate. No mention of the laughing televisual teddy bear. Wise, that.

Shells have been laid beside the stone, and a pine cone, and a little card. Feeling faintly invasive, touristic, ghoulish, I peel apart the damp leaves of the card. 'For all the happy years of poetry, churches and railways, thank you.' No signature. The ink has begun to seep and bleach.

I don't want to go into the church. It will be just another

church to me. I sit awhile above Betjeman's bones. The damp cools my backside. The strengthening sun warms my baldness. A wren appears in the hedge and chirrups, tiny, insistent, loud beyond its size. I am, well, not entranced, but awash with a mix of veneration, association and seaside sweetness.

Take the grave away, and I would not sit amid this golf course. At seventeen years old, and half a dozen counties east of here, I bought the paperback *Collected Betjeman* with its pinkish cover. I learned great chunks of it. I've got the book still. It's sitting at home in New Zealand, its spine stiffened by masking tape. And here is one of the places that Betjeman loved enough to have pickled it in words, words that have already outlasted him by twenty-one years.

A husbands-and-wives foursome comes trundling over the ridge. I watch one of the wives play an iron-shot with the cruel clumsiness of late middle age, her swing a cramped and pitiful battle against fat and hips and the stiffness of time. The ball rises briefly from the turf, then performs a few veering rabbit hops among the hummocks, and is acknowledged with an unconvincing, 'Nice shot,' from one of the husbands (and my bet would be on the one who wasn't hers). I leave.

I climb Bray Hill beside the golf course to find a view as sweet as strawberries. The sea comes in from the north between dark heads, and past an off-centre island. On the far shore, wavelets feather a sandy beach, and Cornwall stretches away behind in greenly gentle slopes before dissolving into greyish watercolour distance. A clump of indefinite buildings to the south must be Padstow. The sands of Trebetherick bay reflect a shimmering hazy sky. A skylark does its invisible tuneful stuff and beside me where I sit, a clump of cowslips droops, the flowers the colour of cheap margarine, the leaves a greyish crinkled wad. And I feel strongly that this is good. Part nostalgia, part literature, part clean air and sky and sea and grass and solitude, entirely good.

*

Back in the Audi and halfway along the coastal road to Tintagel, I see a lad by the road with a surfboard, hitching. I stop. He wants to go a mile or so up the road to Trebarwith. The surfboard is big. The Audi's cabin isn't. He tries to fit the thing in then says not to bother, it isn't far. But he's not getting away that easily. Somehow, and without lowering the roof, we angle the board in and he slithers beneath it with the lissomness of youth that has long since deserted both me and the lady golfer.

His name is Sam. I tell him he's the first hitcher I've seen.

'Hitching's dead,' he says. 'No one does it much any more. It's all right round here if you live here, like, cos people know you, but on the big roads it's a waste of bloody time.'

I tell him that it didn't use to be a waste of time, that when I was his age I hitched all over the country with ease. As I hear the words they sound like an old man's lament, a back-in-the-good-old-days, and I realize that to Sam I am a former, a has-been, a was. At the same time I am aware that when I saw him on the road, saw his outstretched arm and raised thumb, I felt a kinship of similarity, felt that effectively I was stopping the car to pick up myself, my real self, my alone and young and hitching self.

'People are scared to pick you up, I reckon,' says Sam. 'They've read too many stories in the paper.'

When I ask him if he expects to spend his life in Cornwall he says he doesn't think he'll ever be able to afford a house. 'The money men have bought them all up.'

'So?'

'Dunno,' he says and shrugs. I drive him down an impossibly narrow lane to where the surfers gather. Trebarwith is just a steep cleft in the slate, a stream-carved vee that opens to a little bay and giant headlands and beyond them, the surf of the Atlantic's edge.

*

Tintagel proves similar but surferless. To either side of the pebble beach stand a cave and a peninsular crag. On top of the crag are the remains of a castle. The castle is supposed to have been Arthur's, the cave, inevitably, Merlin's.

'Do boys still read Malory?' asked Morton. 'Do they lie on their stomachs in orchards with that book propped up before them in the grass? Do they forget to go home for food and lie on till the harvest bugs set about them and the dusk falls, reading that wild gallantry? Do they still go back through darkening woods, shamefully late, peopling the hush with the splintering crash of steel point on jesseraunts of double mail?'

No, Mr Morton, I don't think very many of them do. But they do play Nintendo. It's much the same.

Steps carved from the rock lead up to a hut where a woman in a thick crew-neck English Heritage sweater takes three pounds ninety from you. If you offer her another three pounds fifty she will give you a guide book. I don't.

Morton had the place to himself. I share it with several hundred people, most prominent among whom are a party of middle-aged Swedes. They are a byword for happiness. On this windswept heap of granite as forbidding as the Old Testament they chuckle and giggle their way around, roaring with joy at sudden gusts of wind that threaten their headscarves and their balance, taking photos of each other, hair streaming, in front of stone remnants of who knows what bits of which castle.

For there have been several castles here, I gather, and I can readily understand that this is an easy place to defend. The natural walls are sheer and the only point of access is the narrow and easily defended cleft leading down from the village of Tintagel. What I don't understand is why anyone should bother to attack it. If I were invading Cornwall, I'd just land elsewhere and march past.

The place feels grim, remote, austere. I wander, peering at stuff, reading the standard informative placards, but taking more pleasure from the gulls that ride the winds and the short seaside flowers whose stalks flatten to leeward, their petals quite undamaged, their roots moored amid the turf. Every time I turn a corner I meet another huddle of Swedes being gleeful.

I'm soon bored, and climb back up through the valley to the little stone village of Tintagel, which knows exactly how pretty it is. It makes a living from that prettiness. Granny Wobblys Fudge Pantry is painted pink.

13
Afternoon Toggles

In Tavistock, birthplace of Francis Drake, something is about
to happen. Morton didn't stop here and I have stopped only
for something to eat. It's Sunday afternoon. On the paved area
between the old church and the not-so-old civic buildings,
people are loitering. You can tell by the way they are loitering
that the something they are waiting for is not an exciting something. But on a sombre Sunday afternoon, when every shop

134

except Superdrug seems to be shut and Tavistock seems drenched in torpor, any something is welcome. There's a firm of solicitors here called Sleep and Co.

A knot of non-Enid-Blyton kids is spitting and swearing and laughing with private malice. The boys have bikes, the girls cellphones. They're all about twelve, I would guess, though the boys look nine and the girls sixteen. The adults loiter well away from them. A couple of policemen turn up in flak jackets and set up road cones, directing the traffic away from this little patch of civic street. There isn't much traffic to direct.

'A Boy Thcout parade,' says one of the coppers when I ask him what's going on, 'for St Georgeth Day.'

'Wasn't that yesterday?'

'Yeth,' says the copper with a flick of the eyebrows and a warm complicit smile.

Two stout ladies arrive and stand by the kerb. Each is wearing a chain of office. One accompanies hers with a grey trouser suit, the other with an anorak and beige pleated skirt.

A non-Enid-Blyton boy shouts, 'Bogey.' The girls snigger. The mayoress turns round sharply. The boy turns his back. 'Bogey,' he shouts again, a few seconds later. This time the mayoress does not turn round.

The dignitaries are joined by two elderly men, one of whom is wearing a suit that shimmers like fresh horse dung. Some distance off a drum starts beating. But still there is nothing to see. More people arrive, mostly old. Some are attended by nurses. Others lean in wheelchairs. Younger adults come slung with cameras.

A beaming scoutmaster, complete with toggle, strides through them to the mayoress. 'Hello,' he exclaims as if he were lost in the jungle and she a rescue party, 'thank you so much for coming.' The word 'so' is underlined with obsequious delight. He pumps her hand, then the deputy's hand, and then, as though his skin is over-crammed with joy that it has no choice but to express, he pumps the hands of both the attendant elderly gents, to the elderly gents' evident distress. He beams. The dignitaries smile effortfully back, then turn back through ninety degrees to face the road where nothing is happening. More nothing now would be upsetting, but the situation is rescued by the band. Somewhere out of sight it strikes up. I'm no fan of public music, but an unseen band playing an oompah tune that I half recognize lends an air of imminence, of joy to come. The mayoress tugs at the tails of her jacket, straightening herself into dignity. The chain is attached by a clip to the geometric centre of her back. The weight of the chain persistently hauls the jacket up, rouching the cloth, exposing the expanse of her backside.

The Tavistock Stannary Brass Band is dressed in green. The players are both young and old. They don't march especially well, but they bang and blow with vigour, exuding an air of festival. People relax and smile. A crumpled woman taps feebly on the arm of her wheelchair.

The scouts follow in troops. Each troop is led by an adult wearing a neckerchief, and the leading scout carries a placard announcing the troop's provenance. They have come from all the surrounding towns and villages. Some troops are only half a dozen strong; others run to thirty. They march worse than the band.

As each troop approaches the dignitaries, the adult leading it shouts, 'Eyes left!' and salutes, raising three fingers to the forehead. Some manage a military snap. Others don't. Most of the scouts look left, but some are distracted by scuttling parents with cameras, or else are consumed with shyness, their eyes yoked to their shoes.

Perhaps twenty troops pass by. The head-honcho scoutmaster maintains an arm-aching three-fingered salute throughout the parade, his smile fixed like a photograph and as wide as a slice of melon.

It isn't only Scouts. Guides, Cubs and Brownies follow, the ages ranging from seventeen to maybe five. The female leaders of the littlies look shamefaced at the militarism. Their 'Eyes left' is barely audible and given in a tone that says, 'To be frank, I'd really rather not.' They salute apologetically too, the elbow of the saluting arm not flung out tautly like a triangular wing but hanging limply by the breast.

And then it's over. The boys and girls are milling en masse outside the abbey across the way where presumably God will shortly get a slice of this event. The crowd disperses. The dignitaries try to do the same but don't escape before the beaming scoutmaster has given them all another pump of the hand and another effusion of thanks to warm them on their journey home. The old are led or wheeled away. The parents join their children. And Tavistock returns to Sunday-afternoonishness. The non-Enid-Blyton children who could have undermined the whole event but didn't, lurking in the background as if cowed by the massed forces of rectitude, reclaim their patch of street, sneering in a vicious private code that's liberally sprinkled with fucks.

There was something brave about the parade, but also something half-hearted. It felt like the tail-end of a long tradition, born of the deeply strange Baden-Powell, and the relief of Mafeking, and stout Victoria, and an unswerving belief in Empire. Morton was part of all that. It's what gives him his buoyancy. But it has dwindled now to almost nothing, the moral mainstream reduced to a quiet backwater.

I suspect that the morality that the scouts were born of is still espoused by much of adult Tavistock, but it has lost its confidence, its willingness to preen in public. Conservatism's gone shy. The *Daily Mail* may shout its headlines, but it's the Cool Britannia, multicultural line that now holds sway as the official national code of ethics, the rosette you can wear with pride in public. The Boy Scout movement is a retreating relic. The parade was an anachronistic straggle, shorn of pomp and self-belief. The bitter-mouthed urchins will inherit the earth, there being no longer a village policeman with slow gait and rosy cheeks to grab a pair of them and quaintly box their ears or bang their heads together or tell them that he knows their dad. Nor will any citizen stand up to them, for that citizen knows he'll just be sneered at or visited by their dad. A pendulum has swung, even in sleepy Tavistock. Or so it seems to me. Ten years from now I doubt there'll be a Boy Scout parade through Tavistock on the day after St George's Day.

Tavistock sits on the edge of Dartmoor. Morton called Dartmoor 'the green Sahara of England, a wilderness of hills and heather' and as I purr across it in the Audi's rich cocoon beneath a lowering sky, I can sense something of what Morton meant. The vegetation is darker than grass and the sudden bursts of weathered rock are gaunt in a way that Sussex, say, is never gaunt. I'm looking for the Warren Inn, where Morton found a fire that had supposedly been burning for a hundred years, but I don't find it. I just follow a road that dives in and out of steep dark valleys and over streams that look as cold as a stepmother's kiss. I stop the car on a ridge and get out.

Except for a distant whoosh of unseen water, silence. It isn't raining. It will. The sky is pressing towards the earth, and I am standing alone in a thin slice of air between land and cloud. I set off across boggy turf towards a nearby tor. Heather sweeps my calves with its resilient wiry stems, soaking my cotton trousers. The cloth slaps with wetness at each step. Even the gorse sits low to the ground here, scrubby and coarse and barely flowering, a starveling cousin to the rampant stuff that flamed and sprouted over Bucklebury.

I go further than I meant to, drawn on by a tor beyond the nearer one, a startling thing that's topped with rocks like tumbled dice. Drawn on too by a strange lust for a dose of the remote. This is a thin skin of moorland stretched over a great bulb of granite like a buried skull. The only comparable landscapes I have seen in Britain were in Wales and Scotland. This place feels stark and elemental, uncosy, undomesticated, unhedged, un-English. Odd sheep stand in the bleakness staring, not running, their coats like badly knotted rugs, their legs and noses just bone and skin.

It starts to rain, seeping rather than falling, the wind casting it across the hills in waves, like wreaths of stage smoke. I zip my jacket, haul the hood up, bury my hands in the pockets. It is darker than late afternoon has any right to be. Deep in a valley the slates of a farmhouse roof meld into the land, surrounded by a few walled paddocks of wet cattle. The rain strengthens. Through its tattoo on my hood, I can hear the cattle lowing.

The scattered dice of the tor's summit are boulders twice my height and more, fissured by centuries of wind and rain. As I clamber I nick the numb skin of a finger. The blood diffuses to a pink wash over the back of my hand. I reach a cave of sorts, the roof formed by a great block of rock that lodged as it fell. Water streams over the walls, and strange shade-dwelling plants cling to the cracks like mussels on a wharf. The relief from the beating rain is delicious, despite the involuntary shudder that scatters water from my jacket like a dog shaking. It is always good to take natural shelter. The place feels like Lear's hovel on the heath where he lay madly ranting in the straw and then slept. I don't rant or sleep but I do think primitive thoughts, Lear thoughts, 'poor naked wretches, wheresoe'er you are, that bide the pelting of this pitiless storm' thoughts.

Somewhere out there in the wet a couple of miles away sits the Audi, its cabin an upholstered leak-proof cave, a Shangri-La of warmth and comfort. The contrast is laughable. I laugh, loudly, among wet rocks. 'Poor bare forked animal.' I wait for the rain to abate. It strengthens.

A sudden heart-startling noise at the cave's entrance and a pony appears, streaming with water. We stare wide-eyed at each other a second, then I move and the pony shies and snorts and wheels and clatters off into the weather, its hooves beating

and slithering on the stone. I am sorry. I would have liked to
share the cave, to shelter with a rich-smelling steaming beast. It
would have felt rough and right and Learish.

It's getting dark, not just storm dark but evening dark.
Fearing disorientation, I head out to find the car. The jacket
sold to me as waterproof defies all my previous experience of
waterproofing by proving waterproof. But my trousers are just
sheets of wet that cling to my thighs like squid. The weight of
water hauls the waistband down and I can feel the frigid touch
of the jacket on my whitely urban flesh.

After perhaps three-quarters of an hour I fear that I have
missed the car and the road, that I am heading away from both
towards the moor's trackless heart. It's dark and I don't recognize the hill shapes and I feel a worm of unease in my gut.
Forcing myself to keep going in a straight line, I crest a rise and
see the cones of headlights sweeping through the rain illumi-
nating sodden tracts of moor. Two minutes later I make out
the Audi as a shape beside the road. I press the button on the
key fob in my pocket and thirty feet away the Audi winks its
hazard lights.

'To stand', wrote Morton, 'on a Dartmoor tor, with all the
world, it seems, falling away to the distant horizon and the
clouds moving just above your head, is to experience in some
measure a kind of panic like the primitive fear felt by many
people for thunder. A man in such surroundings seems so small
and naked. All the pretence goes from him. He drops the mask
of his civilisation and is humbled and afraid. Afraid of what?
He is rather like a rabbit moving in the open beneath the eye of
an invisible hunter.'

I'm not so sure about the invisible hunter, but I know what
he means. And I like it. Or at least I like it when an hour later I
have changed out of my sodden clothes and left them drying
on a radiator in a bedroom in a Princetown pub where the rose-
patterned wallpaper matches the rose-patterned bedspread,
and I am seated downstairs on a bar stool with a pint in front of

me and I am savouring the intense and sensuous pleasure of
dry socks.

The only impediment to further pleasure is seated two bar
stools away. He has worryingly nervous eyes, which keep flicking to me in search of a conversational opening, but then duck
back down to his pint with a sense of trespass committed. In
the end I cut the knot of silence myself, though not without a
nagging sense that I may be unwise to do so.

'Lovely evening,' I say.

'I've been medically retired,' he says.

I can think of no reply to that. I try to say, 'Oh really,' or 'Oh
dear,' but veto both and all I find myself offering him is an
idiot smile.

'My head,' he says.

I do manage a reply to that. I say, 'Oh.'

He looks at me as if the conversational ball is still on my side
of the net. I nod a bit, as though weighing what he said and, on
balance, concurring with its wisdom. But beyond that I can
find no way of carrying on. The pause lengthens. I let my eyes
fall to my glass and then feign complete absorption in its con-
tents. I can feel those eyes.

A minute later I look at my watch, drain my pint and stand.
If this were a play and I the audience, I'd groan at the implau-
sibility of my acting.

'Better be off,' I say. 'Might catch you later.'

'There's only three pubs,' he says. It sounds like a threat.

The rain has not abated. With no more dry trousers in my
pack, and with no desire for another soaking, I sprint along the
one main street of Princetown, vaulting over puddles, and
push open the door of the first pub I reach. I order a pint and
while it pours I scan the clientele for Mr Medically Retired.
Astonishingly he isn't there.

On the wall of the pub is a brass plaque. 'In 1832', it says, 'on
this spot nothing happened.' I'd like to see more such plaques.

This pub brews its own beer. The landlord is a well-spoken

non-local. The dominant character at the bar is from Ayr. A dumpy woman from Cambridge explains why she's fascinated by Spitfires. And the barmaid announces that she would like to become pope.

'No way,' says the bloke from Ayr.

'Why not?'

'They've picked that German bloke, Ratsarse. And anyway you're a woman.'

'It's about time we had a woman pope.'

'You don't speak Latin.'

'Do.'

'Go on then.'

'Paracetamol.'

'Paracetamol?'

'Yeah, it's medical. Everything medical's Latin, innit?'

I have a lovely evening. I learn a few things about Dartmoor but more about the people who tell me about Dartmoor. I drink quite a lot of good beer. I eat a plate of roast meat and vegetables that is quite rightly inexpensive, I laugh a lot, I exchange a lot of words that neither I nor anyone else will ever remember, I don't re-encounter Mr Medically Retired and I galumph happily back along the main street at closing time without noticing whether it's raining or not. In short, on 24 April 2005 on this spot nothing happened.

14

Crusties and Teacakes

Despite the rose-motif wallpaper, the pub bathroom is well appointed. The shower offers a strong and steady stream, there's a cubicle to contain it, an agreeably fluffy bathmat, a sachet of soap for my exclusive use, a little bottle of root-ginger shampoo, and towels that, while not precisely fluffy, do look to have powers of absorption. But the water runs Dartmoor cold.

Beside the shower hose is what looks like an electric water

heater. Naked and shivering, I fiddle with the controls to no effect, then fossick for a switch. I look behind the towel rail, under the sink, inside the little cabinet, and in all the other obvious places that rented bathrooms have taught me over the years. Nothing. I splash myself with cold water, recoil as if bitten, sigh, give up, get dressed and find the heater cord. It's hanging outside the bathroom. Now that's impressive.

It's still early. The pub's asleep. I pad down the dark corridor, not even bothering to look for the light switch which is no doubt conveniently on the roof, and tiptoe down squeaky steep-pitched stairs. The air is rich with last night: stale smoke, stale beer, a sullied, human, lived-in smell waiting for cleaners and opened windows and the antiseptic sweep of cloth and mop to banish it and render the place fresh before doing it all again.

I peep into the bar. Glasses are piled at one end, hooped with dry rimes of beer-suds. The ashtrays have been emptied into one, to form an Etna of dog-ends. The curtains are drawn, the bar-top sticky. I like this sense of heldness, of controlled mess. It's like going backstage. And I like being the only one moving in this elderly warren of a pub. I get a gust of the sense that I have always cherished on the road, the sense that used to keep me moving far more than I do now, a sense of randomness, a sense of arbitrary freedom to savour the ordinary and the soiled and the haphazard, the sweetly meaningless.

A cleaner is waiting outside the pub with an orange bucket, her cheeks flushed by the cold. She stands before a backdrop of fog as thick as sheep's wool. The door between us is locked. Through the glass I mime the act of unlocking it and shrug a question mark. She shrugs back. We stand two feet apart, smiling. She rings the bell. It seems absurd. We both laugh. The bell summons the landlady in a dressing gown, her face still folded with sleep. She starts when she sees me, but lets me out and the cleaner in.

It's ghostly quiet in the fog. The High Moorland Visitor

Centre was built with an EU grant and stars a mannequin of Sherlock Holmes. A worker in paint-spotted overalls stands by a bus stop stamping his feet, the *Sun* rolled up under his arm like a baton. I carry on beyond the village to gaze on the notorious prison. There's not a lot to gaze on. All it conjures for me is the comic incarceration of Paul Pennyfeather and Grimes in *Decline and Fall*, and Grimes's daring escape from a chain gang in the sort of territory that soaked me yesterday. Is there anywhere in this country that hasn't been written about? Morton, who was writing only a couple of years before *Decline and Fall* was published, saw chain gangs here. I see only grim stone walls and razor wire and I pad back into town. The sweet shop sells postcards of the prison.

The morning has started to move. School kids emerge from the fog like wraiths, then dissolve back into it. Opposite the pub, a man and his boy are standing on scaffolding to dig a hole at head height through the wall of an ancient whitewashed cottage. They attack with a drill and a crowbar, like monstrous dentists, hauling out rubble and mortar and letting it drop.

When I emerge after breakfast, the man and boy are still hacking at the wall. The hole they've dug is a foot and a half deep, yet shows no sign of breaking through.

I spend a while in the car park, emptying the Audi of old newspapers and plastic bags, picking brochures and bits of softened digestive biscuits from the foot well and hopelessly trying to sweep the crumbs out of the seams of the passenger seat. Beside me a man has crouched to fiddle with the back of his Mercedes. He's had a prang. The plastic's broken on the nearside lights. As he fiddles, his car alarm goes off. He looks up at me but says and does nothing. The noise is designed to madden. The wall-drillers look round. Still the man does nothing, keeps fiddling with the light fitting. Then he loses patience with it, starts up the Merc, revs it fiercely and drives away. The car-alarm noise does not go with him. With a lurch of embarrassment I realize that it's coming from the Audi.

I've no idea how to silence it. I rush to look for a switch on the dashboard, consider studying the driver's manual in the glove compartment, discard the idea on the basis of previous experience with driver's manuals, decide to drive hootingly to a garage for help, slam the boot shut and the alarm stops.

Morton went from here to Clovelly, which he found self-consciously quaint. If it was all quainted up in 1926 I don't want to see how quainted up it is now. I head instead across the moor and then up to Barnstaple. The moor is fog and fog only. Again I fail to find Warren Inn with the century-old fire. Perhaps it burned down. All I do find is a gift shop in the heart of nowhere. It calls itself Home of the Dartmoor Pixie. Outside the shop are a mass of concrete toadstools, two foot high and painted red with white spots. More remarkably still, they appear to be offered for sale.

At Barnstaple, Morton admired the Pannier Market with its apple-cheeked farmers' wives, their jugs of brown cream, their dressed poultry, their shiny strawberries. The Pannier Market's still there, but the farmers' wives have gone, of course, steam-rollered by time and Tesco and health regulations and battery farming and universal prosperity. In their stead are stalls selling fluorescent fluffy toys that are ninety per cent static electricity, second-hand gold-embossed books by Rosamunde Pilcher, watchstraps, fancy soaps, shiny football shirts, duvet covers and lots of those enormous women's knickers that I missed in Marks & Spencer.

There's also a table of pictures. 'David uses watercolour to capture the colours of the landscape' says an explanatory note beneath a picture of a landscape done in watercolour by David. The prints all have rural subjects: *Farmyard Under Snow* shows a farmyard under snow with chickens; *Solitude* shows a lone fisherman in what I fear I shall have to call a glade; *Westermouth Harbour* shows a small boat, a rib-knit jersey and another fish-erman; *Bluebell Walk with River* shows bluebells and a river but no fisherman, and *Thatched Cottage*, *Autumn Gold* and *Riverside*

Pasture I shall leave you to imagine. There are no pictures of Slough, or of today's Pannier Market at Barnstaple.

I don't know where England got the notion that a suitable subject for painting involves very few people and lots of nature. Do Africans paint pics of solitary black fishermen holding a meditative spear in a glade on a crocodile-free Limpopo? I doubt that they do, and nor did the English once.

Medieval painters, for example, did nothing but biblical stuff. Any natural scenery they included was comically per-spectiveless, so that a badly drawn mountain appeared to perch on the shoulder of a badly martyred St Whoever.

During the Renaissance the painters took to depicting real people, but nature still rarely got a look-in, unless it had been killed and become a trophy.

Around the eighteenth century – and I'm no art historian, but wasn't Gainsborough round then? – the posing aristos liked a bit of landscape in their portraits, but only in order to show how thoroughly they'd tamed it and built impressive things on it.

It wasn't until the romantics popped up that nature really got onto canvas, and it's stayed there since. Constable's *Haywain* – river, thatched cottage, big trees, low sun, acres of sky, a couple of picturesquely impoverished peasants, some hay and one wain – is effectively still the model for every ama-teur painter in the country. The ingredients vary but the recipe doesn't. They paint a thinly populated natural world that offers eye-candy and no threat to the contented people who dwell in harmony with it. In this artistic arcadia, the houses are more like burrows than artificial constructions, and the people are effectively hobbits. It's akin to the rural idyll of the National Trust, an idyll that Morton did plenty to affirm. And it seems that the more urban England becomes, the more entrenched the fantasy.

Barnstaple's got a Wimpy bar. Perhaps I've been inattentive but it's the first I've seen. I thought they'd died. They certainly deserved to. The sight of the Wimpy logo brings a great waft of nostalgia for the England of the late seventies when I was at university and perpetually drunk, and Jim Callaghan was in Downing Street and terminally dull. In his shambling manner Callaghan seemed to embody a country that had no idea where it was going. War pride had long gone, and so had the Beatles, Swinging London and the World Cup. Inflation soared, public services wilted, workers struck and industries died.

Wimpy was the Jim Callaghan of restaurant chains. Its very name was a miracle of bad branding. Its burgers were disastrous, its workers famously disaffected and its restaurants seemingly always empty but for the occasional sheltering vagrant. It was so seedy, so shallow, so bad, it was almost wonderful. And it's still chugging along.

Efforts have been made to smarten the image. The interior is done out in primary-coloured plastic furniture in imitation of American burger chains, but it tries to differentiate itself by stressing its Englishness. The window menu is backed by pictures of the Houses of Parliament, deckchairs, a cartoon Beefeater, the Angel of Light on Tyneside, the RAF emblem, and, as a nod to inclusiveness, a hint of tartan. But one thing remains unchanged. The place is empty.

I get back into the Audi and follow the tyre tracks of Morton, and the footsteps of Joseph of Arimathea, to Glastonbury.

I came to Glastonbury once as a child. I don't remember it, but I do remember a photo in the family album, a black and white Instamatic snap of myself and my eldest brother. I am grinning with an unselfconsciousness that I've since lost the knack of. I am chubby and perhaps four years old. My brother, ten years my senior, looks rather more sensible. We're sitting by the chapel on the summit of the tor. I head straight there.

I climb beyond the last semi-detached, along a muddy footpath, past walkers with dogs as good-natured as they are predictable – apart from one lunatic Dalmatian – past sheep and cornily gambolling lambs, through a herd of dopey cattle, over a stile, round a bend in a lane and into a man in a hi-viz vest. He stops me. I can see the tor and the chapel, and I think I can make out where the photo was taken, but the man won't allow me to go there. They are working on the chapel's foundations, he says. In confirmation, a helicopter comes chugging over the ridge swinging a load of rubble. I wheedle with Mr Hi-Viz but to no effect, and lollop back down the hill into town.

The closer I get to the town centre the more I run into knots of young people of a type I don't remember meeting in any numbers in England before. They are a distinct tribe. They're not quite hippies, nor yet gypsies. The males wear rainbow sweaters, or jester pantaloons, or both. The females wear three skirts each. The material seems to be gauze. Both sexes favour dreadlocks. Some carry old-fashioned satchels made of hemp, and most have facial piercings from which they hang an assortment of quite substantial ironmongery. Several of the accents I overhear are expensive ones.

These young people are numerous enough to be catered for with vegetarian restaurants, a highly practical World Peace Garden and establishments selling crystals, runes and facial ironmongery. In a shop smelling of incense and offering maps of ley lines and books on alternative medicine, I flick through a copy of *Man, Myth and Magik – The Spirit of Mankind*.

I don't know what to call these strange young people, but the owner of a conventional coffee shop does. 'They're crusties,' he says, 'and they're a right royal pain in the arse.' He caters for the other breed of visitor to Glastonbury, the white-haired, who come by the coach-load for the ruins and who sustain themselves on teacakes and jam rather than vegetarian falafel. But both young and old, though apparently so widely separated, come to Glastonbury for similar reasons. There's a totemic quality to the place, stemming from the days when the tor stood in the middle of a vast lake. Glastonbury has been a place of pilgrimage for over two thousand years. And it has to be said that if anyone today resembles Joseph of Arimathea, it is probably a crusty rather than a polite old dear in a C&A skirt.

The Glastonbury Thorn, a tree that supposedly sprouted from Joseph of Arimathea's staff, stands just inside the crumbling walls of the crumbled abbey. I did not expect authenticity, of course, but I did expect something a little more convincing, after two millennia of gentle English rain and warm encouraging summers, than a ten-foot tall shrub. Nevertheless the thing is suitably crippled and is kept erect only by steel girders.

With my entry ticket to the Abbey I get an explanatory pamphlet inexplicably in French. From it I learn that *le tombeau de Roi Arthur* is not in fact *le tombeau de Roi Arthur* at all. It's a fake, a piece of ancient myth-making. Twelfth-century monks claimed to have found the tomb, thus establishing Glastonbury as the legendary Avalon and ensuring the succession of pilgrims that continues to this day. Then, as now, pilgrims meant money. The abbey grew rich and vast.

There are thirty-six acres of abbey land and I wander about them happily enough, peering at bits of wall, and I particularly enjoy the *site des latrines*. Earthily practical stuff pleases me more than unearthily spiritual stuff. On the same principle, I take more pleasure from the abbot's huge kitchen than from the site of the less huge altar. I expect the abbot did too. In the *étang à poissons* I see no *poissons*, but I do sit in the grass beside it for a while to watch a flock of honking *oies*.

I spend the night in Wells, with old friends. One of the nice things about old friends is that they get richer. Twenty-five years ago I often used to crash at Peter's rented flat in London. I slept on a sofa that smelled. Now, in Wells, I get a spare room and a private bathroom.

I don't want kids of my own but I relish small doses of other people's. Peter and Jenny have four. The eldest boy is on the cusp of puberty. His voice swings between squeak and rasp. Soon he will want to break away, to have secrets from his parents, to imagine that the intensity of brooding adolescence is his and his alone. Not long after that he'll move out and on, renting a flat of his own where friends will crash on a sofa that smells.

In the middle of the evening, when the house is noisy with kids not wanting to go to bed, a Conservative campaigner calls. He's the first solid evidence I've met that there's an election campaign in progress. I've sensed no fervour in the streets, heard no discussion of it in pubs. But I did catch the two main parties opening their campaigns where it matters, which is on television.

Tony Blair paraded his entire cabinet before the cameras. 'You recognize these faces,' the gesture said, 'you've seen them on the telly so you trust them.' He and his closest half-dozen stood behind little podiums, the sort of things that a host might use in a studio quiz show. They made sonorous speeches for far too long and answered patsy questions for even longer. As always, Tony Blair spoke with the pained earnestness that makes his abstract nouns appear to mean something. Meanwhile the lower ranks stood silent at the back and shifted awkwardly from foot to foot. It was staged, transparent and ghastly.

For the Tories, Michael Howard opened the innings alone. 'Look,' his launch announced, 'I know we've been a bunch of duds, but I am the new and reasonable face of Conservatism. I shall speak moderately and calmly, with my slightly unusual accent and my hands that somehow wander without reference to what I'm saying. And what I'm saying is that I don't like immigrants any more than you do, apart, that is, from nice immigrants such as my parents were. You know what I mean.'

The other radical Conservative policy with which Michael Howard proposed to take this great nation forward into the twenty-first century was to employ more hospital cleaners. 'My mother-in-law died of a hospital-acquired infection,' said Mr Howard with heart-rending sincerity, 'so I know.'

In short the result seems foregone. All Labour has to do is to avoid gross blunders and to fudge round Iraq. You couldn't call it inspiring. And the country seems uninspired.

The campaigner at Peter's door is almost a parody Tory: green quilted jacket, flat tweed cap, and vowels as rich and confident as Victorian furniture. He burbles a few platitudes, but when I tell him that Peter's busy and I'm not eligible to vote, he just hands me a pamphlet and leaves. The pamphlet is semi-literate.

Late that night, when the kids have gone to bed and I am mellow with wine, I take the family Labrador down through silent streets to the walled cathedral close where the two squat towers of the cathedral are gently lit to the colour of digestive biscuits. No cars, no people, a silence as deep as the thirteenth century, and a cathedral close that is encircled by rubbish bags. Tomorrow must be bin day. The rubbish bags delight the Labrador.

15

The Tethered Goat of Happiness

The shampoo in my en-suite bathroom is made with cocoa-bean extract and silk protein 'for darker shades of brunette hair'. The shampoo promises to reveal 'incredible vibrant shine and glistening luminosity,' and to bring out 'the multi-dimensional richness of brunette hair'. In other words, sorry you're not blonde. I slap the stuff on liberally in the shower and come down for breakfast smelling noticeably of cocoa. No one notices. The house is morning frantic with two parents due at work and four kids due at school, and books and papers and violins and clean sports gear to be found. I marvel at the exhausting energy of it all, I who live alone and selfishly and whose kids are dogs and who wake to silence every morning.

I have an appointment today. I am to take an elderly family friend out for lunch, a woman who went to school with my mother unthinkably long ago. They kept in touch and I met her and her family many times as a child. She's widowed now, her children scattered.

It takes a while to find where she lives. It turns out to be a housing estate that is immediately and incontrovertibly recognizable as English. The architecture is the essence of Barratt, all brick and tile with white wooden window frames, a style devoid of local associations. Some houses are detached, some semi-detached. Each house has a path of concrete slabs that ends in a glass front porch, and a drive of concrete slabs that ends in a corrugated garage door. Each garage is closed like an eyelid. The neat front lawns give onto the pavement that flanks a street called an avenue or a cul-de-sac called a close.

I was brought up in a place like this. And though my childhood was a charmed and happy thing, from puberty onwards I hated the place where I lived. It seemed repressed and sterile, cramping. And right now I get such a blast of the same sentiment that I want to turn the Audi round and just leave. I don't, of course. I draw to a halt on the concrete drive, cut the engine, open the door and feel the awful brooding weight of late-morning suburban silence. It acts on me like a chloroform pad. I cannot tell you why, because I don't know why. It goes back a long time. Though it's probably not, as Larkin knew, the place's fault.

We drive to a country pub for lunch through lanes that are rich with flowers. 'This is a rare treat,' she says. Steak and kidney pie for me, gammon and pineapple for her, dreadful steamed vegetables for both of us, and the genteel reverential hush of an English dining room, as though eating were a slightly indecent sacrament. Behind us, the noise of the bar where I have always felt more comfortable.

She tells me about my mother. 'Joy was very clever, you know, much cleverer than me. I used to get her to do my homework.'

It is odd to hear of a parent as a child. To the infant eye, parents were born as fully-formed adults. Only later do you see the full arc of a life. My mother and she would just have been starting school when *In Search of England* was published. They would have been subject to the same spirit of the times that made the book so popular, a sense of a staunch and potent England, the best place in the world to live, a beacon of justice and democracy to a vast empire. On Empire Day, my mother once told me, all the schoolchildren in Eastbourne gathered at some park to perform mass callisthenics.

What changes their generation has seen: Depression, the war, Churchill, *Carry On* films, long hair, the unions in Downing Street, *Till Death Us Do Part*, Thatcher, multicultural tolerance and the bleating Tony Blair. It must feel as though many of the threads yoking England to its past have snapped, the threads that led directly back to Drake at Plymouth, Alfred at Winchester, Arthur at Glastonbury. Though separated by hundreds of years, they felt spiritually adjacent. So it is perhaps unsurprising that Plymouth, Winchester and Glastonbury are now crowded with the white-haired ones, fossicking for yesterday.

My companion is eighty-something. 'The evenings can get a bit long,' she says, to which I can find nothing to say.

I reach Bradford-on-Avon mid-afternoon and immediately decide that it will do me for the night. The town is soft on the eye, climbing in steep and winding lanes from the river at its foot. The landlady of the riverside pub where I take a room tells me this is the southern tip of the Cotswolds. 'You can tell by the roofs,' she says. Apparently Cotswold roof tiles come in seven sizes, the largest at the bottom, the smallest at the top. Each tile size has a quaint Anglo-Saxon name. And sure enough, as I climb through the narrow streets, my eyes are drawn upwards and I notice that the tiles diminish from tea-tray size at the eaves to little more than palm size at the roof line. The older roofs are mossed and humped and lichened, delicious with age and probably leaking.

Beside the squat, ugly and almost windowless Saxon church that Morton called yellow but that looks grey to me, the ancient roof on a stone shed is slowly collapsing. Now a committed roofophile, I study the ruin. The tiles are rough-hewn slices of stone. Each has a hole drilled in the top. A wooden peg pushes through the hole and the slate is simply hung over the underlying wooden lath, to be held there by gravity and the weight of the tiles above. I realize that I am in danger of boring both roofing experts and those unmoved by roofs, but I find it all delightful.

Morton remarked on a chapel built on a bridge. It's still there, like a stone dovecote built out over the water. It hasn't been a chapel for centuries, but it has been a lock-up for drunks. After nights on the beer I have woken in worse places. I spend a while leaning over the parapet beside it and watching the shifting flickers of tiny trout. Then I follow the river out of town to the west.

A park of sorts gives way to meadows and a muddy track. The river is masked by a wall of alders and willows. I hear the unmistakable sound of a sculler, the clunk of the catch, the expulsion of breath, the pause as he comes up the slide, the catch again. Through a gap in the trees I glimpse the after-swirl, two puddles like a pair of revolving spectacles in the mud-green water, shrinking, weakening, dying as I watch. Sculling looks so serene and swanlike. I had a go at it once. And if a passing writer had tried to describe my progress, neither serene nor swanlike would have been his first choice of adjective.

Ahead of me a youngish woman is walking her mongrel. I have been gradually catching up with her for the last half-mile.

She looks over her shoulder then walks on. I can tell by her gait that she's nervous. There's no one else around. Over recent weeks the papers have been full of the unprovoked assault on a young mother in Surrey, in just such a place as this.

My clothes are travel-worn. I am male, bald and alone. I have no dog with me, no binoculars round my neck, no keep-fit clothing, no reason, in short, to be walking this path at this time of the day. I must look like a lecher.

The woman looks over her shoulder again. She is perhaps thirty yards ahead. I don't know what to do. I feel that to greet her, to wave or shout hello, would somehow make things worse. Her dog trots towards me. I call it. The dog bounds up to me. I hope that my cheery affection for the beast will make things better. It makes things worse. Every pat I give it, every stroke of the hand, feels like lechery by proxy.

'Danny,' the woman calls. Her voice is urgent, but trying not to seem so.

I find myself incapable of acting normally. Weirdly I raise both hands above my head as if at gunpoint, trying to say by my action that no, the dog is free to go, and no, I didn't enjoy touching it, and no, it wasn't a covert means of introduction. My action, of course, says precisely the opposite.

Danny bounds back to the woman, who clips the lead to his collar, then feigns an interest in a tree some ten yards to one side of the track. As she hopes, I carry on past. Or rather I scuttle past. I want to seem all wholesome and relaxed, a whistling boulevardier of the countryside, but I look, I know, like a furtive sleaze.

I decide not to look at her, or to speak as I pass. When it's just too late, I change my mind and say, 'Lovely dog.' Even to my ears it sounds like, 'How about it?' She heads immediately back towards town, jerking the dog. I tell myself not to look back. Twenty yards later I look back, at exactly the same moment as she looks back. She starts to run. You'll be surprised to hear that I do not run after her with an explanation.

The path ends at a wide weir with ducks, moorhens, a derelict mill and a couple of honey-stone houses, half hidden behind willows, but with enough of them visible to suggest a giant price tag.

I climb a short track to thirty feet or so above the river and discover a canal. I find that remarkable. But when I follow the towpath past a couple of cottages and turn a bend I find something even more remarkable. Here's an aqueduct over a river. I am standing on a bridge that carries a substantial body of water over a substantial body of water.

More remarkable still, the aqueduct also passes over a road and a railway. The little railway station down below looks as though it's awaiting the arrival of Thomas the Tank Engine carrying Beatrix Potter.

The place is a wonder, a peace-drenched oddity, sitting unheralded in a steeply wooded valley, with a cluster of stone buildings sloping down from canal to river. They include a pub. The pub has an outside lavatory, which is always a good sign.

The barman tells me that I've arrived on the designated locals' night. The naked accountant may even attend.

'The what?'

'The naked accountant.'

'An accountant?'

'Yes.'

'And he's naked.'

'No.'

'Oh.' I pause. There's a trick here. I choose to fall for it.

'So why's he known as the naked accountant.'

'Now that,' says the barman, 'would be telling.'

I settle in for the evening. The barman is a trainee maths teacher. I offer him my one bit of show-off algebra, a formula that I learned in the fourth form and that for some reason has lodged in my head like gristle in a tooth. The purpose of the formula is to solve a quadratic equation, though what the purpose of a quadratic equation is, I never knew. The barman ripostes with the equation for discovering the area of overlap in a pair of circles.

'What's that good for?' I ask.

'Goats,' he says. 'If you've got two goats tethered close enough to each other to be able to mate, then the formula will tell you the area of shared grazing.'

'Why would you want to tether mating goats?'

'So they don't run away,' he says.

This is a pub as a pub should be. People come in to talk to whoever happens to be there. All have troubles; few bring them in. By not bringing them in they diminish them. The only thing the customers have in common is that they live nearby, several of them in houseboats on the canal. They laugh a lot. There is nothing that cannot be discussed. I spend time with a psychiatric nurse, a socialist who cannot vote for Blair – 'It's the Tony that gets to me. He's like an unconvincing vicar' – and a lovely woman who has spent much of her life on voluntary service overseas but wonders whether she has actually done any good.

I discover that the river down below the pub is full of barbel. I'm not surprised. I fished a fair amount in English rivers as a child but never caught a barbel, or ever saw one except on the pages of the *Angling Times*. For me they were fabled fish, fish to dream of. It seems right they should be found in such a place as this.

Over the course of the evening I learn that a snake goes down stairs like a billiard cue, and that R. G. Hardie Ltd supplies bagpipes to the Queen. I have pub conversations about God, literature and pub conversations. I am happy. Here is the sort of adult family I want, each member bringing a multiplicity of random experience to a single place, to stir it into the stew of chat, to laugh and think and drink. It's a coincidence of paths, a random intersection of lives that will never come again. We meet, we laugh, we go away again. I like that.

'Don't fall in,' says the good-doing woman as I leave her at midnight on the towpath. Apparently the calm canal has swallowed a number of drunks. But it doesn't get me.

The canal is sunk in soft night and mist. The moored narrowboats are darkened, but for one where a youth sits in a cabin without curtains, engrossed in a livid computer screen. Sleepy ducks grumble gently at my stumbling presence and waddle a few steps to give me passage, or else slide into the dark water to bob like dinghies. Horses stand in the fields like statues, waiting the night out. The trees are huge black umbrellas. I am on the road and happy. I sing.

For dinner I had two pickled eggs.

16

Cider with Romance

My room overlooks the Avon. On the path beneath the trees a lout is standing. Flesh like pastry, shaven skull, silly earrings, a face like a punctured football, a tattoo rising over the neck of his T-shirt, and kick-your-fucking-head-in boots. And he's feeding the ducks. He's tossing them bread. When the bread runs out he just stands to stare at them.

I breakfast with a short, plump, nervous, divorced and

161

recently retired local-government administrator from South London. He pronounces south 'souf'. His wife and children gone, he has sold his house in London and is just gently wandering between here and Cornwall to no particular purpose, pootling his money away and hoping it sees him out. He's an amateur student of architecture. He speaks warmly of London sky-scrapers and even of the Royal Festival Hall. He has taken a while to unfurl, so I don't disagree too fiercely. I tell him about Cotswold roofs. He is terribly impressed. Then he asks me questions I can't answer.

I ring friends in Bath, a young couple who came to New Zealand last year and stayed a while at my place. By way of thanking me they cooked a meal on their final night. Lamb shanks and peppers it was, and it was awful. I mean to return the favour.

Tosh gives me directions to their little house on the hill in Bath. 'Second set of traffic lights,' he says, 'then turn right up the hill and park by the fuck-off church.'

The fuck-off church is gauntly Victorian, grimed with neg-lect, emphatically fuck-off. Outside Tosh and Caroline's rented terrace house stands a tiny ornamental pond with a plastic prism floating on its surface for reasons that are presumably ornamental and definitely misjudged. The pond teems with tench, ponderous greenish fish as gloomy as mud.

I first knew Caroline as a shy four-year-old, the daughter of a couple who employed me to teach at a summer school. Now she is waddling, her feet splayed by the last stage of her first pregnancy. To see her like this is not so much a shock as a sudden panoptic overview. I hug her cautiously, taking care not to crush the embryonic daughter. Here are three gener-ations in embrace and I the eldest. One more rung and I'll be the retired local-government administrator pootling down-wards, dispensing what I've spent the years amassing, serving out my time.

Their rented house is tiny. One room wide, no garden front

or back, a sweet view over Bath and worth, I'm told, about a million Kiwi dollars. We toddle down the hill to town, Caroline leaning backwards and holding my arm to resist the tug of gravity. She's only days away from giving birth, from having to live for someone else, from taking a stake in the future that she can never forgo. She seems remarkably at ease.

We amble round Bath's celebrated pretty bits, the stone buildings, their facades as flat and formal as starched shirt fronts. Morton claims to have found the place deeply drowsy. 'A delicious numbness drenches me,' he wrote, with the hyperbole that is beginning to grate on me. He almost always affirms the established image of a place, giving his readers what they both want and expect. 'I go to sleep at ten without counting one sheep and I wake up at seven feeling almost as tired.'

It would be hard to be drowsy in central Bath now. The silent Bath chairs for the frail have been replaced by noisy cars for everyone. But the Pump Room tries to maintain an old-world afternoon elegance. Here where the steaming waters have sprung from the earth's crust for thousands of years to be swum in or drunk, here where the Romans lounged, and where Jane Austen's women paraded and gossiped and fretted, there's a string quartet and tiered cake stands and crustless sandwiches and deferential waitresses in pinafores and elderly women playing out the pantomime of niceness. It's a self-conscious effort to fend off the present, to freeze a fraction of the world in a seemlier time.

The baths are closed, apparently because someone died in them, so I have to make do with drinking a tumbler of the celebrated water. The girl who serves it is sad and French. The water has the consistency and the taste of warm saliva. Outside the Pump Room a man with no obvious disability is playing a xylophone. He is either incompetent or playing jazz. The distinction is a fine one. Of the tunes he plays, I manage to identify only 'Men of Harlech'.

An antiquarian bookshop window shows a French

nineteenth-century map of New Zealand, and I feel drawn to, and oddly moved by, the familiar shapes of the islands that I now call home. I live, I discover, on La Presqu'Isle de Banks. Against the window glass I place a finger to cover the spot where my house is and where my dogs right now are being loved to within an inch of their lives by my devoted dog-sitters.

With ripe Caroline in tow I don't wander through Bath as I would if I were alone. Instead I become as solicitous as a nineteenth-century curate, fretting that she might tire, or dehydrate, urging her to sit and take refreshing cordials lest she should suddenly launch into contractions in the manner that I have seen on television but have no desire to see in real life. But she's fine.

I don't get to cook a revenge dinner. Instead I spend the evening with Caroline's parents, my former employers, Roger and Dorita.

I could write chapters about Roger. He is not typically English but I think he may be distinctively English. There is in his manner the best of the country: a clarity of mind and a tolerance that are a rare combination anywhere in the world, but perhaps less rare here than elsewhere. He is absurdly honest, scrupulously kind, much given to giggling, and, in his own opinion, deeply screwed-up. We sit up till three in the morning with thick wine and old Scotch sorting out everything from gods to cricket.

Outside Tosh and Caroline's place in the morning a cheerful one-eyed woman is watching the tench. She tells me that the floating glass pyramid is a heron-scarer.

'I'd never have guessed,' I say.

'Nor do the herons,' she says. 'One comes every day at dawn. I get up early these days to do the scaring myself.'

I head north out of Bath through spring-lush gentle hills where cattle lie at ease, all ignorant of the abattoir. Almost all of England that is not urban is farmed. It is a factory for food. But the urban English do not expect it to look like a factory. They expect it to be pretty. The farmer's job is not to make a living. It is to maintain hedges, ponds and woods for wildlife, a gentle wilderness with rights of way for ramblers.

The contrast with New Zealand is stark. There wilderness means wilderness, land without people. Farmland is not wilderness. It's a business.

Farmers in New Zealand have clout. They are seen, especially in the South Island, as the generators of wealth. The annual milk-fat payout is broadcast on the evening news.

I was brought up semi-rurally in Sussex but I don't remember any farmers' children at school. Farmers were a remote breed encountered mainly in books. Red-faced they were, with oooh-aah accents, the sort of characters Morton kept either meeting or inventing.

City and country here seem irremediably divorced. It is partly the legacy of class. Farming is still to some degree associated in the English mind with privilege, that very English sense of a landed gentry, the county families whose thousands of inherited acres have been a guarantee of money down the centuries. The Jevington field on which my father played cricket, for example, was rented for a penny a year from the local landowner whom no one ever met but whose name everybody knew.

The recent ban on hunting exemplified that mind-set. It was a sop that Blair threw to the old left-wing to gratify their grudge against the posh. Politically it had nothing to do with foxes and everything to do with tilting at privilege.

At the same time it illustrated an urban English sentimentality about animals, a sentimentality I share, a sentimentality that has found expression in some of the most popular literature in the country's history. How many copies were sold of *Tarka the Otter* or *Wind in the Willows*? And how many million Beatrix Potter books are there, those little white illustrated hardbacks of *Jemima Puddleduck* and *Peter Rabbit*? I loved them.

Today's *Sun* has a story that springs from the same source. Indeed to any researcher on England the *Sun* is priceless. It takes every English attitude and winds it up to something close to parody. Today's top stories are 'Becks: I respect Posh' and 'Schoolkids' Craze for Daisy Chain Sex Orgies'. But on page six I learn how 'Two new-born lambs were saved from Death Row last night thanks to the *Sun*'.

The lambs were born inside an abattoir. 'After RSPCA officials and animal lovers had joined the outcry,' the *Sun* stepped in with money and ensured that the lambs 'would live out their days safely in green fields.'

The hypocrisy is breathtaking, of course, but the *Sun* is one step ahead of mockery. It christened the lambs Mint and Sauce.

The *Independent*, meanwhile, has a three-column obituary of an expert on British fungi. 'He was by nature something of a loner . . . He had decided views on most subjects that interested him. Although he did not suffer fools, he was encouraging and helpful to those who showed a clear interest in fungi. As a field mycologist he was second to none: there were few who could match his eye for the fine detail that separates one small brown fungus from another.'

I doubt that there's another country in the world where you could find the same range of tone in one day's newspapers, the same diversity of irony and wit and crassness and parody and understatement and hyperbole. That's class, I suppose.

I am heading half-reluctantly for Cheltenham, where I spent eight bad months in 1986, months that convinced me to go to New Zealand. I stop at Stroud for lunch, but am sufficiently taken by the place to stay the night, perhaps because Morton didn't come here. I can see the town fresh.

Stroud sits among the Cotswolds like an egg in a palm. The streets wind and climb. I dump my gear at a small hotel. The proprietor's a wonder. Dressed in battered shooting gear – brown waxed cotton vest, muddy green corduroys – he is spectacularly morose. While I fill in the register he sits back and swings his boots onto the desk.

'You a farrier?' he says as he hands me the key. 'We get a few from New Zealand.'

I shake my head. His flicker of interest fizzles. I've been dismissed. When I ask him where my room is he says, 'Upstairs.'

The Liberal Democrat campaign office in Stroud is a single rented room. Painted white, it holds a trestle table, a few pamphlets, a telephone, mugs, sugar, tea, powdered coffee and an eighty-year-old woman. She's been a Liberal for forty years.

'Doesn't it get a bit dispiriting?' I ask. 'You've come third every time.'

'Oh no,' she exclaims, laughing without restraint, 'no, no, no, you've got to keep hoping, haven't you? If you don't hope, where are you?'

'Well,' I say, then bite my tongue.

Her cause is indeed hopeless. It is also strange. Charles Kennedy, the Lib-Dem leader, comes across as the only leader committed to ideas rather than to simply acquiring power. He's personable. When asked a question he answers it. His party has clear principles. Its policies are specific. Those policies don't seem particularly wacky. And yet the Lib-Dems are going to come third again. Everybody knows it, including Mr Kennedy.

The reason, I suspect, goes back once again to class. Though both New Labour and the Tories are ideologically bankrupt, and though the differences between them are now minimal, and though neither party now bears much resemblance to the party it was born as, they sit in the common mind on either side of a wall of class division. Every five years a few people shift from one side of that wall to the other and those few people dictate who assumes power. But most people stay on one side or the other of that wall for their whole lives.

I shift the conversational direction, and with only the slightest prompting the eighty-year-old reels off her autobiography. Raised in London and trained as a dressmaker, she came to

Stroud in 1951, liked it and stayed. Her accent is an unpredictable compound of lazy London vowels and rich West Country ones. She bore six kids in eleven years then her husband died. Life was a struggle.

'I got into debt once. Frightened me silly, it did.'

One of her sons died just after Christmas in 1976 when he crashed a toboggan and hit his head on a stone horse trough. 'I always say, "He was killed," cos he didn't die, did he?'

For the first time she stops talking. Her old eyes are moist. 'It's still hard to take,' she says.

When the last of her kids left home she found she was lonely so she took in troubled youths. 'My boys, I called them. I divided off a bit of the house as my bedsit and they had the rest. They'd all had tough lives. Just needed a bit of love, really. But you can't force it on them, can you? I used to wait for them to come to me. If any of them knocked on the door and asked if I wanted a cup of tea, I always knew they wanted a little chat. But I still always waited for them. Always waited. But I wouldn't want to bring kids up today. It's different now, isn't it?'

I say I'm sure she'd still be very good at it.

'Oh, I did love my boys. I still remember all their birthdays, always send a card.'

She has great-grandchildren in Canada. 'I save up for five years and then I go and visit them. It's nice to have something to save for.'

In the hour or so I spend sitting with this woman one week before the election, the phone does not ring, and the number of visitors totals one. Me. And I only dropped in to pick up the prospectus in the hope of finding something to mock. Yet I emerge warmed. She's a kind woman, a bubbler, a hoper, an unconditional lover of people. I'm not. I don't think I could be. But I can be warmed by proximity to goodness.

I wander through Stroud, past 'England's first fully organic café' and the usual array of shop fronts and jostling school kids, then find myself on Slad Road. My mind fumbles with the name a moment, knowing that I recognize it, and then with a pleasing smack it falls into place. I am surprised I didn't think of Slad the moment I reached Stroud. I set off up Slad Road at pace.

Slad was the village that Laurie Lee left so memorably in the opening chapter of *As I Walked Out*. He left his mother 'caught in the grass like a piece of sheepswool', walked to London, and then through Spain. From Lee's words I have a mental image of Slad. I expect to have it smashed.

Leaving behind the last tongues of housing licking up the valley, I become immersed in a deep steep green. A pheasant crakes like the ratchet on a fly-reel. Wood pigeons coo fatly, crows wheel and a green woodpecker swoops across the valley and clamps to a trunk. I stand a while to watch a horse eat cowslips. I can hear the crunch of the stems. At the valley's foot a brown stream winds. There are farms and barns of stone. Shaggy sheep lie in lushness. The beech woods are pale with leaf. Two middle-aged men with jogging disease lumber past me, their faces purple, their bellies slopping, their running shoes huge and costly.

Surprisingly soon I round a low-walled bend and there's the village, a scatter of stone houses on the valley's flank, a church above the road sunk deep in a gloom of trees. At first glance it seems less compact, less complete unto itself, less remotely rural, than Lee painted it. But a child's world is circumscribed and giants can inhabit hamlets. Even the drab commuter village in which I was raised seemed, when I was six, a place of epic.

The Slad parish noticeboard is wood-framed, glass-covered and penetrated with damp. The drawing pins on the poster for the Painswick Bird Club Field Trip are rusted. A corner droops on the printed bulletin that details Parish Councillor Allowances. A small coloured card plugs the Bushido Academy of Martial Arts 'where the teaching lives on'. The resident sensei is called Richard Weale.

Any one of the little low-tiled cottages could be the one where Lee was raised and I am disinclined to look for it. An open garage by a lane holds a Ford Orion. The walls of the garage are lined with Lee memorabilia – posters for his books, blow-ups of the covers, the books themselves, and a billboard for a stage version of *Cider with Rosie* that I am glad never to have seen.

The Woolpack pub is cramped and six-o'clock busy with a mix of smug BMW accents and slower rural ones. A plaque on a beer pump advertises 'Laurie Lee's Bitter'. On the wall in the end segment of the bar, above an elderly leather pommel horse the presence of which I can't begin to explain, there's a hand-painted notice. 'Try a Cider with Rosie cocktail' it says. I think I can guess one of the ingredients. Beside it hangs a framed and fading reproduction of what for me is one of the great images of the world. It's a picture of Laurie Lee taken in a photo booth in Southampton a week after he left this village.

Here's a young man in old man's gear: a slouch hat, Charlie Chaplin trousers, rough jacket, a pack slung over his shoulder and a pipe in his mouth. He is turning to face the camera, as if in the act of looking back as he heads away. I don't care that the photo was posed, taken in a booth before a canvas backdrop. For me it is a distillation of the romance of going, of moving on, of being self-sufficient, of youth and freedom. It's a romance that I love and that has hugely influenced my life. Though I have never quite believed in it.

17

Back to School

In the little bar and sitting room of the hotel in Stroud a
plaster sparrowhawk perches on a glass case of two stuffed
snipe. The walls carry pictures of stag hunting, fishing, a duck
shoot. An owl above the wide black television has been
stuffed in the act of snatching prey, its wings arched, its talons
tautly spread and stretching towards the television viewers.
There are no television viewers. In a far corner stands a

171

stuffed hen partridge, her broodlings peeping from her breast.

The landlord is dressed for shooting in the same waxed cotton vest as last night. He is taking orders for breakfast. Civility has only the slightest hold on him. 'Full English? Beans? White toast, brown toast? Tea, coffee?' After each question mark he sniffs, expelling disdain for the meniality of his task. He serves without care or desire to please.

"thing else?' Neither I nor the silent couple at the corner table want anything else. He disappears upstairs and returns to swagger through the room with a shotgun broken over his shoulder. It's the visual embodiment of his sniff.

'Good shooting,' I say.

He turns. 'Hopefully,' he says and offers for the first time a glimpse of a smile, like tightly knotted string. A girl appears in a white pinafore. He mutters half a dozen clipped words to her then hastens from the room. I hear a door slam, an engine rev, and he powers past the window in a muddy Land Cruiser.

At the end of 1985 I resigned from a job in Canada and came home with money in my pocket. I would rent a flat and write a novel.

By April 1986 I was broke. I had not rented a flat. I had slept on smelly sofas. I had written two unpublishable poems. I had drunk my money. I applied for a job at a minor public school in Cheltenham..

The headmaster at Cheltenham was a vigorous Christian. When he told me about the school, he beamed. When he showed me round the school, he trotted and beamed. I took the job. Eight months later I went to New Zealand.

The kids were fine, but the school depressed me. There was too much Englishness, and far too much God. I felt cramped. One of the playing fields was called Humpty Dumpty. It used to appear as such on school notices. My head boiled. Individually my colleagues were affable enough, but I found the tone of the place stifling.

One morning break I was seething about something. I forget what, but I was sitting alone at a window, enraged, bitter. The young, bearded, earnest chaplain came over, and laid a hand on my arm. 'Remember, Joe,' he said softly, cooingly, horribly, 'this life is only a rehearsal.'

I could tell so many stories. I had only one close friend. Oliver was a young teacher of classics with aristocratic vowels and an endearing mix of insouciance, courage and vulnerability. We got drunk one night, came back to the school and climbed the scaffolding to the roof of the new gym. A torch flashed below. The beam caught us. We ducked below the roofline.

'Right, you boys,' came the voice of the deputy head, 'come on down.'

We stayed on up, crouching, giggling.

The torch swept the rooftop. 'I'm losing patience. I know who you are.'

We waited half an hour until he went away.

There was chapel every morning, led sometimes by the soft-voiced chaplain, sometimes by the happy head. That next morning, after the hymns and the prayers and the sports reports, the head announced that two boys had been seen on the gym roof. 'They have until eleven o'clock to report to my study. Otherwise they will be fetched.'

I wanted to confess. Oliver just laughed. We were never fetched.

When Oliver married later that year, they set up house by going to every department store in Cheltenham, taking out a store credit card in each, spending it immediately to the maximum, then cutting it in half. At the last store they could find nothing they needed for the house. They bought an electric can opener and spent the rest on pink champagne. When I left Cheltenham I left them my car. It died soon afterwards, apparently.

As I near Cheltenham, all this and so much more comes

washing over me, stories I haven't thought of since they happened. Some are funny, but most are dressed in that same repressive gloom I knew at the time. I find that I am clenching the steering wheel and am tempted to drive on by.

GCHQ, the huge technological espionage centre, has grown huger. It makes no attempt to disguise its purpose, pays no heed to aesthetics. It bristles with razor wire and satellite dishes and surveillance cameras on stalks, a grim spaceship come to earth on the fringe of genteel Cheltenham. It testifies to international distrust, to the thin ice of human peace, to the reality behind the diplomatic rhetoric. It jabs a telescopic antenna into the eye of every idealist. A thousand cars are clustered around it, tiny beside its windowless walls. It's twenty years since I saw it. In that time it must have eaten several billion pounds. Has it done any good? I don't know. It will have kept itself busy.

I park in the tree-lined lane that fronts the school. To my left stretch the playing fields where I coached cricket and pretended to know something about hockey. As I near the school's unimposing front gate, I feel bubbles in my spine. I do half-want to look around the place, but I am nervous of meeting former colleagues – the bitter man who kept his Alsatian in the chemistry lab to guard his chemicals, the historian who lived only to hear his own name mentioned, the ancient linguist who told me soberly that he had stopped buying Proctor and Gamble products because the company was run by Satanists, the organist who, oh, it doesn't matter.

I push open the front door and meet the school smell of disinfectant, linoleum and cabbage. The place is quiet. It's the middle of a period. The secretary is bent over her desk. I scuttle past. Are those the stairs that led to my little attic room where I lay on my bed, marked essays and drank Hungarian wine alone from a thick green coffee mug? I'm not sure.

The school has come into money. The Portakabin where I taught has gone, a swish brick building standing in its place.

There's a new pool, and a theatre named after the joyous Head.

Public schools – the name is deliciously inapt – are effectively placeless. Many are isolated beyond towns. Each is a little civilization complete unto itself, like a monastery. It has a chapel and kitchens and dormitories.

And like a monastery the public school offers something definite and inflexible. That something is a form of Englishness. There is a dress code and a fixed hierarchy. There is compulsory religious observance, though belief is optional and not really expected. There is a code of social behaviour too: deference and courtesy are greatly valued, and enforced by punishment. Great emphasis, in other words, is put on appearance. How you are seen to behave is everything. How you are underneath is your own affair.

The whole code, the package that a public school offers, is presented without apology. If a child comes to the school from overseas, and many do, little allowance is made for his previous culture. He is expected to conform, and to do so swiftly. By and large he does. Though the seas of multicultural tolerance may slop against the walls of these schools, within those walls the code of Englishness is king.

The people within all speak with much the same accent. It is an accent not of place, but of class. And this class keeps to itself. Public schools play sport only against other public schools. By doing so they reflect an ingrained and fundamental class division.

Public schools exist throughout the country, and though they have been under siege for years, they have survived. Many, indeed, have flourished. There are plenty of people who want what they offer and will pay for it. They want the values that the rest of the country has either forgotten, or become embarrassed by, or learned to sneer at. They are values of which Morton would approve.

I don't disapprove. But I found teaching in Cheltenham hard because I came from the other side of the tracks. Not far on the other side – my grammar-school education was modelled on the public-school tradition – but just far enough to make me feel uncomfortable. At the heart of my discomfort was that I simply didn't belong. I was playing a role I hadn't been trained to play.

The bell rings and the place explodes with kids and staff. No one looks at me. The uniform hasn't changed. The kids could be the kids I taught, the same unchanging mix of faces. Teaching is the most stable of businesses. The kids stay always the same age. From one point of view it's invigorating. You are always charged by proxy with the folly and energy and zest and overwrought emotions of the young. From a longer perspective, it's wretched. You, the teacher, are the only ageing creature in a constancy of youth. Look at the photographs that line a boarding house, the housemaster passing from middle age to age in fifteen snaps, surrounded always by unaltering youth. Then he disappears. The middle-aged man who replaces him in the sixteenth photograph is smiling.

Somewhere among these walls there's probably a picture of me, with hair and twenty-nine-year-old skin. I doubt that I am smiling.

'Joe.'

I recognize the face.

'Suzanne,' she says, and I remember her. She was young like me, but she has aged far less than I have. I am surprised she has survived the place. She didn't seem to fit its Christian tone, its stiffly cramping Englishness. But I say only how young she's looking.

I offer to teach her third form Spanish class. I like doing single show-off lessons, surprising the kids, bouncing with energy, making them laugh. Teaching is theatre. Grip your audience, and there's nothing you can't do. Lose them, and there's nothing you can.

My Spanish is shaky, but theirs barely exists. I turn on a show and the kids respond as they always do, puzzled, then keen, then going too far, then settling into the rhythm and some of them clicking. I am sweating. I stop. Suzanne gives them some work to do. We go outside to talk. I ask after a girl whom I remember vividly. Apparently she became a teacher. Suzanne tells me that the girl's brother, whom I remember less vividly, is now a missionary. I leave.

I'm pleased I visited. It was good to stir the memories. But I shall not go back again. The place and I just never found a fit.

From the Prospect at Ross-on-Wye Morton described 'one of the best panoramas I have yet seen . . . I looked down at the bend of the river and out over the green country that lies in calm beauty to the mountains of Wales . . . In the River Wye small, shrimp-pink children were bathing, and in every dark patch of willows stood cows chewing the cud and letting the water ripple past their legs.'

I'm not sure how Morton could see from up here that the cows were chewing the cud, but the view's just dandy. It's threaded these days with traffic, but the land still rolls from the Wye to Wales. Over the distant mountains hangs a fat and purple roil of cloud like the skirt on a hovercraft.

A nurse pushes an old woman in a wheelchair up past the church and graveyard. From all sides come squirrels. They ripple across the grass, their spines undulating like waves along a skipping rope. The woman tosses them peanuts in their shells. Each squirrel snatches a nut, then darts a yard or two away, stops, sits up like an old-fashioned typist, and eats with rapid nibbling jaws, a stationary head and blinkless eyes of black glass, its tail curled like a mirrored question mark.

I tried to rescue a squirrel once when I was eight. It had been struck by a car and lay squirming on the road. As I went to pick it up I had already decided that I would train it to sit on my shoulder.

Squirrels have got tiny Ken Dodd teeth, strong enough to pierce hazelnuts. The maimed squirrel sank those teeth into

my forefinger, buried them to the bone. I screamed and flung
the beast off, back into the road. I should have written to com-
plain to Beatrix Potter.

It's late afternoon. In the butcher's window the chops have
gone grey, and two old men are sitting on a wall by the Audi.
They seem an unlikely couple. One has been dressed by his
wife in fawn with zips. Even his shoes have zips, set diagonally
across their quilted fawn uppers. His face is as round as an
egg, his skull as bald. He looks slow.

The other looks quick. His battered face still twinkles like a
boy's. He wears a modest cravat and a greenish jacket with
corduroy collar, the sort of clothes I associate with drivers of
MGs. He looks, in short, a class above his companion.

'Nice,' he says pointing at the Audi. 'Yours?'

'A friend's.'

'You Australian?' I am used to that. Before I went to New
Zealand, I too could hear no difference between Kiwi and
Australian accents. Now they're more distinct from each other
than Scots is from cockney. The distinction lies in the vowels. In
Sydney, Sydney is Seednee. In Auckland, Sydney is Sudnuh.

'Close,' I say, 'New Zealand.'

'Why would you want to come here from a lovely place like
New Zealand?'

I tell him I had hoped to hitch around the country.

He shakes his head. 'Fat chance. No one picks up hitchers
any more. This country's got too dangerous,' and he gestures
cheerfully at Ross-on-Wye, with its Prospect, its seventeenth-
century market house – now heritage centre – its inn where
some king or other inevitably stayed the night, its wiggling
streets, its dove-rich graveyard deep in wet grass, 'it's all a
bloody mess.'

'What, Ross?'

'Oh, Ross is all right, I suppose, in its way, though it isn't a
patch on what it was. The shops have closed down because of
the council tax, see? And those the superstores have taken over.

Same everywhere. And the cities are turning into ghettos. All the blacks and the drugs. It's impossible. My son-in-law's a big bloke but he was beaten up last year in Birmingham, middle of the day, by six Pakis. They took his phone. You're better off out of it.'

His slow round-faced companion nods at the litany, enjoys it and says nothing.

'And as for phoney Tony – you know who I'm talking about? – well, God help us. I'm going to vote Lib-Dem.'

I say I took him for a classic Tory voter.

'I've voted Tory all my life, including 1945, but Michael Howard's a typical slimy mid-European immigrant trying too hard to be English.'

He delivers all the above with an engaging zest and a manner that is hard to distinguish from pleasure.

He doesn't live in Ross, hasn't been here for fifty years. He came here last in 1953 on the eve of the coronation. 'Had to get out of London because of all the bloody fuss. I had a little Austin, my first ever car. Drove back across the country while the coronation was going on. Had England to myself. It was lovely. Everyone was inside listening to the nonsense on the wireless or watching it on little black-and-white tellies. Whole towns were deserted.

'Di's funeral was the same. I just had to get away again. Went to a Greek island for the fortnight. Place was full of people doing the same as me. She seemed a nice enough girl till she developed a taste for Arabs.' He pronounces Arabs 'Ehrabs'.

A pair of women appear across the car park and wave. Each is carrying several shopping bags.

Both men shake my hand and go to greet their wives. Egghead has not spoken once.

I spend my evening trying to avoid a football match. Liverpool are playing Chelsea for perhaps the twentieth time this season in the second leg of the semi-final of a European competition. The game is on television in every pub and the drinkers everywhere are swivelled on their bar stools staring at the screen in slack-mouthed silence. As far as I can gather the Liverpool team contains one Liverpudlian, a clean-cut keenness who is also captain. Their goalkeeper is the famous Scouser Dudek, the goal-scorer Luis Garcia. The manager is Spanish, and the centre-forward a very black man called Cissé who has bleached hair and a bleached beard and who constantly loses the ball. The Kop cares about him losing the ball but not about his provenance. Liverpool is the group of players who happen at any one time to form a team called Liverpool. The fans believe and sing, full-voiced and whole-hearted, given utterly to the moment, united in faith. I gather from the commentators during a lull that Cissé has bought a country house somewhere south of Liverpool. With it came the title of lord of the manor.

I find a pub at last with no television and I drink a pint beneath a print of Charles II. Next to it is an older-looking print of an ancient yokel. He is besmocked and bewhiskered, his face the essence of bucolic merriment. In his hand, a tankard. Above his head, the legend Carlsberg Lager.

The bar is lined with men in their thirties on bar stools, enjoying the proprietary sense that comes with being at the bar. It's the hub of power in any pub. In order to be served I have to attract attention over them, then reach between their shoulders. Those shoulders separate fractionally to allow me to reach my pint, then close again like a sphincter.

Three nicely spoken people enter in smart clothes: two men, one woman, with brollies. They are daunted by the lined bar, but refuse to appear daunted. One of the locals is talking about 'the cunting Yanks'. The nice threesome laugh nervously at unfunny interludes while their drinks are being poured. When they study the prints on the wall, I overhear the signature middle-class phrase, 'Oh, that's interesting.' It means the opposite.

Having collected their two halves of lager and one of bitter, they retire, oh so rightly, to a far corner table. They are not under threat in this pub, but they are out of place.

Despite myself, I want to know the result of the football and return to a former pub. Liverpool are one–nil up with five minutes to play. The camera keeps cutting to the Liverpool fans in attitudes of prayer. No waving at the cameras for them. They are heart-pure and passionate, in love, in thrall. Dudek, Luis Garcia, Lord Cissé of Bleachdom, these people are Liverpool, and Liverpool is all. A part of me envies them. Belief in anything makes life simpler.

18
Pork Juice

When Morton wanted to view the Mappa Mundi in Hereford Cathedral, he had only to open a pair of oak doors. Now I have to pay, and the thing is displayed in a climate-controlled, specially lit, acid-free, argon-filled, fuel-injected, double-overhead-cam case of technology by NASA. I ask after the old oak doors, and a volunteer woman, who is only too pleased to help, summons the exhibition supervisor, who is only too pleased to take a break from supervising. He tells me that the former doors are hung on the walls of his office and allows me in for a peep at them. They look like oak doors.

The Mappa Mundi does not look like a map. Nor was it meant to be one. Drawn by a thirteenth-century monk, it represents a compendium of knowledge, a sort of visual encyclopaedia of the time, a mix of Christianity, weird mythology, magical tales (though I'm not sure that isn't a triple tautology) and abundant guesswork. Jerusalem's bang centre. Britain is tucked away in the bottom left. Dublin's in Northern Ireland. Across North Africa it says EUROPA. Across Europe, AFFRICA. In short, George W. Bush wouldn't find much wrong with it.

The Mappa gives little detail on Britain except for the cathedral towns. But just north of Hereford it names and even illustrates a place called Clee Hill. Why, I've no idea. The volunteer woman thinks it may have something to do with ley lines but I am inclined to have more respect for medieval monks.

The map is drawn on vellum made from the hide of a single ten-month-old heifer from Lincoln. There are scars from ticks still visible on the animal's skin. I like that sort of unintended detail. It testifies to a sapid actuality, random, bitty, imperfect. Indeed it gives me a stronger sense of the reality of the past than the Mappa does.

The vellum around Hereford is heavily worn. I like that too. It's the equivalent of the 'You Are Here' arrow on town-centre maps that it is always smudged to illegibility. Here are seven centuries of finger marks.

The chained library, next door to the Mappa, is precisely as you imagine it. Every text is chained to its shelf. The monks of Hereford obviously shared my experience of lending books. Here are manuscripts going back to the eighth century, and printed texts going back to before Caxton. 'The Golden Legend' of 1483 contains the 'Lyf of Saynt George Martyr' in English.

It's touching to be able to read it. 'Saynt George was a knyght,' it begins, which is a sound start, straight to business.

Across the road from the cathedral is a fun fair. It seems indistinguishable from the fun fairs of my childhood. Here are the same hoopla games; the same ridiculously short-range shooting galleries with the same easy-to-hit targets, the same fluffy toys and the same bent air rifles; here too are the same elliptical rides to fling you and thrill you, erected by the same tattooed illiterates whom you wouldn't trust to repair your bicycle. And just as when I was young, in the light of morning the whole shebang looks merely tawdry.

Behind wire in the centre of town an archaeological dig is going on. It consists mainly of puddles. The diggers are wide-hipped girls in boots and scoutmaster shorts. A pigeon perches on a bit of presumably Roman wall. 'Hello,' says one of the girls, 'are you lost, darling?' The pigeon stares at her with understandable suspicion. When the dig has been dug the site is going to become a 'shopping and residential complex'. And I'd be happy to wager that that's what it was when the Romans were here.

Morton went next to Worcester, but I have had my fill of cathedrals. I am more intrigued by Clee Hill, especially when I find that my 2000 Bartholomew Road Atlas doesn't mark it.

Clee Hill turns out to be a bit east of Ludlow. It has a village on its flank. That village is called Clee Hill Village. There's a pub called the Kremlin, a school, a quarrying outfit, boggy common land, an eye-watering wind, an abundance of ewes with lambs head-butting their teats and views to the west that stretch halfway to forever. Under a sky of shifting cloud it looks as though Wales is wetly smouldering.

Clee Hill seems to have two summits. The one I clamber up shows evidence of having been both fort and quarry, but it appears to have been appropriated now by the Ministry of Fear. Radars shaped like the blades of snowploughs sweep in silent circles through the wind, and two giant electronic golf balls stand on pylons corralled by razor wire. For all I know their purpose may be innocent, but they exude menace. With unusual restraint, however, the Ministry has held the electronic gear a little off the summit. I clamber up to find rock and wind and a concrete trig point, and perched on the trig point a bird that may be a shrike. I've seen shrike only in books. They are murderous birds who impale their victims on thorns or twigs for later consumption. I sneak closer to the shrike with predictable success and I have the trig point to myself.

Most of England is spread out like a rumpled grey-green tablecloth. The view in all directions is limited only by the power of my eyes or the curve of the earth. To the west, Wales, to the north-west, the north-west. To the east, the Midlands and a man. He's old and bent, climbing over the rocks and heather with help of a stick. When he sees me he stops, and turns to take in the view. He looks the sort of man who'd know his birds and I go down to meet him.

His eyes are weak and watery. His skin is wind-raw and stretched like parchment on his cheeks. I describe the bird's size and shape and what I could make out of its plumage. I pause. He says nothing.

'I thought it might be a shrike,' I say.

'I wouldn't know one if I saw one,' he says. His voice is soft, his accent nasally Midlands. But he seems withdrawn, elsewhere, preoccupied. I am on the point of leaving when he says, 'Special day today.'

I wait for him to go on.

'My wife's birthday,' he says. 'She's been dead over two years now. I always come up here to say . . .' His voice falters. He's going to cry. 'To say a few prayers.' He chokes up. I lay a hand on his arm. I can feel the bone. I can sense him heaving like a troubled child.

We stand there a moment, strangers on a hill. 'Good on you,' I say and leave him to it.

As I go down I try not to look round, but I look round. He

has climbed to the trig point, the highest point of land for a hundred miles, and is standing with his back to me, looking out and away over England. The wind is ballooning his jacket, taking his prayers and scattering them. Anywhere can be a cathedral.

Ludlow's pretty and knows it. The lower end of Broad Street is so Georgian you would not be surprised to meet Jane Austen women wearing BBC costume dresses with the waist just beneath the breasts. The upper end of the street is overhung with exquisite half-timbered houses that belong on a tourism poster. The walls of Ludlow Castle are toothed like something that a child builds on the beach. The three-arched bridge over the Teme is a stone-built loveliness with dandelions sprouting from its cracks. And the butcher by the market square wears an apron and makes his own pork pies.

All pork pies are fine but some are finer. At university they were my breakfast. I was reading English so I had no lectures. Ten o'clock most mornings would find me sitting on the wall of the Fitzwilliam Museum waiting for the tray of hot pork pies to appear in the window of Fitzbillies Bakery. I would come away carrying a brown paper bag translucent with fat. The pastry was a bomb-casing, as thick as a finger, as rich as Trump. And the thing felt heavier in the hand than it had any right to feel. It was neutron-dense. When I bit into the mound of pork, it smoked. Juice ran over my chin, my trousers.

Some years later in France I was living in a hostel full of unemployed Arabs and suicidal Vietnamese. One night I was tortured by worry, tossing and hot with guilt and fear. I forget, as always, the precise cause, but I remember the sleepless desperation, a screaming Vietnamese somewhere along the corridor, and drunks howling in the bitter street below. On a pad of squared French paper I wrote a story about hot pork pies. It took an hour. I've still got it somewhere. It is explicitly erotic. When it was done, I slept.

'You'll have to wait ten minutes, sir,' says the butcher, 'they're just being jellied.' Through the door I can see his aproned assistant tipping a battered saucepan over the ranks of open-topped pies.

Ten minutes and fifteen seconds later I am back. The butcher doesn't recognize me.

'You'll have to wait ten minutes, sir,' he says, 'they're just setting.'

I say that I like my pies unset. He resists. I insist. I carry my prize to a bench in the market square, the brown paper bag translucent with fat. The pastry is a bomb-casing etc. It's a very fine moment. I am in Cambridge. I am in France. I am sticky with juice. Proust can keep his madeleine.

The pie costs one pound fifty. You can get them in Tesco for 25p, so people do. As I eat, a woman in leathers and a motor-bike helmet the size of a diver's bell put-puts across the square on a Vespa. Two ornate and complex bunches of florist's flow-ers protrude from her backpack and rise above her head, bending slightly with her slow progress. I follow her across the square towards the little museum where I mean to use the washroom to wash the pork fat from my hands. I find myself following a wake of scent.

On the desk at the museum entrance there's a copy of *In the Footsteps of St Paul* by H. V. Morton. I ask the quiet, fiftiesish, jacket-and-tie attendant whether he's read *In Search of England*.

'Of course I have,' he says. 'Who hasn't? Lovely man, Morton.'

'Yes,' I say, but I'm no longer sure that I mean it.

In *In Search of England* Morton comes across as the debonair English gent, the patriot, the jovial patrician in a Bertie Wooster car. And for me that pose is beginning to ring hollow. What is particularly beginning to irritate is the way he wheels out anonymous stock characters in order to underline the image of old England that he wants to portray. For example, he regularly transcribes conversations with ignorant American tourists to present, by contrast, an England drenched in history and

quietly proud of it, but far too well-bred to boast. And he gives
us ooh-aah bewhiskered yokels to suggest that England
remains semi-feudal, with a sturdy yeoman stock who know
their place and are happy to occupy it.

I've no doubt there was some truth in the picture he was
painting, but then there is an element of truth in all effective
propaganda. And increasingly it seems to me that this book is a
form of propaganda. Morton was inventing England as much as
he was discovering it. He was giving his audience the England
they wanted to be given. There is a fundamental paradox in a
quest that begins in England and yet goes in search of England.
Morton knew from the outset the England he wanted to find.
No reader would guess, for example, that when Morton set out
from London there was the National Strike going on. In the
England that Morton paints, a National Strike is unthinkable.

Of course all writers select. None offers the entire unpol-
ished truth. Every word carries the imprint of its author, is
selected to confirm a view. But there is about Morton's work a
sort of jaunty insincerity, that is fun in small doses but that
after a few weeks of close acquaintance is beginning to infect
me with doubt. None of which I say to the museum attendant.

Like so many people I've met on this trip, he has a tender
image of New Zealand. 'I thought of going there years ago,' he
says. 'Probably should have. But I don't suppose they're looking for elderly museum attendants, do you?'

The printed guide to 'What's on in Ludlow' offers me a screen-
ing of *Million Dollar Baby*, Paul Snook in concert at the Bull,
and, at seven o'clock at the Arts Centre, 'Poetry Café'. I'm at
the Arts Centre smack on seven.

So are six others, all my age or older. Moira's in charge. She
wears I-don't-care gardening clothes and keeps sweeping a
tumble of white hair from in front of her eyes. She has a pile of
books. When I tell her I've brought nothing to read, she lends
me *The Oxford Book of Modern Verse*.

We start in a sort of cafeteria with beer pumps ('cream flow' or 'classic', both of them ghastly), but three men in suits are discussing business so loudly that we shift to a table in the empty restaurant. *Million Dollar Baby* is playing next door. Occasional gusts of music intrude on our little group, and sounds of characters shouting.

Tonight's theme is roads. We go round the table, reading a poem at a time each. I wonder how long it is before someone reads Chesterton's 'The rolling English drunkard made the rolling English road'. No one does. One man has copied the poems he will read into a clothbound foolscap notebook. Another keeps a list of what's read: Betjeman, Edwin Muir, Kipling, McGough, Derek Mahon, Housman, Edward Thomas, Frost, de la Mare, Graves, and a Russian woman who got the obligatory seven years' penal servitude for writing. To judge by this poem she deserved them. One man, unfortunately, reads a poem he wrote himself. During each poem we sit in heads-down silence. After each poem there's a collective ah, or ah-ha, or a muted chuckle.

The Roger McGough poem is set at a bus stop on the day before the world ends. Everyone at the bus stop thinks what the hell, and gets shagging. It's moderately funny, but the language of the poem would be unacceptable in conversation here. When what I take to be a schoolteacher finishes reading it, there's an exhalation of polite laughter, but it is a head-driven laughter. It doesn't rise unbidden and unstoppable from the gut. Rather it expresses a conscious choice to laugh, a slight and English awkwardness. The laughter says that we are broad-minded enough to cope with this coarseness. The awkwardness says that we'd rather not.

Poetry for me is a private pleasure. The noise exists only inside my head. The best words mesh with my skull, become an intimate possession, a part of the way I see the world. So I have never been attracted to poetry readings. They are private made public.

But here with these gentle, unpretentious, decent people, I am at ease. This tiny gathering is a means to address the stuff that is so rarely addressed in daily Englishness, the stuff you don't say at coffee mornings, in checkout queues, at work, on housing estates where the garage doors are all identical and closed: the big stuff, the death and love stuff, the whether to stay or go stuff, the stuff that can keep you awake at night, the seriously strong meat. Here's a chance for all that to peep from underneath the cloak of everyday civility, not to be solved, because none of it is ever solved, but to be aired, as it has to be aired to avoid it turning rank.

Then a couple turn up and sully the evening. They are dressed like folk singers. It soon transpires that they like folk singing. Indeed they like folk everything. They are here to plug a 'folk weekend' in a nearby village with 'Myths, Music and Mermaids' plus 'story-telling, poetry and prose open session'. They urge everyone to attend. Everyone mutters non-committal politenesses that mean no.

Moira asks the woman if she has a poem to contribute on roads. 'Oh yes, of course,' she says, with the air of one about to unlock a chest of bullion. She reads 'The rolling English drunkard made the rolling English road'. Badly. I fancy I am not alone in drooping. When she finishes she looks triumphant.

After that, it's all over. Ms Folk has burst the balloon. I go to the Bull to see Paul Snook. It's more curiosity than desire. I don't like music in pubs. Pubs are for talking in.

With its sagging fifteenth-century ceiling the Bull is not designed for music. Neither is Mr Snook. He's a down-at-heel shaven-headed Bruce Springsteen derivative without apparent gusto. He plays a guitar, of course, too loud, of course, above an electronically-generated drum beat, of course, and he sings lyrics that, of course, I can rarely make out. When I do make them out I wish I hadn't. 'She was a bad machine,' he sings.

But Mr Snook is more popular than poetry. Perhaps forty

people have come to the Bull, all aged between fifteen and twenty-five. Those who came in groups remain in groups, drinking, occasionally shouting. Those who came alone remain alone, dolefully sipping at their solitary drinks and watching uninspiring Mr Snook without apparent inspiration. The elderly poetry club had more fun.

I last one beer, then wander back through decorous empty streets to the pub where I am staying and fall into conversation, as one is supposed to do in pubs, with a man who used to sell cars. He had a Rover dealership 'in the days when Rover made proper cars. Jap cars then were Jap-crap. They just rusted out, Datsuns especially.'

But the Japanese cars got better and the Rovers kept getting worse. 'Cars used to arrive with bits missing. Can you believe that? Bits missing, all sorts of bits. And they became famous for oil leaks. So I went over to Nissan. Guess how many warranty claims I had on the Nissans I sold. None. Count them. None. There just aren't any decent British cars any more. It's all gone.'

Recently he retired from cars altogether and opened a sweet shop. I noticed it in town today. It's deliberately old-fashioned, displaying humbugs, bull's eyes, Everton mints in big glass jars. It's pure boiled nostalgia, and it's thriving. 'I had a man come into the shop the other day,' says the proprietor happily, 'and he stood in the middle of the floor and he just stared at all the jars. Then he just burst into tears.'

A plaque at the corner of the bar says, 'Reserved. Mr J. Harris first sat here 46 years ago and still does. 2004.' It's empty.

19

Democratic Yawn

The election campaign is over. Over the climactic period, the evening news has shown a confident Mr Blair striding the street, ostensibly canvassing in the good old-fashioned way, his jacket swung over his shoulder and one finger through the loop, a pose simultaneously casual, manly and purposeful. Sometimes he even stopped for an ice cream.

Mr Howard tried to reply in kind. Though well over sixty, on one occasion he discarded his jacket and ran from door to door for the cameras, trying very hard to grin as he went.

On election day I wake to silence in a pub set hard against the old stone walls of Ludlow. Outside my window a Union Jack hangs lifeless in the misty air, but I feel a flutter of mild excitement. For tonight, I mean to be present when an electorate result is announced. I want to see the returning officer mount the rostrum, tap the microphone, cough and then read out the figures in a local accent, with the candidates ranged behind him in a crescent, all wearing rosettes on their lapels and self-conscious looks on their faces, apart from the Monster Raving Loony Party candidate who is wearing a pink rabbit suit and the smile of a dork. I remember it all from television throughout my childhood, with a Dimbleby whispering that this is Huddersfield East or wherever. But first, I nip into Ludlow for toothpaste.

A woman is waiting for Boots to open.

I say good morning.

'Are you Kiwi?' she says.

She was brought up five miles from where I now live, beside a bay where I walk my dogs. She left when she was twenty, has been in Ludlow for twenty-seven years.

'Did you marry an Englishman?' I ask.

'Two,' she says.

She's not especially attached to this country. 'I mean, sometimes I just want to get out of here. Like when I'm stuck in the traffic or when I pay eight hundred quid to sit in a house in Cornwall for a week in summer doing jigsaws and listening to the rain. But whenever I do go back to New Zealand, I feel the need to have somewhere to escape to. You know what I mean?'

I know exactly what she means and I say so. She looks quizzically at me for a moment as if wanting to dig deeper, then decides against it.

'But my husband would go to NZ like a shot,' she says.

'Especially now we're going to get another five years of Blair, God help us.'

Perhaps it's the people I gravitate towards, perhaps it's the places I've been, but I have yet to hear a compliment and the Prime Minister in the same sentence.

Boots has a bewildering wall of toothpastes. They all claim to differ. I buy the one I always buy because that's how shopping works.

To the library to check my email, but the place has been turned into a polling station, staffed by those legions of middle-aged middle-class full-skirted women without whom the charities would collapse, the Ramblers' Club would have no secretary, the wheels would fall off meals.

The men and women exercising their democratic duty do not look greatly excited.

I have a mental image of sleepy Shropshire and I got it from P. G. Wodehouse. Wodehouse is Morton parodied, the idyll of Englishness played for laughs. And yet on this early summer's day, as I take the back roads to Shrewsbury, Shropshire looks much as Wodehouse painted it. The countryside seems drenched in a deep green stupor. The grass could not look thicker, the cattle more docile, the villages more torpid. I would not be startled to see a policeman on a bicycle.

The Severn wraps round Shrewsbury like the tail on a sitting cat. The town centre's a mix of leaning old buildings that please the tourists and spanking new shopping malls that please the locals. The pub where I have lunch is planning a celebration for VE Day. The landlord is going to decorate the place with sandbags and camouflage cloth and he's trying to get hold of an air-raid siren. Bitter will cost the same as in 1945, seven and a half new pence (as he insists on calling it), plus a one-pound-fifty donation.

'I saw a Spitfire in a museum recently,' he says, 'and I came over all misty-eyed. But, do you know, if there was a war tomorrow and my conscription papers landed on the doormat, I'd make for the hills. Do you think that's weird?'

'Well, yes.'

'I'm proud to be English, though. Not enough people are. I mean the Welsh, the Scots and the Irish have national days, don't they, but what about the English? We're scared we might offend somebody.'

I tell him I saw a Boy Scout parade in Tavistock on the day after St George's Day but he doesn't seem impressed.

The pub, he tells me, has problems with the English Border Patrol. 'They're the boot boys of the BNP, all coordinated by mobile phone. My chef got beaten up by half a dozen of them, for no reason.'

'Aren't the BNP proud to be English?'

'No, mate, they're just thugs looking for an excuse.'

And I suspect he's right. But what is the notion of Englishness that this landlord favours? Does it really have to reach back sixty years to find something to celebrate? In the end, I suspect, like every other country, England is just a giant football team. And football teams become teams only when they play against someone else. The landlord is just remembering the last big match.

'You're well out of it in New Zealand,' he says.

'Yes,' says his wife, who gives the impression of having heard her husband's opinions a couple of times before, 'it's all a bit of a mess here. But you have a lovely day, now.'

Shrewsbury's information centre is staffed by a smug and dapper man. I watch him deal with a string of tourist queries. He prides himself on his Salopian omniscience. He reaches for a town map or a hotel guide or a train timetable without looking. He fires off information too fast for it to be absorbed, and follows it with a swift dismissive dealt-with-who's-next? smile. The elderly trippers are too cowed to quibble. They shuffle away from the counter, taking their wad of brochures to a table where they try to make some sense of them.

When I ask him where the election result will be announced, I am gratified to see him stop short. He clearly doesn't know. He is also clearly annoyed that he doesn't know.

'*Is* it announced?' he asks.

'Oh yes,' I say, 'you know, with the returning officer and a microphone and the candidates, like on the telly. I think it happens in the same place where the votes are counted. Do you know where that is, perhaps?'

He dislikes me. He would like me to go away. I do not intend to go away.

'One moment,' he says and goes sourly, primly to a phone that isn't the phone on his desk. He doesn't want to be heard asking questions. He is the man of answers.

'Right here,' he says when he comes back, 'they're counting the votes here, in this building, in the theatre.' He gestures vaguely behind him, doesn't smile, then looks over my shoulder at the next in the queue.

'Thank you so much,' I say.

I go down corridors, round corners, up stairs, past people moving with purpose who pay me no attention. The theatre's deserted, but trestle tables have been laid out for vote counting, and there at the far end is a stage looking just right for a tubby aldermanic returning officer.

'Can I help you?' The speaker is dressed as a waiter in white shirt and waistcoat. He's pushing a trolley-load of orange juice.

It is possible to say, 'Can I help you?' in a manner that sounds helpful. The waiter says it in a manner that sounds like fuck off.

'I'm looking for the place where the votes are counted.'

'It's not open yet.' This too sounds like fuck off.

'Thank you so much,' I say. 'I'll come back later.'

'Got a ticket?' he says.

'A ticket?'

'A ticket.' Then he decides to clarify things. 'You've got to have a ticket,' he says. He lifts the arm of his trolley and disappears.

Twenty-nine acres of grass stretch up one side of Shrewsbury's hill, with a church at their summit and the river at their foot. An expanse of lawn brings out the idle best in people. They dandle children, play pick-up games of football, and throw Frisbees for amusement or dogs. Every town should have such a place.

The air remains chill but the spring sun has brought out the female flesh. Morton would have revelled in it. He admired Shrewsbury girls 'in their best summer frocks'. Today he could admire a thousand midriffs, exposed between hipster jeans and tiny pink tops. Some of the midriffs are taut and tanned and erotic. Most aren't.

I learned in the pub near Bradford-on-Avon that a word has been coined to describe the roll of veinous midriff fat that so many girls now choose to display. The word is gunt. It derives from two words elided, one of which is gut.

A few girls are wearing flimsy skirts of what looks to be curtain netting, with a ragged asymmetric hemline, a sort of ravaged Barbarella look that will be out of fashion, I suspect, by the time I've completed this sentence.

The boys meanwhile welcome the hint of the summer with the style they've worn all winter: trainers, low-crotched jeans, hooded sweatshirts and the slouching gait of the cave dweller.

But the scene is spring lovely. The river is full of crisp fours and eights moving over the water like sleek stick insects, their coaches cycling the towpath and bellowing instructions. One four contains Jack. Jack's coach is merciless. 'Jack, sit up,' he bellows through a megaphone to the whole of Shrewsbury. 'Jack, don't hunch.' 'The catch, Jack, the catch.'

It isn't hard to work out which one is Jack. In a crew of obvious misfits, Jack is the least fitting. And he doesn't mind. He grins. The boat rocks and stutters. The coach despairs.

*

Late in the evening I return to the electoral counting place. I am stopped at the door by security. I have a little speech prepared.

'No,' I say, 'I'm afraid I haven't got a ticket. I don't see that I need a ticket, for surely it is my right as a citizen and a voter in an open democracy not only to participate in the electoral process but also to witness that process in the . . .'

The speech goes down exactly as you would expect. The squat security man listens with the intense sympathetic interest of all squat security men, smug in his status and cruddy uniform and his sense of righteous muscle, and I don't get to see the returning officer. Apparently all the tickets go to party hacks.

I end up watching the election results on television in my hotel room and fall asleep before they get to Shrewsbury.

20

Where they Borrow Whippets

Sixty-one per cent of the population voted. Labour got thirty six per cent of those votes. In other words, they won the election comfortably on the votes of a little more than one British adult in five. I haven't met any of those one in five. Perhaps they're up north where I'm heading now. But first I take a little detour west. I want a peek at Wales.

It looks so different from England on the map. There are

tracts of roadlessness that dwarf Salisbury Plain. In the heart of Wales the contour lines resemble a thumb-print. And the place names are magnificently alien. I head for Llanrhaeadr-ym-Mochnant in the hope that its name will prove longer than its main street.

A bilingual welcome sign indicates that richly grassed and wooded England has become richly grassed and wooded Cymru, and that the legs of the lambs have become slightly more valuable. But up ahead and framed in the windscreen are sharper uplands, taller, more barren, grey blades rather than green curves, suggesting land more like New Zealand than anything I have seen so far.

Llanrhaeadr-ym-Mochnant could not be English, or at least not southern English. It's wedged into its valley as sombre as a corpse: grey stone, black slate and, though the weather is fine, there's an indefinable a sense of rain that's been and rain to come.

Three young mothers are standing outside the little school watching the kids in the playground. 'Oh yes,' says one, her accent lilting like a cork on ripples, 'the kids are taught in Welsh and English.'

I ask her what the place name means. She looks at the others. They look abashed.

'Llan's village, isn't it,' says one, 'but the rest, I don't know. Oh, hang on, Rhaeadr's the river, of course. Have you seen our waterfall? It's one of the Seven Wonders of Wales.' I can hear the capital letters.

The general store has no postcards of the village, but several of the Seven Wonders: Pistyll Rhaeadr, Wrexham steeple, Snowdon, Overton yew-trees, the well of St Winifred, Llangollen bridge and Gresford bells. I have heard only of Snowdon, the mighty mountain you can climb by train.

I drive five miles up a lane that shrinks amusingly to nine inches wider than the Audi, the scenery shifting quickly from cosy English lowland to mountainous Welsh upland. Round a

bend and there in front of me is Pistyll Rhaeadr, a waterfall
like a tress of blonde hair, forming thirteen and a half per cent
of Welsh wondrousness.

A deserted car park, a couple of stone cottages, and a sign on
the gate of the tearooms saying 'Please do not let the goat into
the garden'. I see no goat. Nor for that matter do I see a garden.

I climb paths through slate outcrops that run with water and
through bogs that suck at my shoes. At the summit there's an
ear-roaring wind and a sky as wide as the world with a kestrel
hovering in it, its wings curved as if hugging a column.

I climb down through a copse. No people, no safety barriers,
no notice boards telling me earnest stuff about fault lines and
rock formations. Just rock, wet grass and a tea-coloured stream
that gurgles through a strew of mossed boulders then disappears with the suddenness of a heart attack.

I want to lean over the edge. I want to see the water falling to
hit the pool in a perpetual steam of spray however many feet
below. My head tells me that I am perfectly capable of leaning
without falling. But instinct screams the opposite. And instinct
is infinitely stronger. When I get within two yards of the edge I
feel a physical revulsion in throat and spine. My gut writhes
with spirals of nausea.

I kneel and crawl. I go two foot closer, slowly, as if fighting
the pull of a magnet. A yard from the edge, and I can crawl no
further. So I flatten myself on the grass and shimmy like a
snake, hoping that if my feet stay five foot ten inches back, I can
poke my head over the rim and do my tourist peeping.

I can't. I am thwarted by a certainty that the sight of the
chasm below, its sheer sheerness, its vertiginous vacancy, will
simply flip my legs up and over my body and fling me to my
doom like a thrown starfish.

I shimmy back. Instinct pats me warmly on the back and
calms my guts and lights me a cigarette and says the view
wouldn't really have been worth it anyway. Far down below a
gang of motorcycles comes buzzing up the lane like flies and

clusters round the Audi as if it were rotting meat. I hurry down the way I came up.

The bikies are milling in daunting black leather. They turn out to be middle-aged and Dutch and frightfully polite. They tell me what a lovely spot this is. I tell them that it's one of the wonders of Wales. 'Ooooh,' says one.

As soon as I step out of the Audi into the busy streets of Chester, I realize that I've crossed a divide. I've come north. The accent has changed. The manner has changed. The price of cakes in the bakery has dropped a penny or two. The foods on display are blander, bigger, fattier, heavier, less fancy. Chester's only perhaps fifty miles north of Shrewsbury, but it feels like, if not a different world, a different tone. And to me it's an alien one.

I'm a southerner. Throughout my childhood the Thames was the northern limit of the world. Although the family took a couple of holidays in Scotland, we drove through the north of England as though it were a corridor, something to be passed through on the way to somewhere worthwhile.

The north had improper accents that didn't find their way on to television except as comedy. The north was where the working class came from, and coal and strikes and cutlery. And also, as it happens, my father. He was brought up in Sheffield, but never once in my presence did he speak of it, and never once did we go there. If he'd ever had a Yorkshire accent, he'd shed it by the time I arrived.

In 1981 I spent nine months teaching in Sheffield. I felt more abroad than I ever have when living abroad. The kids said 'reet' and 'thee'. They said 'were' when they meant 'was', and they ate chip butties with no sense of parody. I remember a tall black male bus conductor saying, 'That'll be nine pence, love.' The vowel in 'love' made a sound unheard in Sussex. Even the beer was different. It frothed like accelerated Guinness.

In my head there is still no distinction between Lancashire,

Yorkshire, Northumbria, Cumbria and any other counties that happen to be hanging around up here. It's just the north.

Morton too was a southerner. Three-quarters of *In Search of England* is set south of Birmingham. You can sense from the text that Morton travelled north with some reluctance. The north was the home of industry, and industry despoiled his lovely ancient England. He was unwilling to drive anywhere near it in his shiny new motor car, a car that the north had made.

'The wall of Chester', wrote Morton, 'stands with its arms round beautiful old Chester, while ugly new Chester peeps over the parapet from the other side.'

Things have changed a little. The wall now has ugly new buildings on both sides. Beyond the wall, the winner in the ugliness stakes is a pink block of flats. It looks like a stack of dyed sugar cubes by Bauhaus. It stands hard by a sweet Roman bridge. Set side by side like that they resemble an illustration from the Book of Decline.

Within the wall the trophy goes to the police headquarters, a concrete monolith that's brutal enough in its basic design but whose brutality has been magnificently enhanced by a set of concrete hieroglyphics set into one flank like the remains of alphabet soup. It belongs to what Bill Bryson aptly called the Fuck-off School of Architecture.

The city wall no longer acts as a wall. It passes over both a railway line and a four-lane highway. Anyone can come into Chester and anyone does. The city centre thrums.

The Rows that Morton admired are still there and still admirable. They're covered arcades recessed into medieval timber buildings at first-floor level. You take steps up to them and then shop in the dry. Morton puzzled over their original purpose and even consulted an antiquary on the subject, before concluding that '"The Rows" are one of the architectural mysteries of England.'

I'm not so sure. Call me an anti-mystic but it seems to me that the Rows are a medieval shopping mall. Seven hundred years ago people disliked getting wet every bit as much as people do today. And it's good to see the Rows still serving as a shopping mall in the twenty-first century rather than being preserved as an antique prettiness for people like me to pay to walk over and be bored by.

I enjoy helping a succession of remarkably young mothers lift their pushchairs up the steps, and I enjoy watching the shaven-headed lads sitting astride the balustrades smoking and swearing and leaping down with the lissomness of gibbons, and I especially enjoy a short and almost spherical black man who's got God. Immaculately dressed in tie and overcoat, he shelters from the drizzle under a blue and white golf umbrella, sings a hymn a cappella, rather well and very loudly, then preaches to the passing crowd with enormous vigour, the umbrella shaking with his gestures. The crowd ignores him, of course, but he adds to the gaiety of the place. The man standing next to him doesn't. He's got a face like a wet Sunday in a debtors' prison. He holds an advertising placard on a stick directly behind the loud man of God. The placard says BURGER KING.

The friends I had made in Sheffield were forever telling me that the north was better because it was friendly. There was none of that stand-offish you got 'down south'. Everything north of Brum, it seemed, was like one giant Coronation Street with people constantly nipping in and out of each other's houses to borrow a twist of tea or a whippet, or to gossip about our Nora who was in the family way again. I've never seen it myself. For sure, people who serve you here are more overtly cheerful, and the older ones in particular call you love, pet or m'duck, but I've not found that it betokens any greater intimacy.

I spend the evening in a variety of pubs, some pleasant, some emphatically not, and no one talks to me. Perhaps I've got hostile southerner stamped on my manner, or tourist, or perhaps I have merely achieved the invisibility of middle age, but not once am I addressed in anything other than a commercial capacity. I have to initiate my own conversations, just as I did down south, and few take wing.

Annie's in her forties and lives in Telford. She has come to Chester to 'make a weekend of it', though when I meet her she's sipping wine on her own.

'Isn't Telford the new town?'

'Yeah, you've got to drive everywhere. Not like here. Everything's all bunched together up here. It's nice. Besides, I wouldn't go out in Telford, not after dark. I just go home, lock the door and don't hear a thing. But I read about it in the morning.'

'About what?'

'Oh, stabbings and everything. It's dreadful. They knife you these days soon as look at you, don't they?'

I consider saying that I've been out on the town most evenings for the last few weeks and I've hardly been knifed at all, but I don't. I just make noises of subdued and serious ambiguity.

'My son, he's eighteen, and he works out at the gym – you should see the size of his arms – he tells me what goes on in the clubs and that. He's not scared of anything, my boy, but a knife, I mean, you can't fight that, can you? I don't know what's happened. I mean you're the same age as me, more or less. We just went out, got pissed up and loved everybody, didn't we? But not this lot, not now.'

I'm not sure that I loved everybody. I am sure that not everybody loved me. Indeed I can remember with the vividness of a Rousseau jungle painting being invited to step outside at a party in darkest Brighton some thirty years ago and having a knife drawn on me. I can't remember what the difference of opinion was, but I can remember running.

Has violence proliferated in this country? Statistics and the *Daily Mail* insist that it has, and the statistics, at least, can't be argued with.

Morton's route has taken me to nice places, by and large. I have skirted the great metropolises, seen none of the urban ghettoes or the sink estates, where violence must hang in the air like a miasma. But in the nice places, I have seen no more evidence of violence than I saw thirty years ago. Are the ordinary streets more dangerous than they used to be for the peaceable many, or has fear been fostered by the media? I strongly suspect that the answers to those two questions are respectively no and yes.

I dine on a kebab. My dictionary defines a kebab as 'small pieces of meat, vegetables, etc packed closely and cooked on a skewer'. I'm puzzled by the 'etc' but otherwise the definition sounds right. However a dictionary kebab is not a modern street kebab.

In the Chester kebabbery window stands a cylinder of what purports to be meat but looks suspiciously like etc. It is botulism on a stick. Behind it there's a thing like the gas fire in a cheap bed-sit. I am the first customer of the evening and the cylinder is pearled with beads of white fat, congealed in the act of dripping. The surly Turk at the counter lights the gas fire with the Bic from his breast pocket, and encourages the flames by collecting grease on his finger and flicking it at the gas. As he does so, two of his brothers or cousins or uncles emerge from the kitchen in John Travolta jackets and gelled hair. The swinging door grants a diminishing series of glimpses of a kitchen that I would rather not have had. The brothers, cousins or uncles say something guttural to Mr Happy the Chef and head out into the night, with the evident intention of giving a good time to the womenfolk of Chester.

When one flank of the cylinder has been given a sufficient warming to excite the bacteria, a period that I have spent admiring the extraordinarily undecorative decor of the place, Mr Happy turns the fire off, swivels the cylinder, shears the discoloured outer layer from it with what looks like a Philips Ladyshave, spreads a pitta pocket wide with his fingers, dumps the meat in, decorates it with a sliver of tomato and a wilt of shredded lettuce, threatens to squirt it with a sauce bottle that has a moustache of dried yesterdays around its nozzle until I wave a hand in objection, hands it over the counter and charges me three pounds ninety, all without a hint of smile. I carry the kebab through drizzle to a park bench where I put some of it down my throat and most of it on my trousers. It's excellent.

21

What a Lovely Pier

So far on this trip I have had few conversations over breakfast. It's understandable. Breakfast is the least convivial of meals. There is no booze associated with it and people are still clogged with the selfishness of sleep. Furthermore, only a few minutes earlier every breakfaster was riding the horse of his dreams, a foam-scattered, rearing, shiny-muscled charger that galloped and whinnied through a landscape that was both somehow recognizable and yet transmuted into vivid strangeness. In comparison, the day ahead seems as bland as a donkey ride on Blackpool beach, a trudge along familiar sand in blinkers.

Hence perhaps the whispering withdrawn privacy of breakfast, the murmurings and grunts over toast, the thoughtful intake of tea, of coffee, stimulants to make the flat day possible. We are learning to be sociable again, relearning the rules of constraint. And the little dining rooms of pubs and small hotels discourage intimacy, their tables set primly apart, the chairs aligned away from contact. As guests arrive they seek out by instinctive mental geometry the point in the room that is furthest away from others, installing themselves with newspapers to take in what others have done in a different, more exciting world.

But today I have a substantial breakfast conversation. A skinny Australian couple at the next table are travelling with their plump grown-up daughter. Daughter, it transpires, now lives in London. They're having a lovely time, 'just soaking up all the old stuff', but they've found the English difficult to talk to.

'You say, "Excuse me",' says the wife, 'and just for a second you can see the defences go up. They sort of bristle, you know. Then you ask for directions and they make out your accent and the bristles go down, they sort of relax, because you're not going to ask them anything difficult. Then they're really helpful.'

'But boy,' says her husband, laughing with a piece of marmalade-laden toast halted on its way to his mouth, 'can the Poms talk about the weather! But the weather's always the same. I don't know why they bother with weather forecasts. Changeable would cover it nicely, every bloody day.' He bites the toast. He's spoken loudly. There are several other people in the dining room, all obviously English, and all equally obviously listening. The pages of the newspapers have stopped turning.

'Dad,' says the daughter, turning the word into two cheerfully disapproving syllables, 'shhh.'

'You're turning into a Pom yourself,' he says, and beams
and gives his daughter a toasty kiss.

Immediately north of Chester the landscape changes for the
worse. It did in Morton's day too. 'Here', he wrote, and you can
sense his distaste in the capital letter to come, 'the traveller
enters Industrial England.'

The land flattens towards the Mersey estuary. Among
scrubby fields and the wan remains of reed beds, industrial
parks have sprouted. A bleak wind roars off the Irish Sea, and
on the horizon stands a massive refinery like a boffin's labora-
tory expanded to cover acres. The motorway system, seamless,
swift, in its way beautiful, sweeps me up between the vast
twin conurbations of Liverpool and Manchester. Signposts
offer a whole swag of Rugby League teams – Widnes,
Warrington, St Helens, Salford, Leigh – and Eccles, home of the
dreary cake.

On page 182 of my copy *In Search of England* – the thirty-
ninth edition, printed in 1949 – Morton records how he
approached a man standing in the main street of Wigan and
said, 'This town has been badly libelled.'

'I'm reet glad to hear you say that,' said the man and he
immediately offered to show Morton round the glory that was
Wigan. According to Morton, 'They all do this in Wigan if you
go up and say frankly that the town has a certain attraction.'

It's a typical Morton generalization, a bid to pin a place
down in the way an entomologist pins a grub. I greatly doubt
that it's true. And for once I'm going to test it.

I've been to Wigan before, almost thirty years ago while
hitching to Scotland to take up a job beating grouse. I stayed
here with Dave, a rugby-playing university friend. Before a
rugby match Dave always ate potatoes. After the match he
always drank. When sober, Dave was a pensive, benign scien-

tist. When drunk he was lethal. Round about pint seven, the cloak of civility would tumble off him and he would become exciting. 'Come on,' he'd say, and we'd leave whatever bar we were in and go out to take on the night.

Drunk, Dave would do anything. He had ideas. Most of them were dangerous. He'd climb things, throw scissors, steal. Of course he'd been brought up a Catholic. I have always warmed to Catholics. Dave taught me there's no such thing as a lapsed one.

One evening I went round to Dave's rooms and he said he wasn't coming out. It would be, he said, a sin.

'What?' I said.

'You'll laugh,' he said. I promised not to laugh.

'God held me down in this chair,' he said, then stopped to see my reaction. I said nothing.

'I couldn't move. God said I had a choice. I could go with him or I could go drinking with you. As soon as I'd made my choice he'd let me go. I went with God. I'm sorry.'

I laughed. 'Let's discuss it over a beer,' I said. But Dave was adamant.

He joined the Christian Union, held Bible study groups in his rooms with cocoa. Once I burst in on his Bible group roaring drunk. Dave was all tolerance. I threw up in the sink. Dave swizzled his finger round the plug hole to force the big bits through, then led me gently, patiently back to my room. He was a good man and a good friend lost. We never drank together again. I've had it in for God since.

When I came to Wigan that time, Dave's conversion still lay ahead of him. He took me to see Wigan Pier. 'The words "Wigan Pier"', wrote Morton, 'spoken by a comedian on a music-hall stage, are sufficient to make an audience howl with laughter . . . Wigan, to millions of people who have never seen and never will see the town, represents the apex of the world's pyramid of gloom.'

It wasn't long after Morton passed through that Orwell used

the comic irony of Wigan Pier as the title for his rather different exploration of 'the real England'. And when Dave showed me round in 1978, the irony persisted. The pier was just broken windows, dead sheds, abandoned supermarket trolleys and a canal like foetid soup. I rather liked it.

We spent the rest of the day in cubicled Victorian pubs, which I also rather liked. I remember frothy thin beer, and a dinner of ham barm cakes. These were bread rolls, each stuffed with approximately half a pig. Late in the evening there was a typical Dave adventure with a stolen bicycle.

Now, at ten o'clock on this Saturday morning, Wigan's thrumming. The shops and pavements are packed with young mothers and old couples.

It's almost a relief to be somewhere without obvious anti-quarian interest. The black-and-white Tudor is fake Tudor. You can always tell by the straight edges of the timber. Nevertheless Wigan's got a new information centre with several computer screens, a staff of two women and no customers. I ask one of the women what there is to do in Wigan.

'Do you like drinking?' she says. 'There's lots of pubs.'

'Anything else?'

'Not much, really.'

'What do people come here for, then?'

'Rugby and football, mostly.'

'What about the pier?'

'Oh aye, I forgot the pier,' and she directs me down the hill.

On the way I spot several idling men on whom I could try Morton's opening introductory line, but I feel the need to warm up to it.

The pier has been cleaned up. According to a plaque, the place was revamped in the early eighties and the revampings were opened by the Queen. There's now a Wigan Pier Experience, a Pier Nightspot and a multi-barred pub and enter-tainment complex called the Orwell where you can get married. It's got pictures of old George himself on it.

And soon the place is going to be re-revamped. 'A brand new, heritage-themed attraction' is on its way. The place's ironic origin is sinking irretrievably into the sea of oblivion. Indeed for many visitors it may already have done so. And thus Wigan Pier will have found a permanent home in the chlorinated paddling pool of heritage theming. It will have become an attraction, complete unto itself and divorced from anything resembling the truth, just like Land's End or *le tombeau de Roi Arthur*.

On the way back up the hill a chip shop advertises sausage barms and chip barms and I get a hot gust of yesterday. I believe Dave became a teacher. I buy a prawn sandwich and take it to a bench in a little park. A man in his sixties, wearing the regulation M&S zippered job, sits heavily down on its other end. I lay my sandwich on my knee, breathe in and surprise myself by giving a little introductory theatrical cough like a returning officer coming to the mike. 'This town has been badly libelled,' I say.

The man doesn't look startled. He doesn't move away. Nor yet does he launch into an encomium of Wigan's virtues and offer to show me round them. What he does is nothing at all. He just continues staring across a bed of civic plants. It's as though I hadn't spoken. I can't say I blame him. I revert to my sandwich, not daring to repeat myself.

But I do try once more in a pub. I go in with the sole purpose of trying. I buy a pint and sit at the bar. The place is sprinkled with lunchtime drinkers. Most have newspapers or friends. An office worker comes in and orders lager. About my age, cheap suit, incipient paunch, chubby face and a benign manner. He looks around while his pint pours, catches my eye, nods and says, 'Morning.'

'This town has been badly libelled,' I say.

'Oh aye,' says the man and calmly grants his complete attention to the barmaid. He pays, sips and takes his pint to a distant table, clearly used to humouring the nutter found in every pub. I drink my beer quickly and leave town.

*

Morton saw no reason to stop between here and Windermere, but as the Audi is purring up the M6 I see a sign to Morecambe, and partly because I've never been there, and partly because I haven't yet visited a seaside resort, that uniquely English mix of tackiness and zest, I turn off.

The wind is murderous and thrilling. When I get out of the Audi on the sea front, it whips the cigarette from my fingers. I follow it up the steps of a hotel. An old woman is pushing against the glass door, leaning fully against it, unable to budge it. When I open it for her, pulling with both hands, the wind knocks her back two steps in the lobby. 'On second thoughts,' she says, smiling, and she retreats into the hotel.

The proprietor is young, chubby, well-meaning and deferential. He does me a room for twenty-seven pounds 'and I haven't charged you extra for the sea view, Mr Bennett'. His fat white fingers move slowly over the registration card, gripping the pen as though afraid someone might steal it, applying enough pressure for it to dent the blotter underneath. 'And will you be dining with us this evening, Mr Bennett?' His excessive servility, his vocabulary, is comically out of kilter with his establishment. It's the sort of downmarket seafront hotel that I am familiar with from Brighton – a narrow frontage in a four-storey terrace, Edwardian at a guess, painted white, a dining room and residents' lounge on the ground floor, a warren of narrow stairs and little rooms above.

The wind powers through a gap in the window frame of my third-floor room and balloons the curtain. Beyond the roaring glass, the tip of a lamppost is vibrating like a tuning fork. A flag above the RNLI office has wrapped itself round the pole, its tip smacking itself like a winter bather.

My sea view has no sea. Only sand and glistening mudflats and a scattering of fishing boats lying at drunken angles. This is Morecambe Bay, where according to 'a complimentary brochure and town map for you, Mr Bennett', the tide comes in at the clip 'of a good horse'. Even in New Zealand the news reached me last year of the party of slave-labour Chinese cockle-pickers who were caught out by that tide and drowned.

Far out, I think I can distinguish the last channel of water, whipped by the wind into egg froth. Beyond the bay the mountains of Cumbria stand dark beneath the cloud, like teeth on a blunt saw. I head out into Morecambe.

I like big wind. I like the sense of elemental pummelling. I like to lean on it as if crucified, to punch holes in it with my arms, or to run with it, each stride absurdly lengthened like a moon-walker's stride. This late Saturday afternoon the wind has emptied the promenade, and Morecambe feels withered, bereft. Its prom was designed round holiday crowds. Without them it's a husk.

The Winter Gardens has steel grilles behind its windows and for good reason. The toughened glass has been assaulted by boots, each assault leaving a crater with a whitened epicentre and a radiating web of cracks. The craters reach almost to chest height, almost indeed to the water-stained notice Sellotaped inside the window, announcing plans to restore the building to its former grandeur.

The Midland Hotel, the only building on the seaward side of the prom, is similarly defunct. An off-white, flat-roofed, four-storey art-deco nastiness, it's got broken windows and doors of nailed plywood. Rust blooms on its guttering and stains the walls like urinals. But signs outside show an artist's impression of how this building will look soon, after cash has been poured into it by the North-West Development Agency, the Heritage Lottery Fund, Lancaster County Council and English Heritage.

Morecambe is clearly trying. The prom has been titivated with stone birds, a replica of Cumbria's horizon, a poem set into the path, and a raised statue of Eric Morecambe in plus fours, skipping towards the wind, one hand characteristically behind his back, the other above his head.

The fish-and-chipperies, the souvenir shops and the penny arcades look forlorn and winter hopeless, two steps from abandonment. A tea room that could seat a hundred, seats none. A second-hand book shop is comically overstocked. There is barely room for the proprietor, a hippy marooned on the shores of late middle age, his seventies hair still bunched in a greying ponytail. He is entombed in books. Hundreds have brought him books in exchange for pennies, or just to be rid of them, but too few have made the opposite transaction. If you pulled out the right volume you could bring the lot down, an unstoppable landslide of words, the shop in sudden entropy.

Behind the prom are the remnants of the fishing village that Morecambe was. Here are tight-packed little terraces and lanes that wind, with a pub at each end. In one such back street a party of pre-teens is waiting to get into an early-evening disco. The girls are painted and animated, holding down their hand-kerchief-sized skirts against the rifling wind. The spike-haired boys look shy or sullen, or lurk around the next corner in hud-dles, smoking.

Morrison's supermarket car park is barely habitable. Over this huge expanse of asphalt the wind meets no impediment. The very few shoppers either battle towards their cars as if wading a torrent, or fly away from them as if sucked.

Inside the store you wouldn't know. The aisles are stocked with brightly packaged everything, in air synthetically bright and calm. The butchery is staffed by a man in boater and apron. In front of him are pre-packed trays of meat. Behind him hangs a row of pig carcasses made of painted plastic.

The town brochure tells me that Morecambe does 'some of the best fish and chips in the country', a truth which it proves with an exclamation mark. The haddock fillet that I get looks like the forearm of a burns victim. But it's fine.

The first two pubs I visit are empty. In the next, the music resembles an assault. An oldster shuffles among the sticky tables collecting glasses in silence, his shirt buttoned at the neck. In his ears are the little green plastic dots of earplugs. A lachrymose drunk wanders the bar hugging anyone she can, like a blowsy octopus.

In my last port of call of the evening I get an effusive greeting from a six-year-old girl and a six-stone Rottweiler. Otherwise the pub is busy with the sort of men that might swing a boot into the windows of the Winter Gardens. Two of them are next to me, their elbows on the bar.

'He wouldn't say fucking boo to a goose,' says one.

'Not him. He wouldn't say fucking boo.'

'Then he just fucking stands up and grabs this cunt by the fucking throat.'

'He fucking never.'

'He fucking did.'

'Fuck me.'

'The quiet ones are the fucking worst.'

'Fuck.'

22

Football for Girls

At breakfast the hotel dining room is packed with pensioners. The bulk of them belong to a bus party from Brighton, organized by Age Concern. The proprietor simpers from table to table, plump, unctuous, taking orders for dinner.

'Good morning, ladies. For your dining options with us tonight we have breaded haddock, roast chicken, and a ham, tuna, egg or cheese salad.' The pensioners love him. And boy do they eat. Every one of them that I can see has bacon, eggs, sausages, toast, marmalade. Teeth are getting a vigorous work-out, fresh from their overnight soaking.

In the hotel corridor I meet two elderly sisters. 'Yes, we're from Brighton,' says one.

'Well, Haywards Heath actually,' says the other.

'But we've spent most of our lives abroad.'

'In Africa.'

'Yes, Africa, Barbary Coast mostly.'

'Barbary Coast for thirty-nine years.'

I ask them as politely as I can what brought them to Morecambe.

'Well, it's a trip, isn't it?'

'And we thought we should see something of the country we were born in.'

'See something of the country, yes.'

It's the sixtieth anniversary of VE-Day. A lobby notice announces that there will be a singer in the lounge this evening to entertain the oldies. 'We'll Meet Again', I've no doubt, 'The White Cliffs of Dover', and all the rest. Those songs can't have long to go now. But what will they celebrate when this generation dies? The '66 World Cup, I suppose. Was there a World Cup song? Was '66 the year of World Cup Willy?

Outside, the wind has abated to merely bracing. The bay is half-full, the mud flats enveloped as I watch. A fishing boat goes from slumped to bobbing in ten minutes. Morecambe looks brighter, a few doughty walkers doing the prom with walking sticks of tubular aluminium and little dogs in tartan coats.

I drive south aiming for Blackpool, but hit Fleetwood. I have never heard of Fleetwood. The ignorance was no great loss. It's a wilting fishing port and a half-hearted resort with brightly painted beach-huts still winter-padlocked, the locks weeping rust. There's a stubby pier, and a couple of anglers huddled on the beach in the bone-scouring wind, watching their rod tips nod at each brown wave.

A green-and-white double-decker bus stops in a car park full of coaches. Permanent lettering on the side of the bus indicates that it belongs to a morris-dancing troupe. The doors open and the bus disgorges a stream of girls, excited, squealing and all dressed identically in green-and-white satin. They carry pom-poms, like floppy hedgehogs. Feeling just a little arrestable, I follow them out of the wind and into a community hall.

The foyer is crowded with mums, dads, brothers, push-chairs and several hundred girls in satin. The air is thick with squealing and the smell of chips. Beyond the foyer, the hall is ringed with seats. On the stage at the far end, organizers sit at a long trestle table covered in paper.

A woman leans over the microphone and says Bootle. To an eruption of applause and encouragement, up rises a troupe of a dozen girls all dressed identically in blue and white. They range in age from perhaps five to fifteen. Suddenly disciplined, they assume a close formation in the centre of the floor, like a compressed military band. 'Ready, troupers?' asks the judge, and music starts abruptly.

The girls rise onto their toes and march on the spot, lifting their knees high, shaking pom-poms, crossing arms across chests, turning, wheeling, re-forming, staying always bang central, smiling the fixed smiles of intense endeavour, and faultlessly synchronized. They turn heads right or left with the crisp precision of Guardsmen. One older girl in the middle of the mob is clearly the leader, carrying some sort of staff, initiating every manoeuvre.

I know morris dancing only as a folk revival with all the awful connotations of the word 'folk': knee breeches, bells, puffy sleeves, braces, handkerchiefs, beards, lute music and a sort of self-conscious antiquarianism suggesting worship of the earth goddess or some such. There's none of that nonsense here. The music is thumping disco stuff, played at a thought-killing volume. 'Ra, ra, Rasputin, Russia's greatest love machine,' sing Boney M (and yes, I'm embarrassed by that knowledge) and the girls stomp and swivel and smile, their satin shimmering, their hair and their skirts bouncing, their heels perpetually raised, stretching their legs to a slim provocative tautness.

As they dance, middle-aged women in track pants circle them and make notes on clipboards. The women have hips like buoyancy rings. And in the corners of the dance ring, tots as young as four go through the routine in time with their elder sisters, the coming generation of morris dancers.

The music stops. The girls wave their pom-poms to the applause and leave the floor, breathing heavily and grinning, running back excited to mums, dads, coaches.

The crowd is in constant flux, battling in and out through the swing doors of the hall, fetching chips and hot dogs and bags of crisps. There is none of the preciousness of a ballet class here. The car park is not packed with Range Rovers. It seems a solidly working-class event.

A boy teases his younger brother. His mother grabs him. 'You'll shut that up or you'll get what for.' He doesn't question the sense of the statement, but neither does he shut that up. Less than a minute later he gets what for, resoundingly and twice. No one looks remotely interested or upset. Indeed hardly anyone looks.

The girls are abundantly happy. The husbands and brothers, it seems, look on it as the female equivalent of football. There is no self-consciousness, no posing. It's competitive pleasure, culture in the true sense of the term, meaning what people habitually do rather than what they feel they ought to do, or do self-consciously, or do to be seen to be doing. The whole bizarre business has clearly been going strong for generations. You'll know if it ever weakens because it will apply for heritage cultural funding.

The next song is 'In the Navy' by the Village People. To my utterly untrained eye all the troupes seem as superb as each other.

In the park outside, girls rehearse the tricky bits of their routines on the wiry grass, their skirts pinned or flipped or inflated by the wind. Fifty yards beyond them the brown sea crashes onto unpeopled pebbles and along the dismal promenade another ancient British tradition continues. In the Vauxhall Corsas angle-parked along its length, elderly couples sit behind misted glass with sandwiches in Tupperware, Thermos flasks and the *Sunday Express*, snoozing.

I drive inland, passing under the M6 and into rural Lancashire, and stop at random. I follow a footpath that winds through a patch of woodland then emerges into a rich valley, the turf as sweetly green as Eden, sprinkled with black-faced lambs and pheasants and rabbits. The fields are flanked by drystone walls and the valley stretches grey-green to the south as though Blackpool, Liverpool and Manchester were myths. The farmhouses have thick walls of stone. It all looks as neatly tended as an eighteenth-century painting. A labourer clearing mud from a ditch straightens to direct me to a 'snicket' that leads in turn to the expanse of a fell. The contrast is stark. Instead of turf, here suddenly is bog and heather. Instead of green, here's land the colour of a lion's pelt, treeless, raw, exposed and harsh. My fingers grow numb in the wind. I see curlews and nobody. My boots sink time and again into bogs of stewed black water, like cold old tea.

From the trig point on the domed summit I can see miles of the same to the north and east, fell after fell being swept by cloud-led shadows. To the west, Morecambe is clearly visible, to the south, the giant conurbations are a smudge, and in between the two the Blackpool Tower stands like an abruptly raised finger. I run down the hill leaping from heather clump to heather clump, deafened by the wind, exhilarated by the emptiness.

The hotel down the road is run by a man with a London glottal stop but he's had it with the south. 'It's just friendlier up here, that's all,' he says. 'You can't sit in a pub for five minutes without someone talking to you.'

I tell him that you can in Morecambe.

'Well,' he says, 'that's Morecambe for you, isn't it.'

As if primed to prove the landlord right, the smattering of drinkers in his hotel bar are all eager to talk. One merry woman with a coy smile and breasts to match has just been to a farewell service for the local vicar. 'He can't cope with the stress,' she says, 'trying to run three churches. The congregation was twice as big as usual. I cried. It was lovely. We bought him a new set of robes and a power washer.'

'Lots of the farmers round here are Methodists,' says the landlord. 'Methodists don't drink.'

He asks me if I've seen the cotton mill down the road.

I thought the cotton mills of Lancashire were all dead, but apparently this one's flat out. The landlord goes upstairs and comes back with a square of chequered cloth.

'What do you make of that?'

I don't make much of it. It's too small for a tablecloth, too big for a tea towel. To everyone's evident pleasure I give up, and am told it's a headscarf for Arabs.

'They can't get enough of them. Yasser Arafat wore one, Saddam Hussein, Gaddafi. They're the best in the world.'

Apparently the Middle East doesn't make its own head-scarves, partly because there is too little humidity for cotton spinning, but mainly because 'the Arabs are too bloody lazy'.

This is how Sunday afternoons should be, spent drinking good beer with affable strangers in a country hotel. In the evening I take minor roads back to Morecambe. The tide is out again, and a single cloud hangs just above the horizon, lit orange-gold by the sinking sun. Strands of that cloud break off like hanks of horse hair, joining sky to mountain, sky to sea. The huge bay glistens. Morecambe would be lovely without Morecambe.

I return to the same fish-and-chippery for another blistered forearm of haddock, but avoid my hotel until I judge that the Vera Lynn sing-along is over. I cut it fine. The lounge is empty of old people, but the waitresses are still clearing the tables of lots of little Union Jacks on sticks.

23

Look What They've Done to Mah-Jong

North of Morecambe, the Lune valley is a goodness, a
thick lush green with unself-consciously pretty stone villages and a sunken rural peace. I stop the Audi by an old
stone bridge and ramble along by the river. It begs to be fished
but I have no rod and anyway a rotting sign nailed to a tree
says

ATE
SHING
secuted

I sit beneath a bush by a slight natural weir and smoke two cigarettes while the river slowly overcomes the shock of my intrusion, absorbs my presence, reverts to self. Swallows and martins return to wheel and roll and swerve, and to pick invisibilities from the water's skin. Lapwings settle in a field on the far bank. A goldfinch perches in a bush. Just below the weir, where the outer water turns and slows, a fish rises, its sucking audible from twenty feet away, the ripples floating out and down the stream and fading into calm. Once, suddenly, hammering across the river just inches from the surface, the high-voltage blue of a kingfisher. Beside me is the fresh dug hole of rabbit, fox or badger, moist and crumbly in the chocolate soil.

I pass a herd of unaccountably frisky cows, bucking and writhing as if to unseat invisible riders. Despite the hedge between us, I can feel the cows' half-ton landings. Further along the lane I meet the woman who owns the cows. She doesn't seem at all alarmed by my unexplained presence.

'Nothing happens up here,' she says, 'at least according to the government. Very different from the south. Down there it's all hustle and bustle, isn't it? Oh, they've got some lovely areas, the Cotswolds, some bits of London, but, I don't know, it's not for me. They've moved Ascot to York this year because they're rebuilding Ascot, and oh the fuss they're making down south.'

She draws out the 'a' in 'making' like the bleat of a lamb.

With a social skill that would be admired in Ascot she signals that our conversation is petering out by saying, 'Oh, but it has been cool, hasn't it? All right when the sun's out, but cool.'

Kirkby Lonsdale, just up the road, is a squeezed stone prettiness with swifts in the churchyard and zeroes in the estate agent's window. A wood pigeon lies crippled in the main street.

Two elderly women approach with a collie cross on a lead. The dog lunges and the bird keels over. 'Oh dear, oh dear,' say the women, looking down, then up, then around. A young man crosses the road, scoops the bird up and takes it down an alleyway. He's back in fifteen seconds, slapping his hands. 'Thank you so much,' say the women, 'thank you so much.'

Ruskin judged the vista from behind the church to be 'one of the loveliest in England, and therefore in the world'. Turner apparently painted it. It's nice enough. There's a loop of the Lune, a farmhouse, trees, paddocks, fields, walls, cattle, sheep, and riding behind all this the big bleak moors. But the most prominent feature is a barn. It's painted in virulent random stripes of primary colour that scream for attention amid the melding pastels of the landscape, a spectacular and clearly deliberate act of long-range vandalism. I point out the barn to another walker who's stopped at the bench with his dog. 'It's a long story,' he says.

I say I've got the time if he has.

'Well,' he says. 'The farmer down there asked for planning permission to knock over the barn and put up some holiday cottages, but some little fucking bureaucrat said no 'cos the cottages wouldn't have gardens and the rules said that any new buildings had to have gardens. I mean, who needs a fucking garden here? The whole place is our fucking garden. So the farmer thought fuck you and painted the barn like what you see down there, so it all backfired on the little Hitler behind the desk. And farmers have been told to diversify and all after foot and mouth. I ask you.'

But he isn't asking me. Without waiting for an answer, he trots off cheerfully with his dog.

I feel a duty to rejoin Morton in the Lake District, but I don't much want to. Then as I'm returning to the Audi in Kirkby Lonsdale, I see a sign to Sedbergh. I find a phone booth and an astonishingly intact phone book and ring Sedbergh School.

'Yes,' says the secretary, in a voice tainted with suspicion, 'Michael Raw is a teacher here.' I drive to Sedbergh.

The place is set among great domed fells. They dwarf the small stone village and lend an air of Scottish remoteness. Sedbergh School isn't hard to find. It is most of Sedbergh. I stop a boy, who tells me that Mr Raw teaches in room 13. The boy's accent could come from Cheltenham.

The corridor to room 13 is painted mucus-green, like a hospital corridor. I put an ear to the heavy door. Silence. I push the door open and there, sitting at a table marking exercise books, is what appears to be the father of my old rugby captain, Mick Raw. He looks exactly like Ramsay, the former Archbishop of Canterbury, if you can imagine an archbishop with cauliflower ears. His shining skull is ringed at the back by a loop of white hair like a horse's noseband.

In this high-ceilinged classroom, with its sash windows that grant a view of the austere fells, and its parquet floor that has been worn into furrows by decades, maybe centuries, of children, Mick is presiding over a class of sixteen-year-olds. They are writing practice A-level essays on Alfred the Great. Mick smiles. 'Come back in twenty minutes,' he whispers, 'we'll go to the pub.'

I want to tell the kids that Alfred the Great looked like Billy Connolly. I want to tell them that this fifty-year-old archbishop was once a twenty-year-old student with a mane of black hair, who drank bottled Guinness by the crate. I want to tell them that time passes fast. In other words, I feel the urge to sermonize, but I quell it without difficulty.

A cricket pitch is drying in the cold spring wind. 'Whites or tracksuit pants and white shirts to be worn in nets at all times. Only boys awarded cricket colours may wear colours sweaters. All other sweaters must be proper cricket sweaters. No sunglasses to be worn.'

I know all of it intimately. It doesn't matter what the rules say. It matters only that the rules exist, to establish and enforce a code of conduct, a propriety, a defence against lawlessness, an Englishness.

All the architecture round here sings of a climate to be defied. The school shop is a fortress of stone. Through the window of a biology lab I glimpse a dangling skeleton. I stop a child and ask him to tell me about Mr Raw. He grins. 'He's a laugh,' he says, 'hard but fair. He's really into rugby and theatre.' He was thirty years ago too. All the changes that matter happen in the first twenty years. After that it's the long bloody slide.

Below the school a boggy bit of farmland stretches down towards the valley, and in the middle of a field, as if for the use of amateur painters of the sentimental variety, stands a shepherd carrying a crook. Alfred the Great would have recognized him.

Mick and I lunch in the squat stone pub across the road. Good beer, good pie, low ceiling. Mick's been here twenty years and will retire here. 'I'm too old to shift and too expensive,' he says. 'Besides, I like this place. It's only three hours from London, but go north and east from here and there's hundreds of miles of bugger all.'

But even remote Sedbergh School has had to move with the times. It was traditionally renowned for its ruggedness: fell running and cold showers before breakfast, and then no breakfast, that sort of thing. But such harshness became unfashionable. The school roll dwindled. Sedbergh had to take in girls. As a consequence it had to change its motto. Consultants were brought in to help (as if that weren't an inherently contradictory sentence).

'*Dura virum nutrix*' was the original motto, which Morton would not have had to translate but I will; it means 'a harsh nurse of men' and is a quotation from Virgil. After a lot of hard and skilled consulting, it was replaced with, wait for it, 'Learning and Beyond'.

It is tempting to see the shift from Latin to English, from limpid metaphor to limp vagueness, from classical precision to contemporary vacuity, as symbolic of, well, everything. Tempting but wrong. Both mottos are forms of branding. One is far uglier than the other, but neither tells the truth.

Mick goes to teach the afternoon with pints inside him, and I wander a bit through Sedbergh's cramped and writhing streets, its livestock market, its tiny-windowed shops. The fells rise all around the village with massive, stark neutrality, a belittling indifference. It feels a long way from the cosy south of England. A metal gate through a drystone wall, a paddock of horned and skittery sheep, and I'm back at the Audi. I go to rejoin Morton in Wordsworth country. I'm dreading it.

Dread may perhaps be overstating it, but I certainly feel no eagerness. The Lake District has become so established a place of prettiness that it will be packaged for my delight. And so, I'm sure, will whinnying old Wordsworth.

I don't want stuff packaged. I don't want my way to be eased. I don't want to be funnelled to the prime spots where it is universally acknowledged that I can get the authentic Lake District Experience. One reason is vanity, I suppose. I hate to be part of a herd. But it also offends my sense of travel. What I have always liked about travel is a sense of the random, of being a wandering Peeping Tom, dropping in on places that do not expect to be dropped in on, and just seeing them be as they are. But if a place expects to be dropped in on, it tarts itself up. It presents a false and cheery front to please me, and by doing so, doesn't please me.

And then there's Wordsworth. I can forgive him his thousands of crappy poems. They're largely forgotten and only the dozen or so good ones remain. But what I can't forgive, what I loathe with my very bones, is the image that has grown around the man and his coterie. Somehow he's become a venerable sage of the mountains, the distilled essence of the romantic poet, a sort of injection of earth spirit available to anyone who can board a bus. He's become a high-cultural parody. It's fake and it's horrible.

The Wordsworth industry was already under way in 1926. When Morton turned onto the Windermere road he met a traffic jam. He described all six of the vehicles. I meet rather more. I crawl through Kendal, Windermere and the impossibly sugary, and even more impossibly choked, Ambleside.

The landscape is formidably pretty, of course. I get view after view in the windscreen that just beg to be painted, framed and offered for sale on a trestle table at the Pannier Market in Barnstaple. But I'm not going to describe that prettiness because everyone else has been there before with paint and a plethora of words, including Morton, who did it as nicely as anyone.

Wordsworth's cottage, or rather Wordsworth's Cottage, is marked on my road atlas. It has a coach park the size of fifty cottages. I pay my dosh, decline the guided tour, and wander through the dark little rooms where poetry went on: a slate floor, a rudimentary scullery, Wordsworth's razor, Wordsworth's passport and a seriously bad oil painting of Wordsworth's dog. There are mementos too of the celebrated drug addict de Quincy. Today we'd celebrate him with a prison sentence.

A guided tour of Japanese comes clattering up the narrow stairs. 'This is a card table,' says the guide. The Japanese look at the card table with great seriousness. 'Wordsworth and his friends liked playing cards. But they didn't play mah-jong.'

And I leave. I'm sorry, but I'm silently screaming. Give me the sweet Lune Valley, give me fell-dwarfed Sedbergh, but spare me this synthetic cultural tourism and a guide's jokeless joke.

24

I Will Nae Have a Headache Tonight

Morton's one sortie beyond the boundaries of England was to Gretna Green, where eloping English couples married in defiance of blunderbuss-wielding puce-faced fathers. I follow him, despite the efforts of several children in Carlisle who are keen as lemmings to impale themselves on the Audi's bonnet.

The border country of Scotland is flat, unremarkable and

indistinguishable from England, and Gretna Green could serve as a dictionary definition of unprepossessing. But it has one story to tell, and it knows the potency of stories. Stories lure the tourist. You have only to package them neatly and provide a car park.

'The world famous OLD BLACKSMITH'S SHOP marriage room,' has a vast car park and an even vaster overspill car park. In a field next door are a herd of shaggy Highland cattle, seriously horned and smouldering with truculence. The Highland cattle are here in the lowlands purely, I suspect, for scenic effect. For this is Bonnie Scotland. On the same principle there's a whisky shop built into the old smithy, and the guide is dressed in a kilt. Thus the time-pressed tourist can get the whole of Scotland in Gretna Green and has no need to head further north.

The kilted guide turns out to be a retired animal nutritionist from Ulster. I tell him about Morton. He expresses fascination and asks me to fetch the book from the car, but when I do so he doesn't open it. He merely takes it hostage. It is his way of ensuring that I don't defect before I have been as fully informed as I need to be of the intricacies of the marriage statutes of 1604 and 1764. For a while I keep nodding and saying 'ah ha' and 'I see'. When we move on to the marriage statute of 1940, I stop responding. The Ulsterman is far from discouraged. He understands that my rapt silence indicates my lust to know a lot about the Episcopalian Church, the Church of Scotland, the Church of England and the power of the Church under Mary. We've reached the contemporary civil requirements of European marriage when finally he breaks off to address a sudden influx of visitors from a Contiki bus. But he does not relinquish his hold on my copy of Morton.

There are about forty Contiki people. They are from Australia, New Zealand, Canada and the States. They are happy and they are young. The Ulsterman herds them onto the steps in the little smithy. 'Line up there, please, pretty ones at the front.' The young are as docile as non-Highland cattle. Mr Kilt then selects Gordon from Canada and Rachel from Australia, gives Gordon a top hat, Rachel a bunch of plastic flowers, and conducts an amusing wedding ceremony.

'I will say, "Gordon, dear, I will nae have a headache tonight."'

The young laugh. No, really, they laugh. They give every appearance of enjoying themselves. When Mr Kilt has taken photos of Gordon and Rachel with a backdrop of the happy young, they queue up to fill in forms ordering copies.

Mr Kilt returns to me beaming, aware that I have been admiring his theatrical and organizational talent. 'Now, where were we?' he says.

'You were about to give me my book back,' I say with what for me is terrifying rudeness. He does and I scram. Back to England. It was the young that did it.

I stop at Brampton, just east of Carlisle, to get my hair cut. The barber is the sort of barber I like. He's got a chair of cracked leather, a comb, a pair of scissors and a bottomless fund of talk. He tells me mainly about fish and space rockets.

The space rockets were a top-secret business in the fifties. 'They built the Blue Streak rocket just along the road at Spadeadam. It was cutting-edge stuff. NASA used to come over to pick up ideas. First intercontinental ballistic missile in the world, then Wedgwood Benn pulled the plug on it and the whole business went to Woomera. We could have led the world in launching satellites. Cost the country a bloody fortune.'

'Woomera, Australia?'

'Yeah, Woomera bloody Australia. We lost the lot. Shall I clip your eyebrows?'

I relinquish the chair to an old man. He used to calibrate the instruments at the top-secret Spadeadam. 'Weren't much of a secret round here, though,' he says. 'When they fired the engines up it used to rattle every window in town. Dead short all over.' The last phrase could win a prize for redundancy. The barber has to scour his scalp for anything to snip. Men come here to this barber for social reasons as much as for cosmetic ones.

The proprietor claims that it's the oldest original barber shop in Cumbria. Part of his evidence is the fish tank. It's thick with fish swimming slowly through what looks like urine. He shows me a fifty-year-old photo of the shop with the tank in the same place. 'Never been emptied, never been stocked,' he says. 'The fish keep breeding and every now and then I pull out a dead one.'

I ask about Hadrian's Wall. 'It's in my back garden,' says the barber.

'Really?'

'Yeah, it's in most people's back gardens. Half the garden walls round here are built out of it.' This rare irreverence to antiquity, the cheerfulness of the barber, and the way that the instrument calibrator says, 'Champion,' when the barber holds a mirror to his baldness, combine to make me take a room at a Brampton pub. It's a good decision. Brampton's nothing special, but it's the first place I've met that fulfils the much-attested northern reputation for friendliness. It's got people who say hello, several pubs, an unsquare square, back gardens full of Hadrian's stones and a butcher's staffed by three women in aprons and smiles who want to hear about New Zealand. I also like the accent. It has similarities with Geordie. Yes, for example, is 'aye', and out is 'oot'. It differs from Geordie, however, in that I can understand it.

Tired of driving, I set out on foot to see the remnants of the wall in situ. It takes a while and it's mainly uphill. Several drivers wave cheerily to me as they pass, so I hitch. The drivers stop waving and I don't get a lift. Can it be true that the whole way of life that was hitching is pretty well dead? Ah well. Nothing much lost except generosity, trust, fellowship, the joy of the random and good economic sense.

The first bit of wall I reach is enough for me. Fifty yards

long, a yard or more thick, but less than a yard tall, it comes with a little parking bay, expansive views and a puzzle. The puzzle is what to do when you get there. My solution is to read the information boards, pat the stones a bit, wonder at the labourers who cut and laid them a couple of thousand years ago, hoist myself on top of them, sit and light a cigarette. A Volkswagen Polo pulls up. Two women in their fifties in head-scarves sniff the air, decide after a little conversation that they don't need their jackets on this gentle spring day, stand in front of the information boards for a minute or two, then turn to the wall and pat the stones. Whether they wonder who cut and laid them, I can't tell you. One woman takes a photo of the other standing by the wall, but the other doesn't offer to take a photo of the one. Then they get back in the Volkswagen Polo and head for Brampton and I set off on foot in the same direction.

Downhill is easier than up and I find a rhythm. I keep going past Brampton and round in a random rural circle, past a monument to a tree where five men were picturesquely hanged on Oct XXI MDCCXLVI 'for adherence to the cause of the royal line of Stuart', alongside the sweetest river that has carved a valley through the soft red sandstone of which Brampton is built, and out into a field of lambs where I surprise a deer. The deer is fear on legs, built to eat grass and to run from everything else. At Talkin Tarn, a sign warns people not to let their dogs swim because of an irritant alga. The water is thick with ducks. My own dogs would dive straight in, joyous with hope, driven by lust, single-minded with instinct, never ever getting close to a duck and never discouraged.

On a railway bridge I stop as I always do to watch the lines recede to the point where they blur and join. It's the essential image of going, the pull of elsewhere. A young man is lying on the little platform, his legs crossed at the ankles, his head propped on his bag. Beside him his mobile phone, a plastic cup and a bottle of white wine. There is no one else

about. It feels like Adlestrop. High in the trees rooks caw. I
stay on the bridge and watch, resting my arms on the graffiti
and my chin on my arms. The man is facing away from me,
looking down the line to where his train isn't coming from.
He drinks from his cup, refills it, lights a cigarette. And then,
by that strange sense we all have, he feels that someone is
watching and rolls over and looks up. When he sees me on
the bridge, he raises the bottle of wine aloft like a communion
priest.

There's only the one cup. I drink from the bottle. The wine is
warm. The guy is Nick. He's twenty-eight years old and until
recently a London marine-insurance broker who was engaged
to be married. He lost his job and his fiancée simultaneously.
Now he's trying to get to an interview for a job as a Newcastle
marine-insurance broker, but he missed the train. He sprinted
for it. The driver saw him and just pulled away. 'You could see
him thinking, "brilliant",' says Nick.

On this deserted platform, with rooks cawing through the
late-afternoon trees, we work down through the bottle just
chatting, him with time to kill, me with time to spend. It's one
of the boons of travel. You break all the threads of duty, all the
requirements.

Nick's phone vibrates. He doesn't answer it. We sit and
watch it crawl across the tarmac like a shuddering limbless
beast, then just as it's about to topple onto the rails he snatches
it up.

The dot of a train appears down the line, swelling to a rec-
tangular yellow muzzle, the rails beside us humming. On this
unmanned station a recorded voice announces the arrival in
purest BBC.

'Thanks for helping pass the time,' says Nick and shakes my
hand. He goes his way, I go mine, and we leave the empty
bottle standing on the platform, mute testimony to a random
encounter.

*

The Nag's Head menu features a Giant Yorkshire Pudding with sausage, veg and gravy. When it arrives, the pudding is shaped like an inverted sailor's hat and everything else sits inside it. It's the best meal of my trip so far, perhaps because I've walked ten miles.

Brampton, I discover, is a stop on the Wall Trail, a seventy-mile hike from coast to coast. An American walker comes to the bar to order food and mineral water for himself and his wife and to be silently appalled by the smoke. I chat with a man from Sheffield who works in finance, and is married with kids but who is walking the wall alone. 'Birdsong, no computer, no phone, no kids and if it rains, it rains,' he says. 'My wife understands.' I say that I do too.

We talk about rugby, fishing, God and beans, and then we get on to nationality. I ask him what it means to him to be English. Thirty seconds later we're back to rugby.

It's been that way throughout this trip. I've thrown the question at numerous people and though most have been delighted to be English they've struggled for any sort of definition of what it is to be English.

Mr Sheffield can define English only by what it isn't. 'The one thing English isn't is European,' he says. 'There's water between us, and water is water.' He doesn't know who his Euro MP is, but he's confident it's an incompetent, or a failed cabinet minister or a disgraced MP. 'Or quite possibly all three.'

I cross the road to the Shoulder of Mutton and walk into a packed but silent bar. 'How many MPs are there in the Swedish Parliament?' asks an amplified voice, followed by a sudden hum of discussion.

I like a quiz. I ask around for a team to join and am adopted by 'Waifs and Strays'.

'What sport involves the use of a broom?'

'Curling,' I whisper and am congratulated.

'Waifs and Strays' consists of Grace and Douglas. Our table

is also shared by an elderly couple but I'm unsure whether they're playing or indeed whether they know there's a quiz going on. They sit in front of glasses of ruby wine that I don't see them drink from, and they smile and say nothing.

Grace and Douglas are both plump and troubled. Their biographies unfold between questions, separately, lightly.

Douglas is shy. He has a slight stammer, little presence, an air of vulnerability or even victimhood. When training to become a science teacher he met the love of his life and married. They went to live in Hampshire where he taught at a comprehensive.

I guess what's coming next. Some people just don't survive as teachers. It's in their demeanour, their hesitance, sometimes in their niceness. To a certain type of adolescent they are prey.

Douglas was harried out of school. He doesn't quite say as much, but it's there between the lines. He now works 'in the restaurant business'. Menially, I suspect, sadly.

'How many planes in the Red Arrows?'

'Nine,' announces the old man with the ruby wine in a voice loud enough for the whole pub to hear. It's his first utterance. He doesn't smile, doesn't debate. His ancient wife pats him admiringly on the arm and leans against him, looking into his withered face with big warm eyes set amid wrinkles like ravines.

One day the love of Douglas's life walked out. The kids went with her. He was suddenly without job or family. 'It was my fault,' he says.

He remarried. 'I worked really hard at it,' he says, ' but . . .' and the tail of his sentence droops into his beer.

'With what instrument is Dizzy Gillespie associated?'

Douglas says trumpet. Grace writes it down.

Grace is awaiting sentence. Her crime has been defined as 'white-collar'. She doesn't elaborate and I don't like to ask. She's packed her bag in expectation of prison. She has a piercing, sad laugh. She knows that the first Puerto Rican to top the pop charts in the UK was Ricky Martin. She answers all the soap-opera questions too.

It's a gentle, fragile, very human evening. I like Brampton.

25

Across the Neck

Manchester United has been sold. The purchaser is an
American billionaire called Glazer. He looks like a troll.
I saw footage of him on telly in the Nag's Head last night, smiling inanely at reporters and saying nothing. The darts players
laughed. But Manchester is not laughing. There was a street
protest, scuffling. 'See you in hell, Glazer,' said a sign

supported by a chubby man. The man's church had been sold and he was spitting with anger.

The board of directors of Man U plc, with their desire to make money, and Malcolm Glazer, with his desire to own a football club, have pricked the myth balloon. The myth is that Manchester United has something to do with Manchester, that this collection of expensive childlike athletes bought from all over the world by their terse gum-chewing barely comprehensible Scottish manager represents something greater and grander than money, something to cling to, some sort of identity and sense of place. The sale acknowledges that it is no such thing. Manchester United is merely a business, a franchise, a brand. It was the same with Chelsea: home to pensioners, installation artists and nice girls hunting husbands, Chelsea was bought by a Russian with oil trillions. It was only the name he bought. He then attached a dozen fine footballers to it, few of whom could speak English and none of whom could have located Chelsea on a map, won trophies and gained a fanatical congregation.

The protester doesn't hate Glazer. He hates the truth of his own duping. The struts have been knocked from beneath his faith. The sacramental FA Cup has been revealed as tin plate. The revered jewels are paste. But he and everyone will soon forget. The crowds will re-swell to capacity, the hymns will be sung again. People want to believe.

From Brampton I cross the country's narrow neck. It's a mere seventy miles or so from the Irish Sea to the North Sea and the road follows more or less the line of the Roman wall. The best remains stand on ridges, silhouetted against the sky and crumbling amid sheep. In deference to Morton, whom the wall 'thrilled to the marrow', I stop at Chesters to tour the remains of a Roman fort. I have the place to myself, though the calf-deep grass is still bruised from yesterday's tourists.

The fort is just exposed foundations, but between them and

the sweetly rippling Tyne stand the remains of a stepped bath-house, including (though how they know, I don't know) a steam room. Even two thousand years on it seems as un-English as a bidet.

Morton found the fossilized ruts of chariot wheels. I don't. In the echoing museum there's the jaw of a wild boar whose ancient teeth are whiter than mine, a range of touching domestic items – keys, bridles, coins, buckles, rings, buttons, a balance, a pretty leather shoe – and hundreds of inscribed self-memorializing stones: 'The 4th cohort of the century of Claudius Cleonicus built this' is typical, the Latin equivalent of 'We woz ere'. The tea shop is called Lucullus's Larder.

The Angel of the North stands high above the A1. In an eye-watering wind I walk around its massive base. The angel's arm-span is almost that of a jumbo jet. The whole thing is held in place by bolts the size of telegraph poles sunk into I don't know how many tons of concrete. Gaunt, spare, deliberately built to rust, plated and riveted like the ships they once built near here, it's a thunderously good thing, a marker, an identity-giver. Like a Neolithic barrow, it proclaims the presence of a tribe.

Apparently the man who designed it said he used the form of an angel because 'we have to keep imagining them' but I'll forgive him that. There's a pleasing irony in celebrating a history of heavy industry with an angel.

And I am not alone in thinking so. Cars keep pulling up in the little parking bay, and the ordinary, seemingly local occupants endure the wind's assault to do a little tour of homage round the sculpture's monolithic base, before heading away in the Mondeo with something affirmed.

'Awright?' asks a man with a gut and a plastic supermarket bag. The wind makes the bag rattle like staccato applause.

'Aye,' I say, surprising myself with how swiftly, unconsciously, I've adopted the lingo.

The two of us stand and stare into the wind and away to the clouds. To the north-east, Newcastle stretches as red roofs and outcrops of tower blocks like teeth. To the south-west, the fields roll to the Pennines. Just below us there's a football pitch so steep that the goalkeeper at the top end could leave for a cup of tea. If you won the toss, you wouldn't know whether to play the first half uphill or down. On mature reflection I think I'd play down, then spend the second half defending a fifteen-goal lead by kicking the ball as often as possible onto the A1.

In Durham, it takes half an hour to park the car, but only ten minutes to find the spot where Morton sat to write about the place. It's down beside the wide green River Wear, on a tree-shaded towpath. A duck stands scratching the back of its head with a foot the colour of a road-mender's jacket. No cars down here, nor even any distant noise of cars, only students whirring past on battered bicycles and a grim-faced mother jogging, her infant strapped into a streamlined buggy like an astronaut at take-off. Across the river stands the startling, steep-sided hill of sandstone that is Durham, fortified with castle walls and topped by the vast cathedral. The stone of the cathedral looks leprous. Ravens or rooks or crows launch themselves at inter-vals from the cathedral towers and describe brief pointless circles.

When he sat here, Morton was troubled by 'flies, small winged dragons, and minute centipedes, which paddle drearily through the ink before route-marching all over the paper.' Then, having written ephemera into immortality, he is trans-ported back a thousand years by thoughts of the cathedral's history, producing a breathless romantic paean with which I can't compete.

He calls the cathedral 'stupendous . . . the most wonderful Norman church I have ever seen, not excepting the great church of St Stephen at Caen.' I cross a bridge and climb to take a closer look at it.

Mothers are collecting their offspring from the cathedral prep school.

'Did you have swimming today?' asks one Mum of her son in his purple-trimmed blazer.

'Yeah.' His head is down, his reply a sullen mumble.

'How did it go?' says Mum cheerily.

'All right.'

'Did you have to do lots and lots of it?'

'No.'

Inside the cathedral the choir is practising. A line of tiny choristers processes down the aisle in purple surplices, followed and then addressed by a choirmaster with theatrical arms. He holds one arm poised aloft a moment, then cuts a down stroke with it, and the treble voices burst. The whole cathedral is instantly full, full to the roof, full to the windows, to the doors, with sweet noise. It dives into every corner, ringing over graves, round the backs of columns. The kids are so tiny, the sound so strong. Every one of the smattering of late-afternoon tourists stops momentarily to look up, look around.

The master stills the voices, says something sharp, corrective, then starts them off again, opens the valve for five, ten seconds, then clamps it shut once more. And so it goes on, a stop-start, fragmented beauty, wrought by kids who don't know what they do to older hearts and minds.

A solo. Just one thin voice going to every cranny of the building, tiny, questing, yearning, vulnerable and lovely. The choirmaster stops the lad in mid-trill, hits the note for him with perfect pitch, then sets him off again.

The pub where I find a room is a deliberate archaism – no television, no music, wooden floors, good beer. There's an ornate and ancient till behind the bar, the cash drawer lolling open like a dog's tongue, and the last sale registered as 11d.

I ring a friend in London to wish him a happy birthday. When I tell him I'm in Durham he says that there's one pub I've simply got to visit while I'm here. 'It's a pub as you imagine a pub to be,' he says.

'Not the Victoria?'

'Yeah,' he says, 'the Victoria. It's set in aspic. It's got . . .'

'I know,' I say. 'I'm calling from it.'

I head back into town via the Kingsgate Bridge, designed by Sir Ove Arup. There's a bust of him looking like either a cheerful Philip Larkin or a glum Eric Morecambe. He was, it says, 'a doyen of total architecture', whatever that may mean, and his bridge won a 'mature concrete structure' award in 1993. From it I can see several older bridges, all of them more graceful, their designers anonymous.

The steep and narrow medieval streets of central Durham are busy with students whose accents would fit nicely into Oxbridge but whose exam results didn't. But here are good bookshops, and little annexes inhabited by the Faculty of Oriental Music or whatever, giving a pleasing sense of town and university as one. In the sloping market square there's a bronze of Neptune with Schwarzenegger buttocks, and another of a military horse, also with Schwarzenegger buttocks. The man riding the horse is predictably a plumed Victorian aristocrat whose name means nothing to me. How smug the Victorians were, how confident of their virtues, their place in history, their rightness. And, there's a legacy of that confidence in Morton's prose, a sense of a strong, indomitable England that's got it right and that rightly runs the world.

Morton dined each evening on standard English food and this evening I do the same. I have a curry. For according to a report I read in the paper, the average Brit has a curry twice a week. That's an annual total of more than six billion curries. Forget bacon and eggs. Forget roast beef. Curry is now the national dish of old England. I've never liked it much.

When I was a youth, the Indian restaurants were only busy when the pubs were closed. From eleven o'clock each night they did a brief fierce trade. Throughout that time, neither the lager tap nor the racial jokes stopped pouring, and the owner kept a cleaver under the till. The food itself was not so much a meal as a virility test. Friends boasted of off-the-Richter-scale vindaloos, of food served on asbestos plates.

But the business now has gone upmarket. My restaurant still has tactile wallpaper, hideous paintings and the recording of sitar music that's been doing the rounds since the seventies, but with its napery, its cutlery, its bow ties and its clientele, it clearly has pretensions to posh. I order a prawn korma, stressing that I would like it off the Richter scale at the non-earthquake end. My surprisingly complimentary nan bread looks like diseased skin, and the curry when it arrives in its little silver dishes looks, as every curry I have eaten has looked, like lumps in gloop.

While I eat I read a theatre review in the local free paper. The play by John Godber is described as 'a riotously funny expose of the moral dilemmas of contemporary Britain', so I go.

The audience is middle-aged and middle class, like me. From the stalls I look down on perms and pates. And the subject of the play just happens to be middle-aged, middle-classness.

Two couples take a ferry to Holland. One couple is inhibited and nice. The other isn't. The nice husband composes film music. The un-nice husband acts in porn films, though that has not reduced the ferocity of his sex drive. 'Oh, my fucking knob,' exclaims Porno as he proposes to bed his partner, a line which sends a titter round the nice audience, but appals the nice couple on stage. Porno drinks, shags, swears, threatens, belches, gives voice to the most blatant prejudices, lovingly fondles his crotch and calls red wine 'a twat's drink'.

The nice couple feel shocked. Their repression is threatened. At the same time it is tested. They find something liberating in Porno's frankness. He is a crude parody of the baser self that lies beneath propriety.

The upshot of it all is that Porno is shown to be softer and nicer than he seemed, and the nice couple tougher and nastier than they seemed. It's a terribly English play. Its theme is essentially conduct.

The only difficulty is the sea. Much of the action takes place on board the ferry. The crossing is rough. Lurching across a flat stage in a way that makes the stage seem like a pitching deck is a tricky skill. Lurching simultaneously with other actors is an even trickier skill, and one that the cast doesn't quite master. But I do enjoy the show. It taps into something true about Englishness. And having enjoyed it, having seen my shell of clenched, repressed and timorously polite Englishness exposed and tested, I clap wholeheartedly and withdraw into the night with that shell still firmly in place.

Others do not seem to have such a shell. Durham is Friday night frantic with the young. They are queuing to get into Yates's, the Fighting Cocks, the Coach and Eight and an Australian-themed pub called Downunder that looks about as Australian as Miami. Though the air is seriously cold and the wind severe, and though most of the boys and girls are wearing only short-sleeved shirts or blouses, everyone is notably loud, happy, drunk and planning soon to be drunker.

The queues are controlled by security guards. If there's a growth industry in England it's security-guarding. The qualifications seem to be a shaven head, a neck of the same width and a cast-iron resistance to boredom, born perhaps of hope of the chance to inflict a bit of semi-legal bodily harm. The uniform is invariably a bomber jacket that bolsters the size of the torso and an earpiece that bolsters the ego.

The pub where I am staying does not employ a security guard but is busy with the sort of heterogeneous mix that the best pubs gather. A nervous man does the *Guardian* crossword. A group of older men play dominoes, the pieces clashing together with the sound of strong false teeth. A stroke victim has been wheeled in. When he tries to talk it sounds like groaning. His wife holds a pint to his lips and calls him sweetheart.

I find myself chatting with a man who tells me that there is an ideal size for a town, and that is the size of Durham. 'It's small enough to know people in the street,' he says, 'but large enough to hide if you want to.'

For seventeen years he's been headmaster at a school for delinquent kids.

'Currently,' he says, 'the score stands at ten–all.'

'What do you mean?' I ask, as I am obviously meant to.

It transpires that ten kids from his school have gone on to gain degrees, and ten to commit murder.

There are times when his job seems hopeless. 'One family,' he says, 'I've had all six of the kids. And the only thing that any of them will be any good at is breeding. They'll all have six kids each and I bet I'll get most of them in due course as well. They'll cost the state millions. But what can you do for kids whose parents and whose grandparents have never had a job?' He leaves the question hanging and goes to play dominoes, a game, as far as I can tell, without tactics or skill. If I had his job I think I'd want to play dominoes too.

26

Wot Larx

I drop four pound coins into a slot and press a button.
'Hello,' says the machine, 'my name is Michelangelo.'

If I'd pressed a different button the machine would have
said its name was Leonardo or Rubens or Titian. It would then
have gone on to draw a portrait of me in the style of that
painter. I chose Michelangelo because I fancy a picture of
myself as David with Schwarzenegger buttocks.

The machine is like one of those booths for taking regrettable passport photos, except that here you can watch your portrait being generated. A simulated hand ghosts over the screen, shading your image with a simulated pencil. 'Ooops,' says the machine at one point, 'I made a mistake,' and it erases the error with a simulated rubber. Art historians may be interested to learn that Michelangelo talked like Stephen Hawking.

Sadly I get no muscles. For four quid the machine does only a granular head and shoulders. But it does date the pic for posterity and sign it Michelangelo. Clutching my souvenir of Durham, I point the Audi south towards York.

York made Morton weak at the knees. So much history, so many lovelinesses. I don't feel quite so thrilled at the prospect. And when I discover that York is ringed by expanses called park-and-ride, I simply drive on by. Leaving my car to catch a bus, and then catching another bus to return to my car feels to me like one move too many in the transport business. And besides, there is somewhere I would much rather go. I want to see Hull. Larkin lived there.

It was Jack Smithies, the best English teacher of all time, who introduced me to Larkin. 'I think you might like him,' was how Jack put it. I was a grunting seventeen-year-old at the time with hair to my shoulders. I doubt that I said thank you, but I went to the school library and borrowed *The Whitsun Weddings*. On the train home I read 'Ambulances' and 'Afternoons'. That evening I lay on my bed and read the other twenty or so poems. The following morning I went back to the library and returned the book. The following evening I went back once more, and stole it. I've got it still. Its wine-red boards are frayed, its pages dog-eared, its stitching frail, but in a little pocket inside the back cover the library card remains intact, my adolescent signature crossed out to indicate that the book has been returned.

It didn't feel like theft. Those poems were rightfully mine. They meshed with my skull, gave words to what I had dimly apprehended. They were detailed, dismal and thrilling. They did for me what literature exists to do. They told the truth, and they told it with consolatory beauty.

I know all about Larkin. I've read the early novels, all the poems, the collected letters, the bits of prose, the interviews, the biographies, the kind reviews, the scornful reviews, the obits, the lot. None of it has diminished that first thudding impact of *The Whitsun Weddings* on a train between Brighton and Hassocks in long-gone 1975.

So yes, this journey to Hull is a pilgrimage, no different, I suppose, from visiting where Jane Austen died or where Wordsworth listened to de Quincy giggling, but I feel no need to justify it.

Because of Larkin, I think I know Hull, and nothing I see as I drive into its suburbs does anything to alter my preconception of the place. It's unblessed, unquaint, unantiquated, unvisited, and most un-Mortonish. Un-anything was Larkin's territory.

I dump my bag at a suitably down-at-heel pub and head into the city centre. Larkin wrote of ships up streets, and here, hard by the shopping malls, is a marina, and beyond that the Humber estuary. The water swirls a forbidding milk-chocolate brown and the receding tide exposes the sort of shining silty mud you don't want to fall into. The wharves stretch for miles, some derelict, some active, some revamped. A former dry dock holds thousands of tons of this mud, like an uncooked cake, studded with chip packets, hunks of polystyrene and random broken lengths of timber with nails.

Just beyond stands the Deep, a shark's fin of glass and concrete. It's 'the world's first submarium', and apparently the second most visited purpose-built attraction in the country. For seven pounds fifty you gain entry to the top floor and from there you travel down a system of ramps and exhibition halls, taking you through thousands of years, thousands of fathoms of ocean, thousands of children and millions of fish. The fish are all silent. The children are mostly screaming.

There are hi-tech, super-clever, hyperbolic, state-of-the-art interactive presentations designed to excite and inform at the same time, though they seem to me to do mainly the former. And everywhere among them in lugubrious counterpoint are monstrous multi-level tanks of fish. The fish slide through the water without expression. Kids bang on the glass, recoil from sharks, shout with glee, with disgust, with fear, and the fish just carry on being fish, swimming.

Here, to my delight, are the sea fish of my childhood, the species I spent winter afternoons on Brighton pier trying to catch. The gust of nostalgia is fierce. I can see my short white fibreglass rod propped against the railing, a bell on a clothes peg clipped to its tip, the line angling out into the ugly swell. Down on the sea-floor were four ounces of lead shaped like a lozenge and a hook baited with a single black lugworm. My brother and I either dug those lugworm from the sands of neighbouring beaches, or bought them by the dozen from the tackle shop. They came wrapped in stained newspaper. And even now the taste of Bovril comes to me, poured from a Thermos into a plastic cup. I can feel my hands wrapped around that cup for the warmth.

I never caught much. But now thirty-five years later I spend most of a spring afternoon with my nose against glass, staring at the fish I dreamed of: cod, pollack, whiting, ling. And they are apt fish to view in Larkinland, dull, non-tropical things, grey-brown and unspectacularly English. Before today, I've only ever seen them gasping in air or dead.

The gift shop on the way out is even more crowded than the exhibits. It's doing good trade in foam-filled, velour-covered cuddly sharks.

I head back to the city centre where a giant screen shows the twenty-four-hour BBC News channel, complete with sound. You can hear it from a couple of streets away. Huge pixellated newsreaders overlook the last late shoppers. The accents on the screen are nicely modulated Surrey. The accents on the streets beneath are flat, h-less Yorkshire.

In the corner of the cafe nearby, a man and a woman chat intensely over tea, their heads almost touching. On the floor beside the man lies a battered hard-skinned violin case, and against the wall beside the woman stands a shiny hard-skinned cello case. It's like a casual eavesdropper, a third party. When the man and woman pick up their instruments I watch them go round the back of the town hall and in through a stage door. I go round the front and buy a ticket for a Beethoven concert.

Many of the men in the concert audience wear jackets cut from a local tweed. It is faintly shiny and has a greenish tinge, like pond slime. Across the aisle from me sits a barrel-shaped old man with whiskers, wheezing. He wears a red bow tie, shiny green suit, black waistcoat, no socks and black slippers. The six inches of exposed ankle are hairless white shanks, dappled with a veinous blue, like light bruising. The ankles look too slight to bear his bulk.

The orchestra comes on to tune up and is ignored, except by a woman in front of me who waves eagerly. A bassoonist waves back, which is sweet. Then the lead violinist comes out to room-temperature applause, followed by the conductor to hot-house applause. True to form the conductor has a full head of shiny hair. When he swings his baton to launch the opening piece, his hair bounces and flops.

I find the hair more intriguing than the first piece of music. Ankle-man doesn't seem too entranced either. He mutters audibly to his wife throughout. Rapidly the music becomes aural wallpaper, in the midst of which I drift. I like the theatre with its balcony and colonnades and fussy old-fashioned plaster work. There's a clock of exactly the same design as the ones in every classroom at Brighton Hove and Sussex Grammar School. Instead of shifting by imperceptible degrees, the minute hand clicks and shudders into place. Five past four was the hour of release each day. Scattered through the building seven hundred pairs of eyes would see the synchronized minute hands click, and instantly the bell would sound, and the silent building would explode with noise. I can remember the roll of my first-form class: Andrew, Awcock (who despite being fat was good at the high jump; the PE teacher called him 'my little fairy'), Bennett, Bryden, Bunker, Crosta, Doyle (who went to India and wrote me a letter about the monkeys on his roof), Grant and then the music ends and applause scatters the past, sends Andy Grant and all the rest of them whirling like Doctor Who back down the time tunnel to their home in the classroom of memory.

A flunkey comes on to open the lid on the grand piano, followed by the pianist, who looks like a solicitor's clerk. He gets the most vigorous applause yet. When he plays he doesn't go in for the histrionics I associate with pianists. If anything he looks a little bored. But when he finishes he bows deeply with what looks like profound relief, and some of the audience stamp their feet.

During the interval one of the violinists comes out from backstage to sit with his family in the hall and eat ice cream from a tub. The hall is thick with greetings, large knots of men and women gathering among the plastic chairs, refreshing old acquaintance. I go outside to smoke. The mayoral chauffeur is sitting in a Rover eating mints.

After the interval we get the plum piece, the Pastoral symphony, and even I, a musical ignoramus, am familiar with the lilting loveliness of its theme, though it annoys me that Beethoven keeps buggering it about.

I have long thought that the worst thing that ever happened to music was the ability to record it. If it had only stayed as a live thing, an ephemeral event like this, something that people had to leave their houses to hear, then it would have retained a potency that it has lost. Not only would we have been spared the iPod, the Walkman, muzak, disc-jockeys, hi-fi buffs, the hi-fi mags and the bouncing purposeless sets of lights on hi-fi hardware, but also we would not have become inured to the sudden surprising joy of music, its unique ability to bypass the gatekeepers of the mind and to bang a tap straight into the barrel of emotion.

The Pastoral acts on me like a soft drug. My mental landscape becomes populated with the past. I wallow. It feels cleansing, like a bath, like weeping. But when it stops, I don't much mind. The conductor milks the applause for far too long, then the crowd dissolves into the night, and backstage the dinner-jacketed players pack their instruments into silent wadding and go home to supper, and known furniture and the present tense.

I go to a pub to write notes at a corner table. 'I'm a writer too,' says an elderly woman. I don't encourage her, but she doesn't need encouragement. 'I'm retired now, see. Never had time before. Worked twelve-hour days all my life. "Oh, the stories I could tell," I always said. Then Ron says, "Why don't you, then?" He just sits at home all day studying the form. I could move the flat out around him and he wouldn't notice. So I got myself a little typewriter and the stuff just came pouring out of me. I've got hundreds of stories. I sent some off to a publisher that was advertising for writers in the paper and they said they'll publish them if I send them nine hundred pounds. Do you think I should?'

I explain why she shouldn't, but she barely listens. 'My daughter's got MS,' she says. 'She's all right now, but I'd like to leave her a little something. I'm sixty-seven. I thought the stories might bring in a few pounds, but probably not. I'm thick, me.'

Sunday morning and I drive east to the coast in search of Larkin's 'unfenced existence, facing the sun, untalkative, out of reach'. There's no sun to face, only flat land, green wheat and Sunday-quiet villages with spiky Viking names – Thorngumbald, Skeffling. I reach an acre of snot-green caravans, the remains of wartime defences, a crumbling cliff of clay and then the North Sea. It rolls like muscles under skin. Its edge is foamy-brown with eroded land, but its bulk is rhinoceros-grey. A lone fisherman stands by his rod on the beach, his line puny amid the vastness. Beyond him a gas rig and shipping, static on the horizon. The dog-walkers here have big dogs, dogs that need more than genteel suburban parks. Birdwatchers stride purposefully towards the tip of the land, their jackets all muted fawns and greens, their trousers tucked into their socks, binoculars slung against their chests.

I walk the beach a while, liking the sea's veiled threat, its sense of held power. So does a little girl in a pink jacket with synthetic fur round its hood. She scampers away from her parents to the foamy fringe of the sea, waits for a wave to break with a rich brown roar, squeals with delighted terror, runs back up the beach, clings to her dad, then does it all again. She's playing Grandmother's Footsteps with a trillion-ton ocean.

The place feels desolate and barren, but less remote and more peopled than the picture painted in my head by the first poem in *The Whitsun Weddings*. Perhaps I came to the wrong place. Or perhaps lots of people have read *The Whitsun Weddings*.

I drive up the coast, through more silent villages, all huddling low to duck the wind that must harrow this place in winter. Then back to Hull. Its suburbs too are Sunday quiet. I ditch the Audi and tour the streets. Dying little shops, far from the flash malls, are shut for a day of relief from failure. Amid the breeze and litter, little gangs of Eastern Mediterranean youths gather in leather jackets, outside a minicab office, or a kebab bar, or around a single, highly polished, low-slung car. I go in search of Larkin's home.

For most of his productive years, Larkin lodged on the top floor of a building overlooking Pearson Park. It was at Pearson Park that the young mothers gathered 'in the hollows of afternoons' and let loose their children, while their beauty thickened and something pushed them 'to the side of their own lives'.

And now it is Sunday afternoon, the deepest hollow of them all.

The park is as ordinary as I expected, an acre or so of flat grass and trees and statuary and play areas, surrounded by a quiet suburban road and a ring of houses.

Two vast games of multi-racial football are going on, with sweaters for goalposts and the teams in a constant state of flux. The forwards are mostly black boys, tall and lithe in enormous training shoes. The doughy white boys tend to hang at the back wearing shirts saying Rooney or Beckham, while midfield is dominated by the slick-haired Turks and Arabs, nifty, dexterous and constantly fouling. I want to join in but don't. The Slavs don't either. Recent immigrants by the looks of them, with close-cropped heads and winter skin and shiny track pants, they sit on the benches with cans of lager and their arms round plump, gum-chewing English girls.

Away from the football a man lies wrestling with his Alsatian on the grass, young couples share the pushing of baby-buggies, and knock-kneed donkeys are tethered to a tree offering rides that no one wants. A shallow dirty duck pond is scattered with twenty slices of cheap white bread that the ducks and the wart-nosed geese ignore. They are sated. A thwarted boy with a vexed mother has stopped playing feed-the-ducks and is using his bread to play hit-the-ducks. The ducks avoid his missiles without difficulty.

Just across the road from the pond stands no. 32, where Larkin lived. Three storeys, Edwardian at a guess, with an overgrown front garden and pillars at the gateway. In the second-floor window a man sits in a vest, looking out at Sunday afternoon, smoking. A Mr Bleaney, of course, but there are Mr Bleaneys everywhere. The floor above him was Larkin's. It is completely without interest.

There's nothing to suggest that he lived there. The place just is, its bricks and mortar as unaffected by his tenure as by my visit. This is no shrine. It is an ordinary place and Larkin was an ordinary man. By ordinary I mean a man who writhed with frustrations, fears, suppressions, lust, prejudices, habits, the burdens of family and convention, and all the rest of the catalogue. His extraordinary gift was to distil the ordinary into words. When he died, the gift died with him. To try to trace its ghost here in Pearson Park is absurd, as absurd as the cheap thrill I got from Hardy's pens, from Lee's village, from Betjeman's grave. There was nothing in any of these things, these places, except what I invested in them.

The greatest advertising slogan of all time is 'All you can eat'. It plugs straight in to the high voltage of greed. That greed swamps the voice of experience, the voice that says that the stomach has limits.

May Sum's six pound ninety-five unlimited authentic Chinese banquet smorgasbord includes such Chinese delicacies as chips, deep-fried onion rings, barbecue ribs and jelly. I include none of these things on my plate but I might as well have included them all. Black-bean sauce mingles with egg foo yong mingles with pork chow mein to produce a sludge indistinguishable from every smorgasbord sludge. It tastes like pureed duvet inner, with black-bean sauce.

On the table next to mine sit an old man and a young one, both lapsing in and out of sleep. The old man's chin rests on his hand. As sleep deepens, his chin slides towards his plate. At the critical moment, when the chin is on the point of slipping from the heel of his hand and planting itself in noodles, he starts and shudders and pulls himself round, gives himself a mental slap, sighs, replaces his chin and shuts his eyes again. Across the table the bespectacled younger man sleeps upright. There's a sports bag by his seat. It's seven in the evening.

The young man's head begins to lean towards his left shoulder, gathers momentum and he too wakes. He takes off his glasses, rubs his eyes, leans blearily across the table and shakes the old man's shoulder. 'Dad, Dad,' he says, 'come on. Let's go.'

Dad's eyes open. He looks across at son and heir, regathering information about where he is, who he's with, what brought them there, why they should move. His mind assesses the information and reaches a conclusion. 'Fuck off,' he says and goes back to sleep.

I wander the dull streets, past the BBC screen where huge newsreaders are talking about Iraq to no one, past a municipal garden full of sleeping ducks, past a statue of Andrew Marvell, down a back street and into an old and pretty pub where a man with an eye-grabbing wart on his forehead sits at the bar with lager, listening to the barman talk about his Polish girlfriend.

'She said it were all shite in this country. Work ethic were shite, houses were shite, food were shite, weather were shite,' he says. 'I think she were homesick.' I suspect he were right.

The man with the wart is a local historian who specializes in ghosts. He does a tourist tour called Haunted Hull, a tour that includes this pub. Has he seen any of the ghosts?

'Of course not,' he says.

He gets a key from the barman and takes me upstairs to the Plotting Chamber. It's a fine old room with carved wooden panels, heavy oak furniture black with age, crossed sabres above the fireplace, and a gas fire with artificial logs. According to legend, here, in this room, the plot was hatched that led to the only execution of a reigning monarch in English history. Three hundred and sixty-three years ago, men sat around this table in pantaloons and planned the beheading of Charles I.

'Only they didn't,' says the historian. 'The room didn't exist.'

Back down in the bar I find the bespectacled son who was sleeping. I ask him where his father is. He doesn't seem at all surprised by the question.

'Went home,' he said.

I tell him I saw them both sleeping in the restaurant.

'Yeah,' he says, 'there was no air in there.'

The late-night streets are deserted. I am surprised when I get back to where I'm staying to find the lights still on in the bar. Inside are the publican, his wife and Danny. Danny seems out of place in Hull, and especially in this tired backstreet pub. His accent is public school, his clothes dapper. Small and tightly built, mid-thirties or thereabouts, he struts like a cockerel.

He lives in Switzerland now with wife and kids, but he used to run the club scene in Hull.

'The club scene?'

'Nightclubs. I had a string of them. All sorts. Everyone knows me round here.'

I doubt him, but I don't say so. Behind his bravura I sense a bat-squeak of potential violence. When I ask him why he went to Switzerland he answers vaguely, then suggests we go out on the town.

'I've been out on the town,' I say. 'It's shut. There's no one.'

'Come with me,' he says. It's the sort of 'come with me' that I obey. There's a thrill of some sort here, a sense of dramatic possibility, a sniff of extra oxygen.

We walk a few hundred yards down a street that I would swear I walked up half an hour ago and found deserted. But here's a club, its walls pulsing with noise, a swarm of people outside it presided over by a bouncer with the face of a baboon and the shoulders of an ox.

'Danny,' he says and the baboon face lights up. He hugs Danny then ushers the pair of us through the throng. I don't sense that the crowd knows Danny, but they part for him, sensing his strut, his differentness, his aura of certainty.

Inside is all noise and stage-smoke and sweat and floorboards and swirling lights and sex. It's the sort of place I shun. Because of the noise, but also because of the loss of control it represents, the disinhibition. The reasons are rooted I suspect somewhere deep in a polite Sussex upbringing. Something to do with fear and guilt. Not laudable, but there, ingrained.

Conversation is close to impossible. I gesture to Danny that I'll buy him a drink. He laughs and raises a hand above the crowd. I see the barman's face light like the bouncer's. Two tall pale drinks appear with straws in them and slices of lime.

Danny tries to tell me a story. I lean in close, my ear against his mouth. All I can gather, and probably all I need to gather, is that it involves a difference of opinion between Danny and 'the hardest man in Hull'. Danny illustrates the end of the story by removing his upper front teeth. They are attached to a pink plastic plate.

People are clamouring around Danny, tapping him on the shoulder, smiling, fawning. He drifts away. I drift into the throng, towards the dance floor. I am nervous, edgy, alive. The music is incessant jungle. I don't hear it so much as feel it. I let go, give in, and astonishingly it leads to sex.

Casual sex is always the same. The preliminaries zing. All scruples, all doubt dissolve before the mounting imperative of lust. Hope becomes certainty.

Ten minutes later we're giggling and shsh-ing up the little back stairs to my cheap room with its bedspread of shiny red sateen. The fumble of undressing, the sudden thrilling feel of flesh, always new. Then the franticness subsides into the lull of the business itself, and for me, always, a sense of absurdity, or of boredom, or of being duped. Mentally I detach and look down on myself grunting and clutching and mouthing and writhing, so comically different from my constructed daily self, so simple. I want to laugh or stop. But then comes the final gasping climb of the last few steps to the summit. From there, when I get my breath back, the view isn't always that wonderful.

But Morton never wrote explicitly about sex, and after giving the matter some thought, I'm not going to either.

27

Up the Stump

I wake alone, which is good. I run the mental video of last night, looking for something to wince at, to regret. I find nothing and half an hour later I am heading out of Larkin's dull city over the great grey suspension of the Humber Bridge.

When I planned to walk through England at the age of sixteen, I wrote of crossing potato fields towards the spire of

Lincoln Cathedral. In my mind that spire stood visible for miles, in regal counterpoint to the great flatness. Morton called it 'an inland St Michael's Mount . . . lying sharply cut against the distant horizon at the end of a Roman road.' So it's with a vague sense of knotting a loose end after thirty years that I head south. But the day is against me. The clouds are low flannel.

To Morton the straight road leading to Lincoln was the romantic Roman Ermine Street. It's now the romantic A15. As Morton drove, he 'sang the legions' marching song about Lalage and Rimini'. I don't.

The further south I go, the lower the clouds clamp to the land, squeezing the air between until it oozes mist. Visibility shrinks to a few hundred yards. I don't see Lincoln until I'm driving its ring road. I don't see the cathedral until I'm standing in front of it. And it hasn't got a spire. It's got towers. The final bacillus of the romantic shrivels and dies without protest. Lincoln Cathedral is a wet old barn.

It's a nice barn, of course, and I do the dutiful tour, noting the memorial to Sir Joseph Banks, the botanist who travelled the world with Captain Cook. In New Zealand I pay my rates to Banks Peninsula District Council. The memorial doesn't mention Banks Peninsula. It doesn't even mention New Zealand. According to the inscription, Banks' most prominent achievement was draining the fens.

It's only when I am leaving the cathedral that I realize I was supposed to pay an entry fee. I keep walking, buy a pork pie for lunch, and eat it under a shop awning. When I've finished eating I go back to the cathedral to pay. My reasons have something to do with conscience and my conscience has something to do with last night. But I don't say that to the tartan-skirted woman at the cash desk. I just tell her that I've had a change of heart.

'Bless you,' she says, taking my four quid, 'you'll sleep better tonight.'

*

All I know about the landscape between Lincoln and Boston is that the hundred yards of it to either side of the road are as flat as my singing voice. The rest is lost in the mist. And all I know of Boston is what I saw on the television news the other day. Apparently Boston is overrun by foreign workers, especially Portuguese. A Boston chip-shop owner shook his head at the interviewer and said that you just didn't hear English spoken on the streets any more.

Both the Boston publicans I visit speak English like natives, but neither can do me a room for a night. I go to a bed and breakfast run by a woman who speaks English like a native Scot.

Her establishment aims at the top end of the market. My room is large and immaculate with ensuite everything. The huge bed has an abundance of feather-fat pillows. The curtains meet, a sumptuous dressing gown hangs behind the door, the towels are an inch thick, there's the first effective bedside lamp of my trip, and I feel ill at ease. Luxury always does that to me. I feel it is meant for others.

My clothes are still damp from Lincoln. When I strip, the litter of discarded sweater, trousers, shirt, socks and underpants lies in a heap on the carpet like a reproach.

Jane gives me coffee and biscuits. I mention the news item I saw about Boston. Jane saw it too, knows the chip-shop owner. 'I was appalled,' she says, 'it's just so unfair. I'm never going to buy chips from there again. A pity, though. He does the best chips in town.'

She's lived here long enough to consider herself as much a Bostonian as she is a Scot.

'But not English?'

'Oh dear me, no, not English. The English are hated the world over.'

As I wander through Boston, the clouds are lifting. I like the place immediately. It's pretty enough to please but not pretty enough to be quaint. The buildings along one side of the market square form a terraced hotchpotch of styles, ages, heights, colours. A three-storey building of white plaster abuts a narrow brick thing that's one storey higher but just one room wide. Its roof juts like a crone's tooth. Its bottom storey is a T-Mobile shop. Next door is Millets. The whole square is a typical English architectural accretion, melded over the centuries into a unity that no one could design, a built pragmatism.

Boston is not on the coast, but its river is navigable, and in the Middle Ages when all the trade came from the east and the south, Boston was the country's second largest port. The church reflects that former importance. It is absurdly large.

To step through the church's door-within-a-door you have to tread on the black gravestone of Mercy Whittingham. 'Hic sita est Mercy, uxor charissima. Rich. Whittingham – 1710.' The rest of what Rich wanted to say about his cherished wife has been wiped by two hundred and ninety-five years of shoes.

I climb the church tower, the celebrated Stump. The stone steps wind tightly round a central stem as stone steps should, and they are hollowed as stone steps should be, and the walls of the tower are a mass of graffiti, as the walls of a tower always are. I find a few unlicensed inscriptions in Russian. Of the recent scribbles in English, 'Pissed Neil and Lindy bonked 'ere' is more or less representative. Of the less recent ones 'T. Slingsby 1918' suggests the more formal tone of Morton's era. At the stair head, deeply incised, 'W + Lisons W 1753'. Is that one person or two? If two, I wonder whether they bonked.

The view proves worth the climb. The flannel clouds have become Constable clouds, and the land stretches as flat as a flounder in every direction, dissolving on one side into a seamless smudge, and on the other into the distant sea. The town is roofs and brick. The people are dots, crawling over the earth's vast skin. A silver river, bridges, spires, windmills, a crematorium among trees, the far glisten of the Wash. Peering down over the parapet offers a life-affirming swirl of vertigo. The graves around the church are like black footmarks in wet grass.

Back down among the dots, I sit a while to smoke on a public bench, listening for foreign voices. They're not hard to find. On the next bench to mine, an agitated man clamps a mobile phone to his ear with his right hand. With his left he performs gestures of remarkable vigour. You don't need to hear his accent to know he isn't English. 'You fuckeen eedeeot,' he shouts and his left hand rises above his head, then swings down and across as if slapping a horse's rump. On another bench the skin is paler, the voices subdued and Slavic.

Randy cock pigeons chase hens around my feet, cooing and brooping, their necks swollen like iridescent flotation aids. A John Major spinster cycles past, complete with the authentic wicker basket and long concealing skirt. A man whirrs slowly past in a mobility scooter completely enclosed in a plastic rectangle, as if carrying his own weather system. And a tiny old woman tows her huge and gormless son by the hand, like a withered sparrow with a giant cuckoo nestling. The son must be forty. He shambles. Is it just that I have had time on my hands to observe them, or are these cruel mother-and-son combos more common in England than elsewhere?

The waitress at KFC is from Mauritius. I don't admit that I couldn't place Mauritius on the map. She's startlingly pretty, a new-minted contrast to the weary brightness of the decor.

'I love Mauritius,' she says, 'but is no money there. Here I am saving money. I have been to Scotland. I want to travel. I love travelling.'

I eat three pieces of close-to-synthetic flesh from a bird that never saw the sun. The spicy coating's good. No other customers come in. Miss Mauritius leans on the counter, her chin on her hands and stares beyond Boston with deep brown eyes.

I am in no position to judge whether Boston is overrun by migrants. Nor indeed whether England is. The England I've followed Morton around has been mainly the England of the shires. Yet I have heard any number of middle-class, middle-aged whites, most of them living in towns that are ninety-eight per cent white, telling me that immigration is ruining the country. The landlady of the pub where I spend the evening is one of them.

She's an infectious bubble of good humour until I ask her about the state of England.

'I feel as though the England I know is being stolen,' she says. 'You walk through the precinct and all you hear is foreign voices. On St George's Day a few of us marched through town with the flag of St George and all the oldies came out and shook our hands and said how good it was to see a bit of patriotism.'

'What about the young?'

She laughs. 'They just kept asking if England were playing.'

She says she's thought of selling up the pub and going to Spain. 'I'm a real sun-worshipper, me. I think I've got a bit of Italian,' and she waves her arms about in illustration. 'It's the winters that get to me. I wouldn't mind if they were real winters, you know, snow and sun, but we just get grey.'

It's the middle-aged that make pubs work. The young are no good. They are preoccupied with themselves and their hormones. The old aren't a lot better. But if, as in this fine pub, the middle-aged gather around the bar and welcome all comers and all topics, then the end result is happiness. I spend most of my evening laughing. And I learn essential stuff. I learn that the best car of all time was the Rover P5B. The Queen had one and so did the Kray twins. I learn that the only pure Lincolnshire word left in common usage is 'squaddy', meaning the sort of mud that sucks a boot off. I learn that the Stump is a popular spot for suicide. The last guy to jump bounced so far they had to fetch his corpse out of the river. And I learn that the steps at the door of the church in Keal Coats stand at exactly the same height above sea-level as the top of the Stump. 'So,' says the speaker, a bearded railway worker, 'if you're feeling down, the sensible thing to do is just to go up to Keal Coats, stand on the church steps, take a deep breath, and jump. Then if you have second thoughts you can just step back up.'

As a young man he drove a digger, but he let his ticket lapse. There's an art to digger-driving, he says. 'The arm should move fluid, like, continuous. My dad taught me. I could teach the fucking instructors. But it'd cost me a thousand quid to get my ticket back.' He sighs and grows beerily serious. He's tired of Boston. His wife 'used to have big tits, but the kids ate them'. Those kids have grown up and scattered. He and his wife have now separated. 'The longer I live,' he says, 'the more I like animals and the less I like people.'

He says he'd like to go to New Zealand. When I tell him the population figures he says he'd really like to go to New Zealand. But the flight daunts him.

'I've only flown the once, to San Francisco. I'm not afraid of much, me, but when I got inside that thing and I saw it was like a bus, well, I tell you, I was concentrating pretty hard.'

In a crowded bar in San Francisco he noticed a stool that no one sat on. He asked why and was told that Clint Eastwood had once sat there.

'"Did he shit?" I asked. "No," they said, so I sat on it.'

28

I Twitch

According to the *Independent*, the children of Britain have no trouble identifying a kestrel or a woodpecker, but they can't identify a sparrow or a starling. The reason, apparently, is that Kestrel is a heavily advertised brand of lager and Woodpecker is a cider. There is no Sparrow Bitter nor is there yet a Playstation game featuring the mass murder of starlings. The Famous Five, who could, I'm sure, distinguish a reed bunting from a cirl bunting at dusk in fog, would be appalled.

But the Famous Five, those rural paragons, would be at home in Cley next the Sea.

'We've seen avocets, and swifts and house martins and herons and three types of goose and loads of warblers.' The speaker is a gentle, cadaverous man from Harrogate, sixty or so years old, toting a telescope and tripod. His wife totes nothing. Half her face has been paralysed by a stroke. Man and wife are both wearing camouflage gear. 'We saw a marsh harrier once,' the man continues, 'and there's supposed to be a bittern in there somewhere but we haven't seen it.'

He pauses. I say, 'Oh.'

'We're not fanatics,' he says, as if my 'oh' were an accusation, 'but we are keen.' His wife's face shows neither keenness nor any other emotion.

'It's a long way from Harrogate,' I say.

'Oh, Norfolk's *the* place, you know, for birding.'

I haven't heard it called birding before. It used to be bird-watching, and for non-birdwatchers the phrase carried a derisory hint of timidity. Then it became twitching, which carried rather more than a hint. So you can understand why they like to call it birding. The concrete immediacy of the word is more emphatic, more decisive, more akin to good old-fashioned manly hunting.

Judging by what I see around me, Norfolk is indeed the place to do it. I came via the north coast, past the Queen's Sandringham estate that I hadn't known was in Norfolk, along narrow roads through little flint-cut villages, past miles of desolation and sea and reed beds and inlets and eerily windy land, utterly unlike anything I've seen so far, a sense of land that half belongs to the sea. But land has fought back. Holme next the Sea and Cley next the Sea are not next the sea any more, not quite. In the gap between village and beach, the reed beds have sprouted, their feet in dank water. The birds have flocked to the reed beds and the birders have flocked to the birds.

Ten yards from the roadway, a duck nests on a mound beside a drain. Ten yards from the duck, two movie cameras stand on tripods in plain view of the traffic and of the ducks. The cameras are swathed in camouflage cloth. Behind the cameras hunch two large men. They too are swathed in camouflage cloth.

Round every twist in the boardwalk I meet another birder. Being binocularless, I get looks. Not threatening looks, of course, for these are birders, but displeased looks. I have gate-crashed a party of the like-minded. I am the churl at the feast, the disbeliever at the service. My very presence dilutes the reverence, the sense of holiness, here in the sanctuary where they can perform their act of worship without fear of the stone of derision suddenly shattering the temple window. Or something like that.

I say quiet good afternoons and get quiet good afternoons back, but I don't get warmth, I don't get smiles. The birders note my mustard-coloured sweater and they know I am not one of them. I wouldn't dream of pointing out to these polite men and women in their olive uniforms that among these beds of uniformly tawny reeds, my mustard-coloured sweater is the better camouflage.

And yet I share some of their delight in these little beasts, these feathered signals that *Homo sapiens sapiens* has not yet overrun the whole of these islands. Enough unpopulated land must remain for these shy and frightened birds to have fed and bred, though the way they crowd these marshes suggests that such land is shrinking.

To watch the birds in their instinctive simplicity is to be reminded of what we are and where we live, that we are creatures too, eaters of seeds and beasts and fish and birds, the omnivorous winners.

Swifts dart and wheel like the flung swings on a fairground ride, like radio-controlled spear-heads, impossibly deft. Drab little dun birds – warblers? buntings? – cling puffball-light to the swaying stems, chirrup once and are off, as if challenging the birders to identify them, to tick them off as spotted.

And like the birders I feel an urge to know what each bird is, to pin the proper name to it, to master it, possess it with a word. Meanwhile the bird lives in ignorance of its name. It just does what it does, unthinking, on this last strip of half land, half water, fragile on the island's edge.

In the midst of the reed beds three hides stand on stilts. The roofs are thatched, and the wooden walls are stained the same colour as the birders' clothes. Open a flap and before you is a pond as thick with birds as a terrace is thick with fans at, say, a second-division football match. Avocets, which I have never seen before, assorted ducks and geese, lapwings, black swans, white swans, a heron stalking like a back-street murderer, its beak a dagger, and a slew of indistinguishable wading birds, their knitting-needle legs lifting them above the water, their knitting-needle bills plunging back into it.

Each flap has a ledge beneath it on which to steady binocular-holding elbows. The hide I'm in holds a dozen or so of us, all looking through holes in silence at a peopleless place. It's like spying on Eden on the sixth day. I am the only one without a notebook.

Beyond the reed beds stands a monstrous bank of shingle. As I climb its flank I cause a string of noisy miniature landslides that halve the length of my stride. At the top it's the edge of the world, an arbitrary point where land and water meet. A fat brown sea thumps a rattling beach. No birders, boats or bouncing dogs, only the clatter of the stones and the hiss of the wind and the mewing of gulls and the thud-suck-thud of the sea.

The landlady of my guest house in Cromer is Jamaican, religious and cheerful despite declining business. 'You can fly to Spain now as cheap as coming to Cromer,' she says. 'This road used to be wall-to-wall guest houses, and now, ah well. In August, when we have the carnival, I could rent the Empire State

Building twice over, but the rest of the year I just get by on travelling salesmen and professors.'

I meet neither. I'm the only guest. My room is virginal. The bedspread is white, the walls white, the white-ware white and the towels almost white. Beside the bed there's a Bible.

> *Please keep this Bible*
> *Her in view*
> *The nex guest might*
> *Need it more than you.*

I open it at random. Job Chapter 18 begins 'Then Bildad the Shuhite answered . . .' Chapter 19 begins 'Then Job answered'. Chapter 20, 'Then Zophar the Na'amathite answered'. Chapter 21 sees Job back in the saddle. For Chapter 22 Bildad and Zophar and Job shut up and Eli'phaz takes over. It's an elderly *Lord of the Rings* and the nex guest is welcome to it.

Cromer may be fading as a tourist resort, but it's keeping its pecker up. The pier is a stubby lattice of corroding Victorian ironwork, but the top side is fresh with paint. Here are the little wooden peaks and turrets of ancient bank holidays, the glassed windbreaks where the elderly can sit with rugs and Thermos flasks. The pier is adventure tourism in embryo, a hundred-year-old chance to venture beyond the land, with only planking between you and the alien sea, a little liberating thrill for the urban hordes, a hint of the limitless, a soupçon of abandon, encouraging saucy jokes and kiss-me-quick. Down on the beach, a lad in a wetsuit illustrates why surfing is not an indigenous English sport. His hands, feet and face are blue.

In a pub overlooking the beach my Desperate Dan pie comes with enough chips to feed a horse. Lacking a horse I leave most of them. I also leave the peas, which are processed. What the process was I have no idea, but I can only marvel how it managed to extract all the pea flavour. But the pie is outstanding.

It's the fag-end of the football season. Sky television is

broadcasting Tranmere playing Hartlepool in mud. At half time the score is nil–nil. 'Now sit back and enjoy the second half,' says the commentator, without apparent irony.

I have no idea what division this is. I also have no idea where Tranmere is. But the game still matters to many. The facial expressions of the crowd are raw and unambiguous. One man in a blue-and-white Hartlepool wig is shown biting his fingernails and looking ripe for the psychiatric ward. Perhaps it's only football that keeps him out of it.

Even at this lowly level, the game is a big and multinational business. Tranmere has a dedicated goalkeeping coach. The Tranmere keeper is called Auchterberg. Hartlepool's is Kunstopoulos. The game goes to a penalty shoot-out, which Hartlepool win. The cameras zoom in on Kunstopoulos lying in the Tranmere mud and beating it with pleasure.

29

Whatever You Do, Don't Smile

It's almost June. Summer is here and I soon won't be. In less than a week I fly back to New Zealand's winter. I don't mind. Though I shall never be anything other than English, New Zealand is where I live. But before I leave I want to find a way to end the trip.

In Search of England finishes in a village 'untouched by modern ideas, in spite of the wireless and the charabanc'. It's

276

got all the trappings: roses, cottages, meadows, entrenched local families, a little stone church and an octogenarian vicar who is keen to mouth the sentiments that Morton is keen to hear. The vicar shows Morton round the graveyard where the locals are buried 'ten and twelve deep', gives him dinner at dusk while a hare dances on the lawn, and concludes with, 'That, I'm afraid, is all we have.'

To which Morton replies, 'You have England.'

Neat. By rights, of course, I should drive the Audi to the selfsame village and ferret out the vicar's successor and grill him on how things are now. I would, too, if I knew where it was. But Morton's archetypal sleepy English village comes with no name. I suspect that he embellished it beyond recognition, or else that he simply made it up.

So Morton goes his way and I go mine, through the lowlands of East Anglia to Norwich. The city is clogged with vehicles and seems determined to thwart me, funnelling me down roads I don't want, into suburbs that no one could want. But over the last couple of months I have grown accustomed to dense roads and strange traffic systems and I have learned not to boil. I just ditch the Audi at the first opportunity and walk into town.

I follow the river, then climb the hill by a school playing field where juniors are running half-heartedly round a track and the first eleven are inspecting a seriously green pitch (bowl first, boys, and let the track do the rest). I pass sagging roofs and mossed flint walls, come round a corner at the back of the cathedral and walk slap bang into the *Antiques Roadshow* and the end of this book.

The programme is being filmed on a lawn within the ancient cloisters. There's a queue of people the size of twenty congregations. Rain threatens but the tended grass is lit brighter than any summer's day. Fat black cables snake over flagstones and through time-eroded arches. On the grass are little knots of tables and chairs as if for a garden party, and strutting among them, fully aware of who they are, are people I recognize. I have seen them on television on the other side of the planet.

Here's the moustached expert on oriental ceramics, and the chubby guy who knows guns, and the jaunty furniture man who rubs his palm over old oak chairs as if they were women. And seated at a table in front of a couple of huge, wheel-mounted cameras is the well-spoken woman who names astonishing prices for teddy bears. She has a teddy bear in front of her now, a battered thing, along with the teddy bear's owner, a battered woman. A semicircle of punters has gathered behind to turn the event into theatre. It's a well-behaved semicircle. It doesn't wave to the cameras.

The expert, holding all the power, delays the financial climax. She speaks of German manufacturers and stitching quality, tuts at repairs, makes quaint jokes, knowing that all of this is merely stalling but that the audience is happy to be deli-ciously stalled for minutes, will stay there silently rapt until she unveils the money.

It's a potent formula and it is quintessentially English. I have seen an American version of the show and it just doesn't work. The differences go close to defining Englishness.

The setting is often a country house, by the kind permission of the Duke and Lady, who need the readies to fix the roof and so for one day will let riff-raff track through the gates with their hope and their trinkets and their ready-made shoes. The Duke and his Lady are rarely in evidence, although if they do deign to show the cameras round the house, the presenter fawns to them.

Class is evident too in the well-spoken experts, descending on the provinces with their impeccable suits, vowels and finger-nails, dispensing knowledge and the promise of largesse to the gobsmacked peasants. The peasants in their M&S cardigans know the part they have to play. The current teddy bear's owner, for instance, is doing it bang right. She defers to expertise, nods or shakes her head as required, and accepts patronage without protest, humbled by the unaccustomed glare of attention.

(If, as sometimes happens, the owner of the item gets above his or her station, interrupts the expert or otherwise tries to impress, it all feels awkward, wrong. We viewers sense that here's a Johnny-come-lately who would do better to shut up.)

There is Englishness too in the ungushing reverence for the past. The older the item, the greater that reverence. Unspoken behind the entire business is a suggestion of a better yesterday, a period that was prouder, more ordered, more beautiful.

And how particularly apt is the setting for this show: ancient Norwich Cathedral, a spectacular house of God, which few people use as a house of God any longer. It remains, however, something cherished, something in no danger of demolition, a cultural attraction to be walked through and admired. It's a venerable shrine to the past. And yet it has been given over to that most contemporary of things, television.

To this shrine people have brought their treasures, and they have brought them primarily to have them valued. Most people have come in the hope of a windfall. But it isn't done to admit as much.

Hence the stress on establishing the beauty of the objects under discussion, the rapt attention to the story of their design and manufacture, and the common insistence that the monetary value is unimportant. Indeed the experts often pay lip-service to this insistence by prefacing the value with the phrase 'for insurance purposes'. But it is the money that everyone wants to hear, which is why it is held back until last. And when that sum is announced it isn't done to look pleased. It isn't done to whoop or holler, or to perform a little jig of joy. That would be unseemly. That would be making a scene. Any such jigs are to be done at home in private. Here the emphasis is on dissembling. Indeed one of the great fascinations of the programme is watching two conflicting forces at work on the face of a suddenly wealthy owner. He wants to grin and to yelp with delight, but the more seemly thing is to appear decently astonished. And oh how hard he tries.

The emphasis, in other words, is on that most English of things, conduct.

The teddy-bear expert is approaching the money-moment now. Though everyone knows it is coming, she still approaches it with a touch of circumlocution. 'Have you given any thought to the value?' she says. Of course the owner has. That's why she is here. But no owner ever says as much.

'If it went to auction today,' the expert says, and the camera zooms in. The sum is named and the owner duly gasps astonishment at the price someone will pay to own a cuddly bit of the past.

But she's not quite a good enough actor. You can see that she's actually a trifle disappointed. But she is far too English to say so.